W9-ACD-726

Gramley Library
Salem College
Winston-Salem, NC 27108

Visions of the Land

UNDER THE SIGN OF NATURE

Explorations in Ecocriticism

MICHAEL P. BRANCH

SUEELLEN CAMPBELL

JOHN TALLMADGE

EDITORS

SERIES CONSULTANTS

Lawrence Buell, John Elder, Scott Slovic

SERIES ADVISORY BOARD

Michael P. Cohen, Richard Kerridge,
Gretchen Legler, Ian Marshall,
Dan Peck, Jennifer Price, Kent Ryden,
Rebecca Solnit, Anne Whiston Spirn,
Hertha D. Sweet Wong

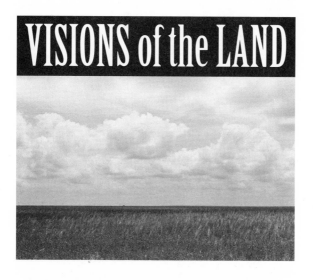

VISIONS of the LAND

Science, Literature, and the American
Environment from the Era of
Exploration to the Age of Ecology

MICHAEL A. BRYSON

UNIVERSITY PRESS OF VIRGINIA

CHARLOTTESVILLE AND LONDON

Gramley Library
Salem College
Winston-Salem, NC 27108

The University Press of Virginia
© 2002 by the Rector and Visitors of the University of Virginia
All rights reserved
Printed in the United States of America on acid-free paper
First published 2002

1 3 5 7 9 8 6 4 2

PHOTO CREDITS: title page—"Kansas Plain," Laura Daniel Bryson;
p. 1—"Antarctica: Man and Plane," Michael A. Bryson; p. 55—"Shiprock,"
Laura Daniel Bryson; p. 103—"Illinois Oak," Laura Daniel Bryson.
All photographs courtesy of the photographers.

LIBRARY OF CONGRESS CATALOGING-IN-PUBLICATION DATA
Bryson, Michael A., 1967–
Visions of the land : science, literature, and the American environment
from the era of exploration to the age of ecology / Michael A. Bryson.
p.   cm. — (Under the sign of nature)
Includes bibliographical references and index.
ISBN 0-8139-2106-6 (alk. paper) — ISBN 0-8139-2107-4 (pbk. : alk. paper)
1. American literature—History and criticism.   2. Environmental literature—
History and criticism.   3. Literature and science—United States—History.
4. Environmental protection in literature.   5. Wilderness areas in literature.
6. Landscape in literature.   7. Ecology in literature.   8. Nature in literature.
I. Title.   II. Series.
PS169.E25 B79 2002
810.9'355—DC21   2001007122

Contents

Acknowledgments   vii

Introduction   ix

· PART 1 ·

Narratives of Exploration and the Scientist-Hero

ONE

"I Saw Visions": John Charles Frémont and the Explorer-Scientist as
Nineteenth-Century Hero   3

TWO

"The Evidence of My Ruin": Richard Byrd's Antarctic Sojourn   32

· PART 2 ·

Imagined Communities and the Scientific Management of Nature

THREE

"A Strange and Terrible Woman Land": Charlotte Perkins Gilman's
Scientific Utopia   57

FOUR

"A Unit of Country Well Defined in Nature": John Wesley Powell
and the Scientific Management of the American West   80

CONTENTS

· PART 3 ·
Nature's Identity and the Critique of Science

FIVE
"The Earth Is the Common Home of All": Susan Fenimore
Cooper's Investigations of a Settled Landscape   105

SIX
"The Relentless Drive of Life": Rachel Carson's and Loren Eiseley's
Reformulation of Science and Nature   134

Afterword   174

Notes   181
Bibliography   201
Index   215

Acknowledgments

Many friends and colleagues read parts or all of this manuscript, provided helpful and insightful advice, and supplied much-needed moral support during this project. My graduate mentor, Susan Squier, provided inspiration and guidance throughout my initial research, on-the-mark criticisms of various drafts, timely correspondence over long distances, and unflagging friendship and professional support far above and beyond the call of duty. Laura Henigman, Don Ihde, and Gerry Nelson helped me formulate and develop early ideas on the topic. Beth Donaldson, Rick Van Noy, Ed Hardin, and Bob Canter gave me perceptive comments aplenty—special thanks to Ed for shoring up my work ethic and to Rick for helping me see things from a different angle. My colleagues at Roosevelt University—in particular, Dan Headrick, Jack Metzgar, Gary Wolfe, Carol Williams, Karen Gersten, Doug Knerr, and Mike Maly—read portions of drafts and supplied valued feedback, encouragement, and intellectual support. Mike Ensdorf's technical and artistic expertise were instrumental in the preparation of the book's photographs. Special thanks to series editors John Tallmadge and SueEllen Campbell for offering superb advice and guiding me through the final stages of revision. Jane Curran provided sterling service as copyeditor. Boyd Zenner of the University Press of Virginia showed faith in this book before it was finished, and for her support, advocacy, and hard work I am most grateful.

ACKNOWLEDGMENTS

My wife, Laura, tirelessly read every draft, provided invaluable editorial and conceptual criticisms, and bolstered my enthusiasm for this project at every twist, turn, and dip in the road. Without her advice, love, and unfaltering support, I never would have completed the journey.

I also would like to acknowledge the library staffs at SUNY Stony Brook, Virginia Tech, and Roosevelt University for helping me locate and retrieve materials. Roosevelt University kindly provided me with a Summer Research Grant in 1997 and a Faculty Research and Professional Development Leave in the spring of 2001; both were instrumental in the book's completion.

Two chapters were published previously and have been revised for inclusion here: Chapter 2 appeared as "Antarctic Interfaces: Science, Human Subjectivity, and the Case of Richard Byrd" in the journal *Science as Culture* 5.3 (1996): 431–58. Chapter 4 appeared as "Controlling the Land: John Wesley Powell and the Scientific Management of the American West" in the volume *Science, Values, and the American West*, edited by Stephen Tchudi (University of Nevada Press, 1997). A sincere thank-you to Taylor and Francis, Ltd. (www.tandf.co.uk) and the Nevada Humanities Committee, respectively, for permission to reprint this material.

I dedicate this book to my parents, Ralph and Pat Bryson, who gave me my love of books, woods, and quiet lakes; and to Laura, my best reader and favorite naturalist.

Introduction

This book investigates the connections between the representation of nature and the practice of science in America from the 1840s to the 1960s, as explored in the texts of seven American writers: John Charles Frémont, Richard Byrd, Charlotte Perkins Gilman, John Wesley Powell, Susan Cooper, Rachel Carson, and Loren Eiseley. In one sense, it is a study of how environmental attitudes have influenced and been shaped by various scientific perspectives from the time of western expansion and geographic exploration in the mid-nineteenth century to the start of the contemporary environmental movement in the latter third of the twentieth century. In another, it is a literary-critical analysis of how selected writers of different backgrounds, scientific training, and geographic experiences represented nature through various kinds of natural science—from natural history to cartography to resource management to ecology and evolution—and, in the process, explored the possibilities and limits of science itself. Fundamentally, *Visions of the Land* examines the varied, sometimes conflicting, always fascinating, ways we've defined the relations among science, nature, language, and the human community. Ultimately, it is a meditation on the capacity of using science to live well within nature.

Several key questions motivate and provide a conceptual basis for this study: How have we described and represented the natural environment? How have our attitudes about and methods of science shaped those representations of nature? How, in turn, have our investigations of nature affected our views of science and even provided a basis of critiquing our scientific methods and assumptions? In what sense have various cultural and historical factors, such as literary conventions or attitudes about gender and race, impacted our views of nature and science? How does the changing notion of the scientist—whether in the specific role of explorer, frontier hero, natural historian, ecologist, or anthropologist—figure into the relation between science and nature? Finally, how do our attitudes about science and nature shape our notion of community—the relation among people, their ideas and institutions, and the landscape?

Visions of the Land examines a diverse array of writings—including exploration narratives, technical reports, natural histories, scientific autobiographies, fictional utopias, and popular scientific literature—united by the thoughtful examination of science and nature. These texts speak—in some cases implicitly, in others directly—to two defining tensions within our views of nature and science: first, the conflict between the use, control, and exploitation of nature versus the recognition that nature should be conserved and protected; second, the recognition that science has in many cases provided the intellectual and technical tools to modify, dominate, and possibly destroy nature versus the potential for science to cultivate a rich and rewarding knowledge of the natural world and foster a responsible environmental ethic. Consider one example of these related tensions. The establishment of the national parks in the late nineteenth century and the subsequent conservation movement in the early twentieth century signaled our developing awareness that the earth's natural resources are limited. Despite this change in attitude, however, the twentieth century saw the most massive use and abuse of natural resources in human history, through activities such as logging, mining, oil drilling, waste disposal, dam building, urban development, monocultural farming, and the indiscriminate use of pesticides and other chemicals. These actions, largely (though not entirely) at odds with the spirit of conservationism and environmentalism, reflect the nation's still prevailing attitude that nature is ours to be used and exploited at will. How do we make sense of this contradiction, one that is at the heart of the relationship between scientific practice and environmental stewardship?

No doubt we will struggle with these basic questions in coming decades, as our scientific and technical capacities grow much faster than our ability to assess their ethical and social import (e.g., cloning and genetic engineering) and serious environmental problems persist and in some cases grow worse (global warming, deforestation, loss of biodiversity). Confronting these challenges effectively requires not only technical know-how, economic resources, and political moxie, but also a keen and historically informed sense of how we conceptualize both nature and science. The writers I discuss investigated the complex relationship between scientific practice and the environment from many different perspectives and in different contexts—from exploring the vast spaces of the unsettled American West or the icy interior of Antarctica to studying the natural history of a New England community to imagining a fictional utopian society to articulating the important concepts of ecology and evolutionary biology. What emerges from a careful examination of their writings is neither a singular relation between science and nature nor a definitive answer as to how we may resolve these longstanding tensions between exploitation and preservation, between science as a means of technical control and science as a mode of empathetic understanding. Instead, these readings foster a deeper awareness of how past ideas about nature and science have shaped our current attitudes and assumptions, and how they may indeed offer insight and guidance in facing present and future challenges. We should study these explorations of science and nature carefully, listening to past voices for echoes of present tensions and contradictions, for murmurings of wisdom and foresight that can facilitate a scientific outlook in harmony with an engaged and pragmatic environmental ethic, rather than one rooted in the desire to control and manipulate nature.

The historical frame of *Visions of the Land* spans an approximately 130-year period from the apex of the scientific exploration of North America in the mid-nineteenth century to the advent of the contemporary environmental movement in the 1960s. Overall, the book's organization follows my subjects' mode of scientific inquiry, moving from geographic exploration (Frémont and Byrd) to the scientific management of nature and the human community (Gilman and Powell) to natural history and the ecological perspective (Cooper, Carson, and Eiseley). While this arrangement stresses similarities and conjunctions in theme and perspective over chronology, the structure roughly parallels key developments in the history of American science from the 1840s to the 1960s: the push to explore and map the continental United States and, when that was done, to move on to new territories such as Antarctica, the deep ocean, and eventually space; the transformation of science from a mostly amateur and individualized undertaking to a complex, professionalized, and largely government-sponsored endeavor; and the emergence of twentieth-century ecology out of nineteenth-century natural history.

These seven authors are united first and foremost by a shared thematic interest: they investigate the characterizations of and complex relationship between nature and science, either as the explicit purpose of their text or as an important narrative theme. Second, their works represent a diverse selection of perspective and genre: as men and women, professional scientists and self-taught naturalists, government bureaucrats and radical social critics, their written work cuts across many categories and rhetorical approaches. Juxtaposing these different sorts of texts produces connections and insights unlikely to emerge from studying a particular literary genre—say, exploration literature, nonfictional nature essays, or poetry. Further linking these diverse writings is a shared audience of the general educated reader—despite significant structural and rhetorical differences, each of the primary works analyzed here addresses a nontechnical readership, albeit readers in different historical contexts and with varying expectations about what they were reading. Fourth, by analyzing less-well-studied figures (such as Frémont rather than Lewis and Clark, or Cooper rather than Thoreau) or works by a particular author (for example, Powell's policy analysis rather than his more famous exploration narratives) I hope to revisit some relatively neglected works as well as to glean insights from novel combinations of sources. Finally and most importantly, these seven authors' works collectively represent an ongoing conversation, both speculative and critical, that transcends the subject and style of individual texts—an exchange of ideas about science and technology, nature and culture, heroism and progress, gender and identity, individuals and communities.

Part 1, "Narratives of Exploration and the Scientist-Hero," discusses two of America's most celebrated geographic explorers, John Charles Frémont and Richard Byrd. Archetypal figures of scientific exploration, Frémont and Byrd traveled great distances, endured harsh, risk-filled conditions to gain empirical and cartographic knowledge of new landscapes, and employed various technologies to codify information about the natural environment into scientific form. Frémont's exploration narratives and Byrd's autobiography tell contrasting stories of the American explorer and in the process raise interesting questions about the character of nature and the methods of science. Frémont's nineteenth-century journals and government reports, analyzed in chapter 1, facilitate the Euro-American conceptualization, mapping, and settlement of the trans-Missouri region. His narratives devise a heroic persona for the scientist-explorer that is rational and unabashedly masculine, a western hero set in opposition to an explicitly feminized, passive nature. Chapter 2 focuses upon Richard Byrd, a career naval officer, promoter of scientific exploration, aviator, and pioneer polar explorer. Byrd's adventures in Antarctica as detailed in his 1938 autobiography, *Alone*, provide a surprising counterpoint to the mythos constructed by explorers of Frémont's generation. In a Thoreau-styled experiment in self-isolation on the forbidding Ross Ice Barrier, Byrd attempts to harmonize with rather than "conquer" the Antarctic environment, a project that unfortunately degenerates into a fight for mere survival. His story redefines the myth of the scientist-hero and symbolizes the limits of scientific practice and technical mastery that were unacknowledged by previous generations of explorers.

Part 2, "Imagined Communities and the Scientific Management of Nature," shifts the emphasis from the individual and somewhat antagonistic engagement of the natural world to the process of reforming the human community through the guidance of science. Charlotte Perkins Gilman, the subject of chapter 3, serves as an appropriate bridge for this transition: her 1915 utopian novel, *Herland*, offers a polemical and gender-based critique of Euro-American exploration science in general and the male explorer-hero persona in particular. Yet Gilman's text is not anti-science—her fictional Herland society maintains great faith in their rational capacity to order both the natural environment as well as their daily lives. Indeed, "nature" in Herland is a carefully monitored, scrupulously controlled entity, an island of ecological engineering within a largely uncharted wilderness region. Consequently, Gilman wrangles with conflicting impulses: despite her radical critique of the masculine explorer-hero, she retains an abiding faith in benevolent scientific management and the myth of unlimited progress. Gilman thus echoes some of the key beliefs and assumptions of a nineteenth-century scientific icon, John Wesley Powell, particularly those surrounding the control of nature. A geologist, ethnographer, and second director of the nascent United States Geological Survey, Powell is best known for directing explorations of the Colorado River region in the 1860s and 1870s. Chapter 4 analyzes Powell's *Report on the Lands of the Arid Regions of the United States* (1878), which sets out his ecological philosophy and practical blueprint for the scientific management of the American West. In his progressive vision, human communities must embrace science and technology in order to adapt to the arid West by controlled irrigation projects, wise management of natural resources, and reform of land distribution. Though the *Report* contains a nuanced representation of nature as an independent, self-adjusting natural system, Powell's reliance upon the scientific method as the ultimate problem solver encourages the control of nature specifically for human use. Taken together, Gilman's fictional utopia and Powell's fusion of policy with science both contain traces of an ecological world view, but these impulses are overshadowed by visions of nature managed and improved by science.

Part 3, "Nature's Identity and the Critique of Science," highlights an important counter-discourse to the narratives of nature's conquest and environmental management; namely, the empathetic engagement with nature embodied in scientifically oriented works of American nature writing. Chapter 5 shifts back to the mid-nineteenth century to examine Susan Fenimore Cooper, a prolific writer and skilled naturalist, within the context of the rhetoric of natural history. As a contemplative piece of nature writing that synthesizes natural history observations with social commentary, Cooper's seasonal journal *Rural Hours* (1850) is a paradigmatic proto-ecological text: her natural history suggests that Americans should see themselves as merely one part of a large and complex ecological community. While this perspective anticipates certain twentieth-century environmental attitudes, *Rural Hours* also exemplifies the nineteenth-century conflict between our enthusiasm to cultivate the land and our obligation to protect its resources and beauty. Finally, chapter 6 jumps forward one hundred years to discuss two important and influential scientist-writers of the post–World War Two period, Rachel Carson and Loren Eiseley, whose work integrates the natural historian's ethos with the theories and practice of modern ecology and evolutionary biology. Their writings capture the essence of a new ecological perspective and environmental ethic, one that emphasizes the complex, interconnected cycles of nature, the importance of evolution in our understanding of nature and ourselves, and a critique of the fruits of scientific progress and the technological domination of nature. Carson and Eiseley eloquently stress the need to study nature with respect and humility; to appreciate the complexity, indeterminacy, and interconnection inherent to nature; and to question science's status as the ultimate problem solver.

By illustrating how our ideas and assumptions about the character of nature and scientific practice have been inscribed, challenged, and revised, these case studies suggest a multi-stranded argument about the scientific study of the environment. First, they dramatize the preferability of the scientist as "plain citizen" (to use Aldo Leopold's phrase) of the earth rather than an all-confident hero or a faceless technocrat, for the heroic or even managerial stance toward nature is closely linked to gendered or mechanistic views of the environment, respectively—both of which in turn lead to the notion of nature as resource. Second, they demonstrate how such culturally inscribed representations of nature are linked to scientific practices that stress objectivity over subjectivity, control over connection, efficiency over ethics. More positively, they show that resistance to these powerful ideas about nature and science, a collective critique amounting to a rejection of science as the ultimate problem solver and of nature as a mere object of study and exploitation, can come from a variety of places: a seasonal exploration of a New England village's natural and cultural history; a feminist social critic's utopian society; a rejected vision for reforming the settlement of the American West. Ultimately, these critical explorations of the past, especially as synthesized and artfully expressed in the writings of Carson and Eiseley, are models for recognizing the limits of scientific knowledge and progress and for rethinking the potential for science to forge a responsive and vital environmental ethic.

At its heart, *Visions of the Land* is a work of ecological literary criticism, an interpretative approach that "takes as its subject the interconnections between nature and culture, specifically the cultural artifacts of language and literature" (Glotfelty xix). At one time scholarship on the relation of literature to the environment consisted mostly of genteel commentary upon pastoral poetry or the nature essay; today, ecocriticism is necessarily interdisciplinary and wide-ranging in its methods; explores a wide variety of literary, scientific, and environmental texts and practices; and derives from a late-twentieth-century concern for the health of the environment as well as the human community's evolving relationship to nature. As an ecocritical study, *Visions of the Land* applies ideas and insights from environmental history, ecology and biology, and literary criticism to the study of texts' rhetorical, ideological, literary, and scientific characteristics.[1] Underlying this approach is the belief that studying past representations of nature and science can contribute to our efforts to understand the evolving American landscape as affected by ecological change and human impact, improve our present relationship with the environment, and foster positive and ecologically sound models of scientific inquiry.[2]

Like ecocriticism itself, this book has been informed by three other closely related areas of scholarship—science and literature studies, the cultural study of science, and feminist critiques of nature and science. Though the first of these dates from at least the nineteenth century, the past twenty-five years have seen literary critics, scientists, historians, sociologists, and philosophers blur the boundaries between what C. P. Snow famously characterized as "The Two Cultures," and challenge our assumptions about the relationship between science and literature.[3] Their work has shown that science and literature not only influence one another, but also are embedded in and shaped by the larger culture; that the rhetoric of scientists gives us valuable information about their theories, methods, and assumptions; and that the literary analysis of metaphor, persuasion, and narrative in scientific texts is a necessary counterpart to the interpretation of scientific themes in literary works.

Closely associated with science and literature scholarship is the multidisciplinary cultural study of Western science, an approach perhaps best defined by an example: Donna Haraway's *Primate Visions: Gender, Race, and Nature in the World of Modern Science* (1989), a detailed historical and theoretical analysis of twentieth-century primatology. Studies such as Haraway's ask, How does a science come into being? What are its explicit and implicit goals and ideologies? What degree of objectivity does it claim, and how valid is this claim? What kinds of stories does it produce? How is it rooted in, or independent from, the social sphere at large? The cultural study of science, in basic terms, seeks to examine a particular scientific practice from a larger perspective than that of science's own rules, traditions, and procedures.[4] The primary assumption of such an approach, inspired by Thomas Kuhn's *The Structure of Scientific Revolutions* (published in 1962 and now one of the most influential books of the twentieth century), is that science is fundamentally a social process.

No less important has been the work of feminist philosophers, historians, and literary critics, who have examined the contributions of women to literature, science, and the study of nature, challenged the notion that science is a bias-free, objective process of acquiring knowledge, and stressed the need to highlight gender as subject for critical analysis.[5] One line of inquiry examines how women have been excluded from the formal channels of scientific education and practice, as well as assessing the important contributions women made from their marginal position.[6] As historian Londa Schiebinger notes, scientific "knowledge has been molded historically. . . . Knowledge was shaped by patterns of inclusion and exclusion from the scientific community and . . . the social and political struggles shaping those patterns" (*Nature's Body* 210). Another approach is to look carefully at how the very language and method of science has been shaped by assumptions and values about gender: to analyze how, for example, nature in Western society has been characterized by feminine metaphors, while science has been cast as a masculine endeavor.[7]

This project synthesizes insights from these diverse areas of inquiry within an ecocritical context. I have had the blessing of learning from previous high-quality work, the challenge of finding new things to say, and the opportunity to find connections where none were seen before. In more personal terms, researching and writing this book has confirmed for me the necessary connections among various parts of my own life: my early scientific training as an undergraduate biologist, my longtime appreciation for and present professional interest in the study of literature, and my fascination and reverence for the outdoors—aspects of learning and experience that are too often compartmentalized, too seldom reconciled. Exploring American representations of nature and science, from Frémont's vision of the western frontier to Eiseley's philosophical musings on humanity's origins, has shown me the value and necessity of an integrated approach to science, literature, and the natural environment. How else to see nature through the eyes of science?

Visions of the Land

Narratives of Exploration and
the Scientist-Hero

"I Saw Visions"

John Charles Frémont and
the Explorer-Scientist as
Nineteenth-Century Hero

I
n nineteenth-century America, science was not confined to the laboratory, bound up in a mythos of isolation and otherworldliness, in-
accessible to the public mind. Rather, science quite often denoted
"action" in the rapidly expanding United States. The practice of natural history and, later on, narrower and more professionalized disciplines such as geology, cartography, and paleontology facilitated our
engagement with the frontier, the wilderness space that has gripped
the American imagination since the earliest times of European colonization. This chapter focuses upon John Charles Frémont (1813–90),
an explorer-scientist who made major contributions to the surveying
and mapping of the American West, who hypothesized about the natural processes of the land he explored, and who as a representative of
the U.S. government was deeply involved in the political process of
westward expansion. Frémont's journals from his first two trans-
Missouri expeditions (published together as *Report of the Exploring Expeditions to the Rocky Mountains in the Year 1842, and to Oregon and
Northern California in 1843–44*)[1] are fascinating hybrid texts. In them,
the discourses of science and of literature meet and interact creatively—data points are juxtaposed with straight narrative, geological
speculation with rhapsodic description of the landscape, botanical observations with buffalo chases.

Frémont worked within a long tradition of wilderness exploration in America by the Spanish, French, and English, dating back to the late fifteenth century. Christopher Columbus (1451–1506) brought the American exploration narrative to a European audience with his *Journal of the First Voyage to America, 1492–1493*. Another important Spanish explorer of the New World was Álvar Núñez Cabeza de Vaca (1490?–1556?), whose *Relation* (1542) is perhaps the first in a long tradition of North American captivity narratives. Among the French explorers of the seventeenth century, Samuel de Champlain (1570?–1635) provided an early account of contact and conflict between Europeans and Native Americans in the territory of present-day New York State and southeastern Canada in *The Voyages of Samuel de Champlain, 1604–1618*. The English, in contrast to the other major European powers of the early modern era, were latecomers to the New World, and their initial exploration and colonization efforts were on a far smaller scale. Nevertheless, exploration narratives in English date back to the early seventeenth century with the publication of Captain John Smith's (1580–1631) *A True Relation of Such Occurrences . . . in Virginia* in 1608.[2]

The leap from these multivocal beginnings to the mid-nineteenth century is substantial; why isolate Frémont from two and one-half centuries' worth of Euro-American exploration? One answer is that the scientific practice of nineteenth-century explorers differed dramatically from that of their predecessors, due to developments in the broader culture of Western science. They include an increasing emphasis upon quantitative rather than simply qualitative information about nature, the professionalization of the American scientist, and the growth of the national project of American science. Frémont, Alexander von Humboldt, Charles Darwin, and others are part of a historical trajectory in which scientific exploration strove for empirical rigor in an attempt to objectively map and describe the natural landscape. Improvements in technology and scientific instrumentation replaced the naked-eye observer's fallibility with the controlled and standardized methods of data collection. Quantitative, empirical practices—such as chemical analyses, elevation measurements, precise astronomical observations, and specific calculations of geologic time—competed with and eventually overshadowed older modes of qualitative description.[3]

Additionally, the deployment of organized scientific exploring expeditions (most importantly, those of Lewis and Clark, Frémont, Clarence King, and John Wesley Powell) was a motive force behind an aggressively expanding American nation. Historian William Goetz-mann, who suggests this relationship in the very title of his important study, *Exploration and Empire: The Explorer and the Scientist in the Winning of the American West* (1966), argues that nineteenth-century exploration "helped to create in the centers of dominant culture a series of images which conditioned popular attitudes and public policy concerning the new lands" (ix). In short, the nineteenth century was a period in which American science (and, by extension, exploration science) took on key characteristics that have formed an important part of its identity ever since.[4]

Frémont's reports use a variety of rhetorical strategies to bring the unexplored spaces of the American West into the realm of the known. Empirical information about nature forms the bedrock of his narrative, providing a day-by-day quantitative assessment of the landscape as well as raw information for topographical maps. Artful descriptions of the territory's natural history and potential for cultivation and settlement made Frémont's reports powerful political as well as scientific documents. In particular, the maps produced from his expeditions aptly illustrate how Frémont's scientific view of the West dovetails with his political objectives of establishing safe and efficient migration routes for western settlement and assessing the country's economic potential. As represented in map form, nature is static, seemingly without a past—but although the map in one sense freezes nature in time, it also provides the foundation for future exploration, more detailed map-making, and eventually settlement of the land. Frémont's maps and reports thus provide a powerful and influential vision of the western landscape in the mid-nineteenth century—the Great Plains, the Rocky Mountain region, and even the arid stretches of the Great Basin constitute a grand and spacious resource for an expanding nation.

Second, Frémont's narratives transform the scientist-explorer into a western hero, a distinctly masculine figure who strives to "conquer" a feminine nature. By revising the identity of one of the most recognizable male hero-figures in nineteenth-century literature, James Fenimore Cooper's Natty Bumppo, Frémont appropriates manliness and adventure for the rhetoric of exploration science. Equally significant is how Frémont objectifies nature as female, a passive space to be conquered by science. While feminizing nature ostensibly creates distance between the scientist-explorer and the environment, this separation conflicts with yet another of Frémont's metaphors—the sexualized desire to know and conquer the feminized landscape. The technologies that Frémont's party brings to the frontier—their scientific instruments—are powerful signifiers of this tension. Frémont's narratives thus suggest an uneasy and somewhat antagonistic relation between nature and the science of exploration. On one hand, observations and measurements done in the field, away from the protected and artificial confines of the laboratory and out in the unpredictable and physically challenging western wilderness, connect the explorer-scientist with nature—natural history, geology, and cartography provide detailed, useful, and intimate knowledge of the land. On the other hand, the subordination of science to overarching goals of political and geographic conquest as well as the gendering of both nature and the scientist-hero contribute to the powerful and still-influential vision of environment as resource.

Mapping the American West: Frémont's Rhetoric of Scientific Exploration

Scan a typical high school textbook of United States history, and you most likely will find John Charles Frémont described as a "dashing . . . explorer-soldier-surveyor . . . [a] flashy young adventurer" (Bailey and Kennedy 369). Frémont was the glamour boy of America's westward expansion, according to standard histories celebrating the imperial march of white civilization. He is an archetypal American hero of nineteenth-century literature and history, an amalgam of Thomas Jefferson, Daniel Boone, and Natty Bumppo. In his introduction to a volume of Frémont's narratives, Allan Nevins describes him as a "lithe, well-proportioned man, clad in deerskin shirt, blue army trousers, and thick-soled moccasins. . . . His remarkable feature is . . . his air of intense energy" (2). Historical accounts place Frémont at the leading edge of expansionism, a man who literally married into the superstructure of manifest destiny when he became the husband of Jessie Benton and son-in-law of Benton's father, Missouri Senator Thomas Hart Benton, who was the congressional voice of 1840s expansionism. Frémont's chief objective, Goetzmann notes, was to "dramatize the West as the American Destiny" (241). Through explorer-scientists like Frémont, science collected data and natural specimens on the behalf of the nation; geographical and scientific concerns were inseparable from the political issues of the day. Summarizing the influence of Benton and Frémont, historian Henry Nash Smith notes that "the further expeditions of Frémont, leading him eventually into California at the outbreak of the Mexican War, were a conspicuous and carefully publicized phase of the burst of expansionism that extended the boundaries of the United States to the Pacific by 1848" (27).[5]

Frémont was not only well connected politically—he also received first-rate training as an explorer-scientist under the tutelage of the noted scientist J. N. Nicollet, who imported advanced methods of surveying from France to the United States in 1832. Nicollet was the first, for example, to use a barometer to measure altitude (Nevins 10). Frémont's thorough apprenticeship gave him a working knowledge of chemistry, botany, geology, and surveying. He accompanied Nicollet as a civilian assistant on two expeditions of the territory bounded by the Missouri and Mississippi Rivers in 1838. After he was commissioned as an officer in the Topographical Corps, Frémont embarked upon his life's work—five exploring expeditions to various regions of the West from 1842 to 1854, during which he covered more ground than any explorer before or since. His major scientific achievements include supplying information for the most comprehensive map of western territory of its time; exploring the Great Salt Lake and the surrounding region; providing detailed surveys of paths through Oregon, California, and the Sierras; and, perhaps most importantly, describing in detail the existence and parameters of the Great Basin, a largely arid region between the Wasatch Mountains and the Sierra Nevada (Nevins 21–22). As a historical figure, however, Frémont is probably best remembered for his controversial role in California's "Bear Flag Revolt" of 1846 and his failed bid for the presidency in 1856 when he ran on an antislavery platform as the first Republican Party candidate.

Frémont's written output was considerable. He submitted major government reports detailing his first two expeditions, *Report of an Exploration of the Country Lying between the Missouri River and the Rocky Mountains, on the Line of the Kansas and Great Platte Rivers* (1843), and *Report of the Exploring Expedition to Oregon and North California in 1843–44* (1845).[6] Late in his life, he published a comprehensive overview of his life's work, including his later expeditions to California and the Great Basin area, in *Memoirs of My Life* (1887). His expedition accounts, written in chronological, journal form, were highly influential documents in the 1840s. Nevins notes that "Joseph E. Ware's *The Emigrant's Guide to California* (1849), much used in gold rush days, was largely founded on Frémont's narratives, reproducing whole sentences verbatim[.] While Frémont's reports gave scientists a wealth of new information, they served also—circulated in tens of thousands of copies—as the readiest popular source of information on the trans-Missouri West" (20).[7] Frémont's narratives truly fulfill a dual function: like the natural histories of William Byrd, John Brickell, William Bartram, Thomas Jefferson, and John Filson, they are both scientific report and popular literature. In this sense, Frémont differs considerably from later scientist-explorers, such as Clarence King and John Wesley Powell, who published both formal scientific reports and informal popular accounts. Frémont thus did much to define and describe the trans-Missouri West to both the scientific community and the lay public—he gave it shape, sketched its parameters, described and quantified its inhabitants (mineral, plant, animal, human), and mapped it two-dimensionally.[8] His audience—the scientific elite, government officials, and lay public of America in the period of Manifest Destiny—read his documents voraciously, suggesting that Frémont's writings were an integral part of American expansionism in the 1840s and 1850s.

In what sense do Frémont's reports provide scientific information about the landscape? What distinguishes them from the exploration narratives of previous centuries? One key characteristic is the inclusion of empirical data made available by the substantial improvements in instrumental technology since the eighteenth century. Such improved technologies included the barometer, thermometer, compass, artificial horizon, sextant, telescope, and chronometer; the last, for example, was crucial in the accurate determination of longitude. Although not all data are collected through the use of instruments (qualitative and even quantitative information can be gathered without artificial means—for example, the type and number of bird songs heard in a given time period in the morning), the new and more dependable technologies did facilitate the gathering of reliable numerical data, such as latitude, longitude, and altitude, for survey work.

With Lewis and Clark's exhaustively detailed journals as his model, Frémont made a concerted effort to include as much data—however minute, disparate, or potentially mundane—within the structure of his narratives. This citation of data is supplemented in greater volume and detail in comprehensive tables of botanical specimens, position readings (latitude, longitude, etc.), and meteorological observations that Frémont and his scientific co-workers assembled and included with the various expedition reports. Frémont records data with great frequency as well as accuracy. He regularly gives the reader a report of temperature, position (latitude and longitude), altitude, and geographical orientation; he provides a wealth of botanical information, with rich passages of nomenclature and morphology reminiscent of William Bartram; and in the area of geology, he speculates on the processes of the formation of rock strata. Frémont is hardly unique in this respect—naturalists had long provided botanical and geological information, previous explorers such as Lewis and Clark attempted to fix geographical positions via astronomical observations (albeit less accurately than Frémont), and scientists such as Humboldt and Darwin liberally incorporated quantitative information within their exploration narratives. Emblematic of this move toward synthesizing quantitative and qualitative data about nature, Frémont's reports present numerical information both within the narrative sections and, especially, in the lengthy tables included as appendixes. Almost every day, he provides abstract data points—temperature, barometric pressure, position—that serve to frame the narrative and give it a definite, though understated, shape. Furthermore, though Frémont organizes his information in the form of a daily journal, it is his various data points that serve as landmarks and prevent us from getting lost in the monotonous stretches of prairie. A progression of latitude and longitude gives distinctive character, a linear and logical flow, to the western plains, where acre upon acre appears similar.

This narrative approach is picked up on one of the key maps produced after Frémont's first two western expeditions, the "Topographical Map of the Road from Missouri to Oregon . . . ," a large-scale rendering of the Oregon Trail constructed from the field observations, notes, and sketches of Frémont and his assistant, Charles Preuss, a gifted cartographer and valuable expedition member.[9] Compiled by Preuss and published in 1846, this extraordinary document was a touring map of its day, for it provided invaluable information about what would become the most significant migration route for western settlers. Along the expedition's path, Frémont and Preuss note the location of each campsite as well as the noon halt, and each of these locations are keyed to a table with records of temperature, altitude, and weather information. Without these and other data, Frémont's journey would be worthless in objective terms—a series of entertaining hunting and military adventures might grip a lay audience but would hardly advance the knowledge of western geography, Frémont's (and the government's) primary purpose. In short, empirical data anchor Frémont's narratives—their authenticity as well as practical value are strengthened by numbers.[10]

Yet another key aspect of Frémont's rhetoric of exploration is his penchant for close, careful, highly detailed description that complements the quantitative elements of his reports. Consider Frémont's description of a spring:

> In an opening on the rock, a white column of scattered water is thrown up, in form like a jet d'eau, to a variable height of about three feet, and, though it is maintained in a constant supply, its greatest height is attained only at regular intervals, according to the action of the force below. It is accompanied by a subterranean noise, which, together with the motion of the water, makes very much the impression of a steamboat in motion. . . . The rock through which it is forced is slightly raised in a convex manner, and gathered at the opening into an urn-mouthed form, and is evidently formed by continued deposition from the water. (*Narratives* 221)

The passage is immediately followed by additional chemical data on the composition of the rock. On one level, Frémont speaks as a scientist, in a voice that is precise and unsensational. He emphasizes analytic description, breaking the geyser formation down into its component parts in order that its structure be more easily apprehended. But this brief passage also contains imprecise yet evocative phrasings ("scattered water," "subterranean noise," "slightly raised") as well as deliberate metaphors ("in form like a jet," "a steamboat in motion," "urn-mouthed form"). This artful combination of analytic and poetic elements makes Frémont's narratives distinctively readable even though they are information-dense. The accumulated weight of detail is best appreciated, perhaps, in the lengthy botanical and geological catalogs, astronomical observations, and meteorological tables attached to each of Frémont's reports.

The interesting interplay between description and quantification is evident in this passage from Frémont's report on his second expedition in 1843, when he was moving from the Great Salt Lake area toward Fort Vancouver:

> I subjoin an analysis of the soil in the river bottom near Fort Hall, which will be of assistance informing some correct idea of its general character in the neighboring country. I characterize it as good land, but the analysis will show its precise properties.

Silica	68.55
Alumina	7.45
Carbonate of lime	8.51
Carbonate of magnesia	5.09
Oxide of iron	1.40
Organic vegetable matter	4.74
Water and Loss	4.26
	100.00

(*Narratives* 262)

This passage exemplifies the give-and-take, the tension between the qualitative and quantitative elements in Frémont's writing. As an adjective, "good" is imprecise—an overused value judgment, laden with subjectivity. In the accompanying table, "good" becomes a function of many variables—organic vegetable matter, silica, and so forth—and their relative proportions. "Good" thus has a chemical analog, and the word's meaning appears to be stabilized by the table, since chemical substances are objects in nature. The table even gives the reader a satisfactory sense of closure: all the soil constituents nicely add up to 100 percent! Frémont, quite deftly, has transformed a vague adjective into a seemingly indisputable (and rather abstract) fact.

The table's data, however, are not transparent—their meaning is closely tied to a particular reader response. A nineteenth-century chemist would interpret the list and percentages of substances differently, no doubt, than a literate layperson of the same era. Only the chemist would be equipped to dispute Frémont's interpretation that the data indicate "good" soil; the layperson is forced to accept Frémont's word just as he or she accepts the data—at face value. Furthermore, a very important question remains unanswered: good for *what*? In fact, "good" has for Frémont a highly specific denotation with regard to his overall mission—as he states a few journal entries earlier,

Gramley Library
Salem College
Winston-Salem, NC 27108

"A military post and a civilized settlement would be of great value here; and cattle and horses would do well where grass and salt so much abound. The lake will furnish exhaustless supplies of salt. All the mountainsides here are covered with a valuable nutritious grass . . . which has a second growth in the fall. The beasts of the Indians were fat upon it; our own found it a good subsistence, and its quantity will sustain any amount of cattle and make this truly a bucolic region" (*Narratives* 258). Here we see the connection made in explicit terms: "good" denotes fertility and abundance, the prerequisites for agriculture-based settlement. The purpose, then, of Frémont's exploration rhetoric is to map the prospects for future settlement, to convince the readers of Congress and the public at large that portions of the western lands are fertile, supportive of the defining aspect of white civilization—agricultural production. In doing so, Frémont creates a counternarrative to the pessimistic descriptions of the "Great American Desert" made by previous explorers such as Zebulon Pike and Stephen Long, who doubted the arable potential of the land (H. N. Smith 175). This is not to say that Frémont ignores or misinterprets ecological realities; in his efforts to provide a comprehensive portrait of the land through which he traveled, he comments upon dry conditions and barren soils quite frequently, and he also takes note of grasslands that would support grazing as well as places where "a farmer would delight to establish himself" (*Narratives* 283).[11]

Frémont's quantitative data and verbal descriptions eventually coalesce into a concise expression of geographic knowledge, the map. Frémont's summary of the mapmaking process aptly illustrates this point: "Indeed the making of a map . . . must be exact. First, the foundations must be laid in observations made in the field; then the reduction of these observations to latitude and longitude; afterward the projection of the map. . . . Specially it is interesting to those who have laid in the field these various foundations to see them all brought into final shape—fixing on a small sheet the result of laborious travel over waste regions, and giving to them an enduring place on the world's surface" (*Narratives* 75). Frémont produced several maps in collaboration with Charles Preuss, a surveyor, illustrator, and cartographer who accompanied Frémont on his expeditions during the 1840s. These maps codify geographic knowledge gained by Frémont and previous explorers, direct future explorations by pointing out gaps and blank spaces in the grand picture of western terrain, provide a practical road map for over-land travelers to the West (who would begin to come in great numbers in the 1840s), and represent the vital first step in assessing political boundaries and determining potential routes of trade. In the plane of the map, space is bounded and presented for instantaneous interpretation and thus enables the potential exercise of power and control by the map reader. As environmental historian Carolyn Merchant notes, "Through the scrutiny of the surveyor, the land is seen as a bounded object. A spatial perspective leads to its management and control" (*Ecological* 51).

Two of Frémont and Preuss's maps, both highly significant documents of the mid-nineteenth century, illustrate these functions in different ways. The first, the "Map of an Exploring Expedition to the Rocky Mountains in the Year 1842 and to Oregon and North California in the Years 1843–44 . . ." (otherwise known as the 1845 map, denoting its year of publication) synthesized geographic information about the trans-Missouri West. This map relied mainly upon firsthand observation and surveying of the landscape, rather than the reports and maps of previous explorers, a fact evident in the abundant white space on the projection. The careful delineation between what was known and unknown not only enhanced the map's credibility and accuracy but also served to set the agenda for the next generation of western explorers, who would strive to fill in the blanks. And as historian Donald Jackson notes, the map effectively defined the vast geographic entity of the Great Basin, giving a cartographic identity to the somewhat mythic "Great American Desert" described much less concretely by previous explorers (13). Another key map produced by Frémont, the previously mentioned "Topographical Map of the Road from Missouri to Oregon . . ." of 1846, was a large-scale road map of the Oregon Trail carried by emigrants on their journey west. The 1846 map provided travelers with a detailed look at the trail's route, including surrounding topography and vegetation, paths of rivers and streams, approximate locations of the expedition's campsites, miles from point of origin, discussion of needed resources such as timber and game, meteorological observations and a record of altitude, and commentary on the location and character of Native American tribes. The scale of the map allows an amazing amount of detail to be included; for example, dozens of small islands within the Platte River are clearly defined. Finally, the map has an outstanding narrative component: selections from Frémont's journals are reprinted at the point on the map corresponding to that date in the expedition. The 1846 map is thus a beautiful example of how Frémont's reports combine empirical and narrative information—readers can get a good sense of the explorer's journey simply by reading the journal excerpts as they follow the trail west.

The maps of the Frémont expeditions also provide implicit evidence of how nature was conceived, defined, and represented by mid-nineteenth-century exploration science. In contrast to the forward-looking qualities of the maps with regard to future surveying and settlement patterns, the representation of land in spatial terms implies a static understanding of the environment, a snapshot of the western landscape frozen in time. This spatial narrative, once stripped of the context of its production, seems to erase history. In this sense, map-making shares with the discourse of natural history (itself a vital part of the Frémont expeditions) a fundamental spatial consideration.[12] Within his narratives, Frémont employs geologic observations not only to gaze back into time but also to stake out the presence of geologic structures in the here and now. When he discovers "strata of fossiliferous rock having an oölithic structure," for example, he is satisfied that he has found "repeated the modern formations of Great Britain and Europe, *which have hitherto been wanting to complete the system of North American geology*" (*Narratives* 213–14, emphasis mine). Here, the accumulation of geologic knowledge could be represented by a spatially organized grid, the overall structure of which is predetermined (much as the Great Chain of Being underpins Linnaeus's binomial naming scheme). For Frémont, the job of the geologist is to find evidence and fill in the gaps—the explorer's duty is to "complete the system." This spatial, rather than temporal, emphasis of mapmaking and natural history facilitates the view that nature is a passive space awaiting systematic description and, by extension, organized settlement and political control. The natural history of an area is simultaneously a description of its flora, fauna, and geology as well as a catalog of its potential natural resources.

Second, the map embodies a visual perspective toward nature: to see the landscape—whether in totality or in minute detail—is to know it and control it. Philosopher Don Ihde, in his discussion of the role of technology in navigational science, explains that a "chart or map is read literally *from above*. Insofar as it represents the terrain, that terrain is seen *from* the heavens. It is to 'see' the earth *from a position I do not actually occupy*. And because this is so, to make chart reading intuitive—to constitute the intuition—I must learn to make a *hermeneutic shift*" (Ihde 67, emphasis his). Thus, Frémont—as well as any explorer or surveyor who constructs a map—performs a perceptual shift, a gestalt, in assuming the visual stance from on high. The map view implies a "God's eye" perspective: looking down, seeing all. But for explorer-scientists like Frémont, this perceptual transformation is not merely metaphorical. It has an analog in the very concrete action of climbing a high point in order to survey the land-space, to "gain perspective," to see what is ahead. Again and again in exploration literature, the narrator describes the view from an elevated vantage—often, the moment is not only scientifically informative but also emotionally exultant. Frémont's excitement at seeing a map coalesce before his eyes corresponds to the emotional impact of his first view of the Great Salt Lake: "[A]scending to the summit, immediately at our feet [we] beheld the object of our anxious search—the waters of the inland Sea stretching in still and solitary grandeur. . . . It was certainly a magnificent object, and a noble terminus to this part of our expedition; and to travelers so long shut up among mountain ranges a sudden view over the expanse of silent waters had in it something sublime" (*Narratives* 243).[13]

The perceptual shift described by Ihde may seem quite obvious to contemporary readers—what other way can there be of gaining comprehensive knowledge of a particular space? Other modes of spatial perception exist, however. In his explorations of the American Southwest in the 1870s, John Wesley Powell (the subject of chapter 4) writes of a moment in which he becomes acutely aware of how his perceptions of the terrain (rooted in vision and map reading) were inferior to those of his Native American companions:

> It is curious now to observe the knowledge of our Indians. There is not a trail but what they know; every gulch and every rock seems familiar. I have prided myself on being able to grasp and retain in my mind the topography of a country; but these Indians put me to shame. My knowledge is only general, embracing the more important features of a region that remains as a map engraved on my mind; but theirs is particular. They know every rock and every ledge . . . their knowledge is

unerring. They cannot describe a country to you, but they can tell you all the particulars of a route. (*Exploration* 299–300)

Powell suddenly recognizes that he is operating from the perceptual stance of the map reader, the God's eye view. His knowledge is scientific, topographical, vision-mediated, abstract, general. When he says that the Native Americans "cannot describe a country," he means only that they do not, as far as he knew, formalize their knowledge in terms of a map. They may not engage the space from above, nor are their perceptions limited to the visual; their particular knowledge may include impressions from other senses. (In fact, Native Americans have long produced various types of maps, which have received more scrutiny from cartographers and historians since the early 1990s).[14] Powell's example of the Native American perspective illustrates the artificiality of the map-oriented view: the latter is by no means a "natural" mode (or the only mode) of spatial perception. The map-oriented view has its blind spots: it cannot represent the crucial minutiae, the tricky trail along the unanticipated gulch. It orients in terms of miles, not in feet, not in the sense of guiding his steps along a narrow ledge in the near dark. Powell is stunned by his revelation, not merely because the Native Americans know the land better, but also because they know it *differently*.

Maps thus signify Frémont's scientific perspective on the West as well as his rhetoric of exploration: they combine qualitative and empirical information in a concrete and concise representation of the landscape; they are instruments of political power, as they facilitated settlement of the West; and they tell us a great deal about how Frémont conceptualized nature itself—as a static, spatial entity best known through a visual perspective. To see nature, to catalog the shape and contents of the landscape, is the foundation of understanding. But to pursue Frémont's representation of the environment further, we also must look carefully at how he portrays himself in his narratives.

The Heroic Persona of the Explorer-Scientist

In early-nineteenth-century America, the relationship between the profession of science and the values associated with masculinity was both unclear and contested. Such a statement seems odd when we consider the themes of ruggedness, manliness, bravery, and love of adventure that pervade the narratives of Frémont and other explorers. But although adventure and manliness typically were linked in nineteenth-century American culture and literature,[15] authors such as James Fenimore Cooper (1789–1851) developed scientifically inclined characters to serve as foils for the hero-protagonist, or even as problematic anti-heroes (as with Nathaniel Hawthorne's pathological and poison-obsessed Dr. Rappaccini in his macabre 1844 short story, "Rappaccini's Daughter"). Cooper's 1827 novel, *The Prairie*, which takes place on the western frontier and chronicles the last stage of the colorful career of Natty Bumppo, provides both context and counterpoint for Frémont's scientist-hero persona. In *The Prairie*, Cooper portrays a scientist among his cast of characters—the bumbling, comedic, and effeminate naturalist Obed Bat, a.k.a. Dr. Battius. The naturalist's conversations with the wizened and resourceful frontiersman Natty Bumppo, as well as their series of misadventures, not only are some of the book's funniest moments but also serve to underscore the gulf that separates Natty the hero from Battius the fool.

Frémont, unsurprisingly, bears little resemblance to the bumbling Battius; instead, he liberally partakes of and rewrites the Bumppo hero persona in his accounts of scientific exploration. His narrator is a complicated hybrid of frontiersman, soldier, aristocrat, and scientist. In Frémont's narratives, that last role is not contradictory—there is no tension, as in Cooper, between the discourse of natural history and the heroic elements displayed by crack shooting or the rescue of the endangered white damsel. In the character that is Frémont, the hero contains all. Ironically, this revised Bumppo persona encompasses the values of expansion and scientific progress, values Cooper critiqued rather than celebrated. Meanwhile, the potential "danger" of effeminacy represented by Cooper's naturalist is quietly subsumed within Frémont's manly hero persona.

His courage sporadic, his speech comedic, Battius is a buffoon whose hyperbolized scientific rhetoric starkly contrasts with the unaffected country speech of Ellen Wade as well as the no-nonsense, backwoodsy talk of Natty Bumppo. Compared to the three other male protagonists—Natty, Paul the Bee Hunter, and the dashing army officer Middleton—Battius is a weak-willed scientist. Self-absorbed in the process of naming, describing, and cataloguing new species of plants and animals, he places complete faith in the project of taxonomic rationality, the concept of a world ordered by the Linnaean system. Though not a wholly unsympathetic character (Ishmael Bush fulfills the role of Cooper's primary antagonist), Battius is an absurdity, a person out of his element in the frontier ecosystem, where a different type of manliness and "reason" are needed. He embodies the intellectual East's ineffectiveness in dealing with the concept of wilderness. Battius represents in a negative sense the encroachment of white civilization upon "uncivilized" space. For Natty Bumppo, the ideal frontiersman, nature's logic in inherent in *things*, not names—the science of western space consists of being attuned to the vibrations of the land and the language that *it* speaks, rather than applying the artificial schema of taxonomic classification to the study of living things. The loss of mystery, of emptiness, that results from scientific scrutiny is something to be mourned.

From Cooper's narrative, a neat dichotomy summarizing these conflicts and oppositions emerges: scientist/frontier hero, feminine/ masculine, rational/instinctual, East/West, Old World/New World, passive/active. By contrasting the effeminate Battius with the aged-but- still-manly Natty, Cooper separates the scientific from the heroic and further suggests that science is irrelevant to living well within the western frontier. These distinctions, however, do not apply to Frémont, who appropriates the manly characteristics of Natty Bumppo while rejecting the effeminate and decidedly unheroic Obed Bat.[16] In his re- formulation, the explorer-scientist is heroic, active, and thoroughly rational.

As an icon created by his own narratives as well as by subsequent historical portraits, Frémont's physical appearance and bearing reflect that of Natty Bumppo, Daniel Boone, and others. In a passage more than reminiscent of Cooper, western historian and Frémont scholar Allan Nevins describes him as "a lithe, well-proportioned man, clad in deerskin shirt, blue army trousers, and thick-soled moccasins, with a cotton handkerchief bound around his head. His remarkable feature is not his curling black beard, aquiline nose, or high forehead, and not even his piercing eyes, but his air of intense energy. . . . He was a lover of action, a man of intensely kinetic temperament, craving outdoor pursuits" (2–3). Such an overly dramatic physical portrait is largely a construction of subsequent historians and biographers; rarely does Frémont describe himself in such detail. Nevertheless, several features of his exploration narratives contribute to the overall portrait of the scientist-hero. Part of this heroic posture consists of demonstrations of courage in the face of obstacles—Frémont narrates these moments of uncertainty and tension with relative understatement. On his first expedition, when Sioux representatives inform him of the danger of proceeding into a country plagued by drought and lack of available food and water, a member of the party urges him to call off the expedition. "In reply," Frémont writes, "I called up my men, and communicated to them fully the information I had just received. I then expressed to them my fixed determination to proceed to the end of the enterprise on which I had been sent; but as the situation of the country gave me some reason to apprehend that it might be [dangerous] . . . I would leave it optional with them to continue with me or to return" (*Narratives* 151). As legend has it, a frontier hero never quits in the face of potential physical hardship; indeed, he embraces it as the ultimate test of manliness. A stubborn devotion to physical endurance is a classic hallmark of exploration literature, whether it be of the West or of the polar regions.[17] The narrative's appeal is often in direct proportion to the degree of the hero's suffering, imagined or realized. Frémont's stalwart persona perfectly fits this requirement of the heroic explorer-scientist.

Frémont's narrative model proved useful for subsequent explorers of the American West, including geologist Clarence King (1842–1901), best known for conducting the "Fortieth Parallel Survey" in 1867, in which his party explored a hundred-mile swath along the planned route of the transcontinental railroad. In *Mountaineering in the Sierra Nevada* (1872), a popular text that recounted his surveying experiences in California, King plays the danger theme to the hilt. The scientist as mountain man takes the ultimate risks, and a potential fall from a precipice is even more gripping than the threat of gradual starvation on an empty prairie. Quite a large portion of King's heroic persona rests on his almost manic need to confront danger; more than Frémont, King paints himself as hungry for a challenge, for ways to prove his manhood in the mountains. His narrated exploits include everything from practically daring his companions to follow him on a dangerous climb to escaping several thieving desperadoes. In considering whether or not to attempt to climb a series of peaks that he considers to be the highest in California, King receives a "verdict of impossible" from two of his scientific companions. He then fashions a test of sorts for the remaining man in the party: "[T]aking Cotter aside, I asked him . . . whether he would like to penetrate the Terra Incognita with me at the risk of our necks, provided Brewer should consent. In a frank, courageous tone he answered after his usual mode, 'Why not?' Stout of limb, stronger yet of heart, of iron endurance, and a quiet, unexcited temperament [,] . . . Cotter was the one comrade I would choose to face death with, for I believed there was in his manhood no room for fear or shirk" (51). In this world of "do you dare?" scientific curiosity is closely associated with the confrontation of danger, with personal discomfort, with pain, with death-defying stunts—far indeed from Cooper's spineless Obed Bat, who runs in horror from a charging and obstinate mule, which he misclassifies as a hitherto unknown vicious beast of the prairie. A scientist of the West, according to these narratives, must be willing to risk his neck in order to achieve the God's eye gaze necessary to construct a map of the terrain.

The challenge taken and the risk survived, another aspect of the Frémont hero-persona comes into play—the statuesque and highly romanticized heroic pose atop a mountain: "Here, on the summit, where the stillness was absolute, unbroken by any sound, and the solitude complete, we thought ourselves beyond the region of animated life. . . . We had accomplished an object of laudable ambition. . . . We had climbed the loftiest peak of the Rocky Mountains, and looked down upon the snow a thousand feet below, and, standing where never human foot had stood before, felt the exultation of first explorers" (*Narratives* 176–77). Like the map-mediated perspective of the landscape, the heroic power of the explorer-scientist is based upon vision—the expansive gaze afforded by a climb is an act of possession, of initiation into the wilderness, of surveying the quiet landscape. The edict of the explorer-hero is to go where no one else has gone—Frémont feels he is the "first" and simultaneously takes communion with other explorers, such as Lewis and Clark, whose work he has read and admired. His mind captivated by undreamt-of space, Frémont sees himself operating within a tradition of heroic explorers. The male quest for adventure, as Richard Van Orman recognizes, has always been a search for an "instant of exalted vision" (138).

The vision metaphor is so powerful, Frémont evokes it as he explains his personal stake in exploring the West: "Shut in to narrow limits, the mind is driven in upon itself and loses its elasticity; but the breast expands when, upon some hilltop, the eye ranges over a broad expanse of country, or in face of the ocean [sic]. We do not value enough the effect of space for the eye; it reacts on the mind, which unconsciously expands to larger limits and freer range of thought" (*Narratives* 37). To see the landscape is to fulfill a psychological need—the sight of nature expands and sharpens consciousness. The passage glosses over the more tangible motivations for a nineteenth-century American explorer like Frémont—fame, adventure, potential political power, scientific accomplishment, patriotism—but it resonates with the belief that being in nature is a beneficial mental and emotional experience. In more theoretical terms, Frémont effectively links the God's eye visual paradigm and the psychological impulse to explore a wide-open space. His explanation also suggests that a profound desire to contemplate nature (an idea I pick up on and consider more carefully below) is an initial and thus important condition of scientific exploration.

Perhaps the most significant qualities of Frémont's heroic persona are those of detachment, self-control, and rationality; the scientist-hero legitimizes his stature and gains respect through the controlled use of knowledge and power. Reason is an analytical and observational tool, as well as a strategy of consistently choosing a reasonable course of action. The hero takes chances, but they are measured and calculated. Moreover, the hero has his emotions reined in—he is the cool observer; he advises moderation. Frémont achieves this effect by speaking "reasonably" from the position of unquestioned authority and by exploiting a foil hero of another stripe, that of Kit Carson.

Frémont portrays himself as a central but unobtrusive character in his recounting of a day-by-day journey overland. In his narrative voice, we can detect a certain reasonableness; a degree of restraint; a tone of objective authority reminiscent of "Steddy," William Byrd's amusing (and somewhat disingenuous) narrative persona in *The Secret History of the Dividing Line* (1728), an early American exploration narrative set in the swampy border country between Virginia and North Carolina. This perspective is evident, for example, in Frémont's stance toward Native Americans, whose culture and mode of existence he systematically assesses in terms of their physical environment. As Frémont notes,

In much travel among Indians I have had a fair opportunity to become acquainted with different tribes and learned to appreciate and comprehend the results of the differing influences brought to bear upon them. . . . I saw how their differing conditions depended upon their surroundings. In the Great Basin I saw them in the lowest stage of human existence, . . . differing from that of wild animals only in the greater intelligence of the Indians. . . .

Going upward, I saw them on the great prairie plains in the higher stages to which the surrounding facilities for a more comfortable and easier life had raised them. . . . And afterward in the nearer approach to the civilized life to which the intermittent efforts of the Government at agencies and reservations . . . had brought them. (*Narratives* 33–34)

Here Frémont describes the cultural distinctions and level of "advancement" against the normative standard of white civilization, a perspective reflective of nineteenth-century Euro-Americans' attitudes toward indigenous tribes and consonant with his opinion that Andrew Jackson's forced removal of the Cherokee nation from their southeastern homelands was "a wise and humane measure" (32). He attributes the quality and sophistication of the native cultures to both environmental influences and level of contact with white civilizing forces—the assumption here is that the Indians lack the capacity or motivation to significantly alter their environment, perhaps through lack of sophisticated technologies.

Accordingly, the Indians' stories and philosophies are mere superstition; Frémont recounts them with the air of a scientific authority whose basis for knowledge is assumed to be correct. His position needs no defense or elaboration—it is the standard against which irrational fear and beliefs can be measured and shown to be inadequate. He wryly notes that "The Indians have a belief that the Spirit of the Red Pipe Stone speaks in thunder and lightning whenever a visit is made to the Quarry. With a singular coincidence, such a storm broke upon us as we reached it, and the confirmation of the legend was pleasing to young Renville and the Sioux who had accompanied us" (*Narratives* 43). Frémont's paternal, somewhat amused attitude applies to the white trappers who accompany him as well: "As is usual with the trappers on the eve of any enterprise, our people had made dreams, and theirs happened to be a bad one—one which always preceded evil—and consequently they looked very gloomy this morning" (246). As the cool-headed, "steddy" leader, Frémont sees beyond the merely superstitious. Moreover, his position in the narrative voice almost fades into the background, muted and understated. Frémont's voice is unmarked because it is normative and authoritative: the scientist speaks from the position of knower. By contrast, it is the relatively nonscientific characters—the trappers, the Native Americans, and brash frontier figures such as Kit Carson—whom we glimpse most clearly.

Carson's subsequent fame in American popular culture has been attributed largely to Frémont's character sketches (Rolle 39). Within the exploration tales, Carson is the rough-and-ready renegade, responding emotionally to a given situation, taking out his restlessness on a wayward buffalo chase or aggressive posturing with perceived enemies. As the reasonable hero, Frémont must monitor and occasionally bring into line the mountain men like Carson. Frémont's complimentary descriptions of Carson echo John Filson's portrait of Daniel Boone, who in Filson's *Discovery, Settlement, and Present State of Kentucke* (1784) became larger than life. Frémont tells of Carson's inherent honesty as well as his skill as a plainsman: "Mounted on a fine horse, without a saddle, and scouring bareheaded over the prairies, Kit was one of the finest pictures of a horseman I have ever seen" (*Narratives* 97). But Carson functions as a foil for Frémont because his heroism has a troubling side: a distinct propensity for violence. On the second expedition of 1843–44, Carson and another man named Godey pursue Indians whom they believed had stolen horses and, finding them, punish the offenders by taking scalps—one of them from a man who was still alive. Frémont offers merely a mild criticism of the event: "Two men, in a savage desert, pursue day and night an unknown body of Indians into the defiles of an unknown mountain—attack them on sight, without counting numbers—and defeat them in an instant—and for what? . . . I repeat: it was Carson and Godey who did this . . . both trained to Western enterprise from early life" (404–5). In doing so, he maintains distance between himself and men such as Carson, whose brand of heroism is without measured judiciousness, and whose violent tendencies seem rooted in the land itself. The Frémont/Carson opposition, finally, accomplishes a more subtle rhetorical effect than merely providing the scientist-hero with a "subjective" foil: the scientist-hero and outlaw figure are mutually dependent, reinforcing one another's position as the exploring expedition enacts the process of westward expansion. When Frémont is forced to confront the ugly side of "Western enterprise," he contains the gratuitous act of violence by emphasizing, "it was Carson and Godey who did this." The scientist-hero thus transforms the otherwise inexplicable and inexcusable brutality involved with "winning" the West into a minor misadventure of the romanticized frontier outlaw.[18]

Feminine Nature, Masculine Science

The masculine scientist-hero is not the only gendered aspect of Frémont's exploration accounts, for the hero sits opposite an explicitly feminized nature. To conceive of the environment as woman was conventional both in literature and public discourse from colonial times onward; in his use of these metaphors within his exploration reports, Frémont thus represents commonly held views of nature in mid-nineteenth-century America.[19] Within a male-centered scientific perspective, this process of feminization is a means of objectifying nature, of increasing the distance between the scientist-hero and his object of study, of defining the natural world as that which is not me.[20] Just as Frémont must maintain distance from the frontier outlaw to avoid the potential contamination of irrational violence, the observer must separate himself from nature in order to better comprehend its characteristics and limits. But this impulse toward separation (i.e., toward a kind of objectivity) conflicts with the explorer's repeated and insistently sexual desire to know and conquer the feminine landscape. The highly emotive and erotic descriptions that pervade the texts of Frémont relentlessly refer back to the male scientist-hero and thus narrow the rhetorical gulf between man and nature.

At this point in which gender becomes central to my analysis of Frémont's narratives, I want to stress that his reports were not simple rehashings of his travel journals—they were careful revisions done in creative collaboration with his wife, Jessie Benton Frémont. The process was largely oral, with John sifting through details, anecdotes, memories, and scientific data and then dictating to Jessie. As Frémont notes,

I write more easily by dictation. Writing myself, I have too much time to think and dwell upon words as well as ideas. In dictation there is not time for this and then, too, *I see the face of my second mind*, and get there at times the slight dissent confirming my own doubt, or the pleased expression which represents the popular impression of a mind new to the subject. This invites discussion—a form of discussion impossible except *with a mind and purpose in harmony with one's own and on the same level*—therefore the labor of amanuensis, commencing at this early time [the winter of 1842–43], has remained with Mrs. Frémont. (*Narratives* 182, emphasis mine)

Clearly, Jessie Frémont, a highly prolific writer herself (her publications easily outnumber those of John), functions creatively in this relationship.[21] As the "face of [his] second mind" she gives feedback, draws out details, and chooses among particular phrasings and rhetorical tropes. Frémont's writings are the product of a dialogic process between two intellects that are, as he says, "in harmony." The collaboration of the Frémonts is noteworthy in at least two respects. Throughout much of her life, Jessie worked to uphold the heroic image of Frémont, even in their troubled times during the latter half of the century, long after Frémont's heyday as an explorer had waned and his reputation was damaged by a failed presidential bid. Discussing the genesis of Frémont's *Memoirs*, Jessie Benton Frémont's biographer Pamela Herr notes: "In her own writings she reined her desire to vaunt him, but she dreamed of producing a book that would make him a hero again.... [S]he wanted to restore his name, his image" (422). Thus we might conclude that the heroic persona constructed within Frémont's narratives owes as much, if not more, to Jessie Frémont's collaboration as to Frémont's view of himself.

The close collaboration of John Charles and Jessie Benton Frémont also disrupts the easy clichés about masculine and feminine literary conventions in nineteenth-century America, particularly with regard to the use of gendered metaphors. The gendering of nature and the romanticization of the explorer-hero have often been dismissed as mere rhetorical window dressing, designed to "lighten" the narrative. Such a claim is made, for example, by most commentators on the collaboration of Jessie and John Charles Frémont.[22] This assertion is based upon rather clichéd and sexist assumptions about male and female authorship in the nineteenth century—namely, that men write "rationally" and women write "emotively."[23] It also makes little sense of the above quote, in which Frémont describes himself and Jessie acting as one mind during the writing process. The fact that the gendering of the text may have had much to do with Jessie's creative powers raises interesting (and thorny) questions of authorship, intention, and cultural ideology. Most importantly, it suggests that mid-nineteenth-century conventions linking gender, science, exploration, and nature were not rooted exclusively within the sex of the author, but rather were part of a wider set of cultural assumptions and metaphors, which attributed feminine qualities to the natural world while ascribing masculine qualities to the practice of science.

Frémont's narratives partake of these cultural conventions not only in the portrayal of the explorer as hero but also in the characterization of nature as a virginal female, a wilderness that entices the scientist-explorer:

> The thought of penetration into the recesses of that wilderness region filled me with enthusiasm—I saw visions. . . . It [the expedition] would be travel [sic] over a part of the world which still remained the New—the opening up of unknown lands; the making unknown countries known; and the study without books—the learning at first hand from Nature herself; the drinking first at her unknown springs—becomes a source of never-ending delight to me. I felt that it was an unreasonable pleasure to expect that it might happen to me to be among the very few to whom the chance had fallen to work with Nature where in all her features there was still aboriginal freshness. (*Narratives* 76)

This passage is remarkable for its expression of the "manly" exploration impulse, the desire to explore unknown space; it would be difficult to find a more erotically charged description of the scientist's relationship with nature. For Frémont, scientific-sexual union with a feminine territory is a mystical experience, filled with both heady excitement and immense pleasure; the conjugation must be with virginal land in order to be meaningful. The acquisition of scientific data mirrors sexual penetration, where the pleasure of discovery is the primary impulse. Note, too, how Frémont contrasts the (sexualized) act of exploration and the (asexualized) abstract study of books. True science, as well as manliness, demands concrete observation via the senses, rather than merely abstract theorizing.

As in romance, the explorer's object of amorous attentions presents certain obstacles in the path of love's consummation. While overlooking a "deep valley, which was entirely occupied by three lakes" and surrounded by steep cliffs, Frémont remarks that "[i]t seemed as if, from the vast expanse of uninteresting prairie we had passed over, nature had collected all her beauties together in one chosen place. . . . [T]he green of the waters, common to mountain lakes of great depth, showed that it would be impossible to cross them. The surprise manifested by our guides when these impassable obstacles suddenly barred our progress proved that they were among the hidden treasures of the place" (168). Here nature is a charming female, who tantalizingly lays obstacles in the path of scientific knowledge. Such challenges, far from discouraging him, pique Frémont's desire; the formidable obstacles display a provocative beauty but also present a titillating challenge to the skills of the manly scientist-hero. Moreover, Frémont is confident that what he finds once those barriers are overcome will be equally fascinating: "The depths of this unexplored forest were a place to delight the heart of a botanist" (168), who thrills at the expectation of being the first to encounter a plethora of plant and flower species to observe, name, classify, and collect. Against the challenge of dwindling food supplies during his second expedition, Frémont and his companions speculate "on what tomorrow would bring forth[;] . . . we fancied that we should find every one of the large islands a tangled wilderness of trees and shrubbery, teeming with game of every description that the neighboring region afforded, and which the foot of a white man or Indian had never violated" (245).

The gendered motif of a bewitching, female nature actively placing obstacles in the way of male knowledge can be traced in the writings of geologist and explorer Clarence King as well. For King, the feminization of a landscape is a variable phenomenon, dependent upon the season and the local climate; he is obsessed with contrast, the extremes evident in nature's design. At a mountain pass in the Sierras, King is able to view two extreme climatic systems simultaneously, a green humid valley to the west (California) and a barren desert to the east (the Great Basin). The latter inspires him to observe: "There is no sentiment of beauty in the whole scene; no suggestion, however far remote, of sheltered landscape; not even the air of virgin hospitality that greets us explorers in so many uninhabited spots which by their fertility and loveliness of grove or meadow seem to offer a man a home, or nomads a pleasant campground" (*Mountaineering* 78–79). Here we are presented with a space defined neither maternally nor virginally, though King explicitly recognizes both metaphors. In King, the lack of sentimentality, receptivity, or beauty seems to threaten the very project of exploration by erasing the necessary force of male desire. In the terms of eighteenth-century English philosopher Edmund Burke, King sees in the desert the essence of the sublime, the potential horror of a tiny, exposed human struggling to survive within a vast field of desolation. Such a scene contrasts mightily with the view to the west, where the aesthetics of the "beautiful" (sublime's opposite) are apparent. Notably, in this passage, King reserves his gendered metaphors ("virgin," "fertility," "loveliness") for the landscape of pastoral beauty.

The feminine beauty of the environment is not always comforting, however. Like Frémont, King thinks of nature's aesthetic beauty as an obstacle set in the path of the scientist-hero. Unlike Frémont, though, whose "botanist's heart" is stirred by the pastoral vision of the land, King believes that it is primarily in the "shattered fronts of walls," the "broken crag and cliff," where knowledge follows the most direct route from observed to observer. In the spaces of land where cataclysmic forces have wrought fissures and chasms, tremendous outcroppings of rock, and cross-sections of the earth's crust, feminine nature's secrets are most readily ascertained: "In this cold, naked strength, one has crowded on him the geological record of mountain work, of granite plateau suddenly rent asunder, of the slow, imperfect manner in which Nature has vainly striven to smooth her rough work and bury the ruins with thousands of years' accumulation of soil and *débris*" (*Mountaineering* 134). For King, the landscape is only informative if the scientist-hero can view nature in a naked state, imperfect, without (to use his metaphor) cosmetic alteration. Thus, the virginal pastoral vision, articulated by Frémont as a source of desire for male consciousness, itself acts as a mask of geologic processes. For King, the aesthetically unified scene can be inviting, because this vision offers shelter and sustenance to the explorer. More importantly, however, nature in its virginal garb hides the truth, the book of geologic change: "the magic faculty displayed by vegetation . . . [redeems] the aspect of wreck and . . . [masks] a vast geological tragedy behind draperies of fresh and living green" (184). It is only the imperfect, jarring scene that provides valuable knowledge about the earth. King is hardly writing as the enchanted lover when he effectively equates the "rough work . . . of soil and *débris*" with the "magic faculty . . . [of] vegetation." Both aspects conceal the truth about nature. The metaphor of nature as woman thus has a dual effect for King: on one hand, the virgin female's aesthetic beauty is appealing, even compelling; on the other, the deceptive female who hides her true appearance is threatening, profoundly unsettling.[24]

In contrast to Frémont, King's desire to contemplate nature's beauty can conflict with the scientific impulse, a tension evident not only in the descriptive passages quoted above but also in King's more introspective moments. When a paleontologist questions King's dedication to science and his tendency to idly gaze upon natural scenes, he wonders, "Can it be? . . . has a student of geology so far forgotten his devotion to science? Am I really fallen to the level of a mere nature-lover?" (*Mountaineering* 178). But the tension is less between desire and science and more between two different *kinds* of desire. In science, "you hold yourself accountable for seeing everything, for analyzing, for instituting perpetual comparison, and as it were sharing in the administering of the world"; but in the more spiritual contemplation of the landscape, "Nature impress[es] you with those vague indescribable emotions which tremble between wonder and sympathy" (126). Here the emotions stimulated by contemplation of the sublime in nature conflict with the practice of science (i.e., the intellectualization of nature). King evokes the traditional opposition of reason versus emotion: in contrast to Frémont, King's emotional responses to nature, whether provoked by the sublime or the beautiful, conflict with the attitude of scientific detachment.

Finally, instrumental technology serves as an intriguing link between scientific exploration, the characterization of the scientist-explorer as a hero, and the representation of nature as female in Frémont's exploration accounts.[25] Barometers, thermometers, chronometers, and sextants are the means by which the explorer-scientist extends the range and amplifies the sensitivity of his normal bodily perceptions, especially the visual, a relationship between body and technology that philosopher Don Ihde calls an "embodiment relation."[26] For Frémont as well as for other nineteenth-century explorers, instruments are not neutral tools merely to be used casually and put away. Their importance is difficult to overestimate—Lewis and Clark's expedition, for example, suffered from inconsistent chronometers, and thus an important component of their survey work (longitude) was suspect.

Instruments provide concrete, quantitative information with which the scientist-explorer can objectify a feminine nature. Read figuratively, instruments are the means of sexualized "penetration"—without them, the scientist forever remains on the surface of things, observing forms and cataloguing shapes; with them, the scientist gains empirical knowledge needed to construct a map, to bring the land into the realm of the known, to define pathways through the landscape that facilitate white settlement and control of native populations. Instruments perceive the empirical "truth" behind nature's "fresh and living green." But owing to the phenomenon of "embodiment relations," they also reflect Frémont's construction of the scientist-hero persona. Repeatedly he writes of his anxious concern for the instruments' safety, discusses the necessity of repairing the barometers, or mourns the accidental destruction of an instrument—indeed, one suspects that Frémont values the technology more than his own health (*Narratives* 137, 148, 152, 206). Moreover, the instruments gain an erotic charge; the same sexual metaphor employed in his descriptions of nature applies when discussing the human-instrument relation, as a passage from Frémont makes clear:

> I met with a great misfortune in having my barometer broken. It was the only one. A great part of the interest of the journey for me was in the exploration of these mountains . . . and now their snowy peaks rose majestically before me, and the only means of giving them authentically to science, the object of my anxious solicitude by night and day, was destroyed. . . . The loss was felt by the whole camp— . . . all had looked forward with pleasure to the moment when the instrument, which they believed to be true as the sun, should stand upon the summits and decide their disputes. (165)

Frémont's tone is of a disappointed, frustrated lover—his suit has been in vain. The metaphoric leap from barometer to phallus is propelled by the sexual imagery: the feminized mountain peaks, the tone of thwarted desire, the loss of pleasure, the denial of knowledge. Moreover, his admission that the barometer represents "the only means of giving them authentically to science" further cements the close relationship between instrumentally mediated science and the construction of a male heroic persona. In Frémont, the two concepts are inseparable. And, one page later, we see the resourceful Frémont cleverly repairing (reforging) his barometer (sword)—the conquest of the land will continue, we are assured.

John Charles Frémont was the archetypal scientist-explorer of the mid-nineteenth century, a watershed time in American history. The country was expanding west at an ever-accelerating rate, forming new communities and bringing new areas of land under cultivation. The line of the frontier itself had shifted from what is now the Midwest to the plains territory, the trans-Missouri region. The science of exploration was changing as well, with new improvements in surveying technology and cartographic representations fostering ever-more detailed and realistic depictions of the landscape. Frémont played a central part in this national expansion, and his work reflected the impact of emerging technologies and emphasis upon the empirical study of nature. Even more significantly, Frémont crafts an appealing public persona in his exploration narratives—the quaint naturalist of earlier times is replaced by the heroic figure of the scientist-explorer. This representative of science looks to conquer the American landscape by bringing it within the range of his vision. Frémont's narratives incorporate the conventional view inherited from previous eras of nature as female and set this opposite the cool rationality of science, as embodied in the explorer-hero. Such metaphors create a psychological distance between humanity and nature, as the land becomes an object to be studied, catalogued, and mapped.

TWO

"The Evidence of My Ruin"

Richard Byrd's
Antarctic Sojourn

Nearly a century after Frémont's 1842 expedition to the Rocky Mountains, aviation pioneer and polar explorer Richard Evelyn Byrd set out to do some serious science on the Ross Ice Barrier in Antarctica. As part of his second expedition to the southernmost continent, he stayed alone at a remote weather station—named Bolling Advance Base and located at 80° 8′ south latitude—during the polar winter of 1934, the season when darkness becomes total and temperatures routinely dip below −70 degrees Fahrenheit. The station was a rudimentary, claustrophobic structure: a prefabricated hut buried in the ice, its presence marked only by a radio antenna and a compact instrument shelter. Over the course of several months, Byrd recorded meteorological data to correlate with those collected at the Little America station—his expedition's main base—approximately one hundred miles to the north, in an attempt to "throw a highly revealing light on the facts of atmospheric phenomena in high southern latitudes" (Byrd, *Alone* 13). Byrd planned to conduct a more personal experiment as well: "Solitude," he felt, "is an excellent laboratory" in which to test the self-sustaining powers of the human mind and body in extreme environmental conditions (139). His efforts, however, proved costly, for during his stay he was slowly poisoned by the fumes of his generator and cook stove that built up in his poorly ventilated enclosure. Byrd was rescued on the verge of death by his companions, after they interpreted his garbled and nearly unintelligible Morse code radio messages as a cry for help.

This plot line suggests that Byrd's published account of his experience, *Alone*, can be read as a moving tale of human bravery and perseverance in the face of a brutal and unforgiving nature, an interpretation invited by the 1939 appearance of an abridged version of *Alone* in the widely read repository of inspirational literature, *Reader's Digest*. Such a take on Byrd's story is right in step with his own conclusions about his stay at Advance Base: "Part of me remained forever at Latitude 80° 8′ South: what survived of my youth, my vanity, perhaps, and certainly my skepticism. On the other hand, I did take away something that I had not fully possessed before: appreciation of the sheer beauty and miracle of being alive, and a humble set of values" (295). Beyond the affirmation of human fortitude and the celebration of life regained, however, Byrd's musings suggest that a tremendous loss occurred as well as the obligatory gain of spiritual enlightenment. He lists the things he learned, or took away, from Advance Base—the joy of life, the value of living simply and honestly—but just as eloquently cites what was taken away from him.

Alone is, of course, much more than an inspirational story and a good yarn, though it is certainly both of these. The *Reader's Digest* portrait of Byrd, however appealing, does not adequately address the complex relationships among Byrd, nature, and the science he claims to serve. In fact, *Alone* provides us with something much more substantial—an ongoing account of an experiment, reported in exceptional detail and with great candor, that tests the relation between one explorer-scientist and his environment, the extreme conditions of Antarctica. Though Byrd fashions his adventure partly as a scientific quest and partly as a Thoreau-styled attempt to live in peaceful, soul-replenishing solitude, the Antarctic environment overcomes Byrd's best efforts at living harmoniously within nature: an inexorable process of disintegration and dissipation results in Byrd's near destruction. Thus while Byrd's scientific efforts succeed in terms of the meteorological data set (the weather record his instruments gather, we learn, is complete), he fails to reach his secondary goal of living efficiently and productively in an enclosed, artificial life-support system within the polar environment. In ironic contrast to the Frémontian hero's mastery of scientific instrumentation, Byrd's authority is usurped by the technology he brings with him. Rather than being symbolic instruments of nature's conquest by humanity, the barometers, thermometers, wind meters, and radios dictate the terms of Byrd's day-to-day existence and expose his lack of technical mastery. If control exists at Advance Base, it is within the workings of the meteorological instruments rather than Byrd himself. *Alone* thus portrays a transformed and psychologically complex explorer-hero: one who embraces the prospect of harmonizing with nature even as he grapples with almost unimaginably difficult living conditions, who questions his position and authority as a scientist, and whose faith in rationality and the scientific method belie his struggle to maintain control over his surroundings.

Polar Exploration in Context: Technology, Geopolitics, and Colonialism

The ice-encased continent of Antarctica has held a fascination for explorers and scientists for the last several centuries, an interest inspired by Antarctica's status as both a pristine landscape and an area of impressively barren sterility. Antarctica's exploration history is singular— it is one of the few instances where an indigenous human population has not been displaced, divided, or conquered by an invading group. As historian Stephen J. Pyne notes, the process of exploring the southern continent "would not be encumbered by the spectacle of clashing cultures, but neither would it be enriched by their interchange" (68). This is not to say, however, that issues of nationalism, borders, and cultural difference have not come into play below sixty degrees south latitude.[1] For example, the historical claims of possession established by Great Britain, Chile, and Argentina (currently unrecognized by the Antarctic Treaty Organization) overlap geographically, a situation that has caused considerable international friction in the past.[2] Moreover, during the flurry of Antarctic expeditions undertaken by various countries in the early part of the twentieth century, explorers from ostensibly "neutral" nations such as the United States made symbolic claims of possession, even as other nations—including Britain, Argentina, Chile, and Norway—were making explicit territorial claims and counterclaims (Pyne 336).

Byrd is the major U.S. figure within this geopolitical setting, and he proved adept at combining personal achievement in exploration and aviation with the impulses of nationalism as well as the work of science. The Advance Base mission was only one component of the much larger "Discovery" expedition Byrd organized, funded, and led from 1933 to 1935.[3] The Discovery effort was, in fact, Byrd's second major Antarctic project, the first being the "Little America" expedition in 1928–30, during which Byrd and his crew became the first to fly over the South Pole.[4] Yet even before the much-publicized events of the Little America project, Byrd had established himself as a popular American figure with his flight over the North Pole in 1926 and the nonstop trans-Atlantic flight the following year (Rodgers 10–12). Both flights reflected Byrd's interest in promoting the fledgling aviation industry by demonstrating the capability and safety of aircraft.

Little America—the name Byrd gave to the base his group established near the edge of the Ross Ice Barrier—functioned as an important media buzzword for Byrd's first Antarctic trip, which was closely covered by the press (to that end, the expedition was equipped with a full-time correspondent for the *New York Times*, Russell Owen). Up to the point where the expedition was disembarking and unloading supplies onto the Barrier surface, press releases had referred to the landing site as Framheim, Amundsen's name for the base he established on his run to the pole. Byrd, at someone else's suggestion, chose the name Little America to offset use of the old name and to imbue the expedition with a stamp of "American-ness" that he hoped would endear him to his benefactors at home (Rodgers 70).[5] The name endowed the expedition with a pseudo-colonial function—by implication, the Antarctic continent became an extension of U.S. territorial possessions and political concerns. Here we get some idea of Byrd's position within the complex geopolitical problem that Antarctica presented in the first half of the twentieth century. The U.S. position on Antarctica at the time of Byrd's expeditions had been articulated by Secretary of State Charles Evans Hughes, who argued that any nation's claims of possession (including those of the United States) were meaningless unless supported by "effective occupation." In other words, "The U.S. would not advance any claims in Antarctica, but neither would it recognize the claims of anyone else" (Pyne 335).

Despite this pronouncement by the United States, Byrd—America's most powerful link to the Antarctic continent—staked a type of claim when he described the newly reestablished Little America II as the "capital city of Antarctica" and extolled its "boom town" growth (Byrd, *Discovery* 113). Indeed, Little America represents Byrd's early efforts to establish effective occupation and thus secure a leading-edge position for the United States in Antarctic exploration and scientific research. His expedition flights frequently featured the dropping of claims documents upon the surface of the Antarctic interior, and he proved to be fond of naming geographical entities after his family, friends, and benefactors (e.g., Marie Byrd Land, the Rockefeller Mountains). The American government did not designate these activities, performed under the rubric of scientific exploration, as formal acts of possession. Nevertheless, naming territory and landforms and establishing Little America represented for Byrd significant symbolic gestures that would provide, in his view, a basis for any future American claims upon the Antarctic.[6]

The first two Byrd expeditions occupy a key transitional point in the technological history of Antarctic exploration and scientific efforts (Fogg 134–46; Pyne 99–108). Byrd's large-scale efforts were the most visible of scientific expeditions in Antarctica between, on one hand, the "Heroic Age" of Amundsen, Shackleton, Scott, Nordenskiöld, Mawson, and others in the first two decades of the twentieth century, and, on the other, the post–World War II era of "big science," as signaled by the proliferation of research stations and the multinational coordination of scientific work in the International Geophysical Year of 1957–58. Byrd's programs introduced the use of key technologies that remain a staple of Antarctic research and logistical support to this day: effective radio communication, mechanized ground transport, short- and long-range aircraft support, and aerial photography.[7] All of these fundamental technologies were crucial in establishing the *scientific* basis of Antarctic exploration. Though many of the earlier explorers, such as Scott, gave considerable priority to performing scientific research, their scientists' efforts were necessarily limited by their inability to communicate over distance and the slowness of traveling by dogsled or man-hauling sledges. In their case, survival—not science—became the primary focus of activity while traveling. The contrast is articulated by Byrd in his description of the South Pole flight: "A wing, pistons and flashing propellors had taken the place of runners, dogs, and legs. Amundsen was delighted to make 25 miles per day [in his journey to the South Pole]. We had to average 90 miles per hour to accomplish our mission" (*Little* 329).

Byrd's implementation of "modern" technologies anticipates the thoroughly technology-dependent state of Antarctic science since the late 1950s. Reliable and efficient electronic communication, routine ground and air transport, and the establishment of self-contained, self-regulating, life-support stations characterize the human presence in Antarctica today. With the advent of computer and satellite technology, data collection can be accomplished by automated, unmanned stations and remote devices; bits of information may then be relayed to researchers at larger bases or at laboratories and universities thousands of miles away (Fogg 151–52). In a very concrete sense, then, science in Antarctica now has much less to do with individual heroics (with the notable exceptions of the daring rescue flights undertaken in recent years to evacuate sick researchers at the South Pole Station): mere survival is taken care of by a combination of life-support and logistical technology and a massive superstructure of specialized support personnel. Scientists, consequently, are able to spend a great deal of their time and energy performing research tasks rather than eking out a tenuous existence in the inhospitable conditions.

Such comparative luxury was not the case, however, in 1934. Like the Heroic Age explorers (such as Scott, Amundsen, and Shackleton) of a generation earlier, Byrd combined an interest in discovering new lands with perfecting the techniques of survival. Staying alive in the world's driest, coldest, and windiest continent was still a task not to be taken for granted in the 1920s and 1930s. Even so, Byrd approached the question of survival from a decidedly *experimental* standpoint: his Advance Base was a testing ground for cold-weather gear and survival techniques as well as a site from which to gather weather and astronomical data. Moreover, the scientific ambitions of the Byrd expeditions were impressively comprehensive in scope and detail. Indeed, Byrd's claims for the scientific utility of his missions foretold the formulation of Antarctica as a giant outdoor laboratory ideally suited to studying globally scaled natural processes and scientific problems.[8] He enthusiastically summarizes the role of science in his account of the Discovery expedition:

> Looking at it in the broad way, there are few divisions of science, or sections of human knowledge, that cannot be profitably explored in Antarctica.
> Geology, glaciology, meteorology, botany, biology and zoölogy,

astronomy, physics, geography, terrestrial magnetism, oceanography, geophysics and paleontology—these and many others hold open broad avenues of research. In all, the second expedition was equipped to investigate and did investigate some 22 divisions and subdivisions of scientific research. . . . I believe that we all pride ourselves on having achieved, by a fair margin, the most complete program of scientific research in the history of polar exploration. (*Discovery* 4–5)

Within this vision, *Alone* is part of a grand scientific narrative Byrd began writing in 1930 (with the publication of *Little America*) and continued working on during the 1930s and beyond. The autobiography represents, in some sense, a mere fragment of Byrd's overall Antarctic experiences—we must read it as one chunk of Byrd's narrative of scientific exploration. Yet, of all his prose, the text most poignantly and informatively depicts the complex relationships among science, nature, and Byrd himself.

An Experiment in Living: The Thoreau Connection

In his preface to *Alone*, Byrd announces that what we are about to read is a "story of an experience which was in considerable part subjective" (vii). He thus contrasts the subject matter of *Alone* with that of his other books, *Little America* and *Discovery*, which are "factual, impersonal narratives of my expeditions and flights" (vii). Byrd's convenient dichotomy of subjective versus objective prose, though, is probably a bit too quick and easy. Both accounts draw (and quote) freely from Byrd's personal journals, both are told for the most part from the first-person point of view (albeit a rather authoritative first person), and both examine at length not only the raw sequence of scientific and logistical activities of each expedition but also the social aspects of daily life at Little America I and II. We might more accurately state that Byrd uses the term "subjective" here to flag *Alone* as a personal story—part of yet separate from the larger, comprehensive narrative of the accomplishments and movements of the Discovery expedition. *Alone* is a subtext to *Discovery* in this respect, an articulation of events hidden in the silent spaces of the larger narrative.[9] The voice of *Alone* promises disclosure, the revealing of events, issues, and thoughts not contained in an "objective" account. And for Byrd, disclosure means bringing unpleasantries to the surface instead of suppressing them: "I appreciated that

I should be obliged to discuss matters of personal moment in a way that would be distasteful. But . . . I shut out the doubts and agreed to go ahead" (viii). In stating that by its very honesty, *Alone* "represents the simple truth about myself and my affairs during that time" (viii), Byrd promises both a revealing autobiographical portrait and a historically accurate account of his mission. Nevertheless, Byrd finds that a detached perspective on the recent past is impossible—telling the story necessitates a painful emotional involvement, a reliving "of some of the bitter moments of Advance Base" (vii). What intrigues me most is not the issue of whether Byrd gives us a historically "accurate" account.[10] Rather, it is important to note that *Alone* is both a day-by-day account of scientific practice and a personal, autobiographical meditation, an exploration of the self as well as of nature.

Byrd's self-imposed isolation is a variation upon the theme of Henry David Thoreau's two-year sojourn at Walden Pond, a connection that Byrd invites by his occasional references to the iconoclastic Massachusetts pencil maker, writer, and social critic. Like Thoreau, Byrd sees his project as a spiritual as well as scientific endeavor and, to this end, finds intrinsic value in voluntary solitude. As leader of the Discovery expedition, he could assign any of the men to the Advance Base post; yet Byrd chooses to go himself. His decision is largely motivated by "one man's desire to know that kind of experience to the full, to be by himself for a while and to taste peace and quiet and solitude long enough to find out how good they really are" (*Alone* 4). Solitude enables one to look inward and examine the soul's spiritual workings and capabilities. Like Thoreau, Byrd sees the "complexities of modern life" as a source of distraction, a hindrance to the attainment of self-knowledge. He looks forward to establishing a simple routine, while indulging a few pleasurable distractions such as reading long-neglected books and listening to music on a gramophone. Thoreau's command, "Simplify, simplify" (Thoreau 173), mandates the rejection of material luxuries, economic concerns, standards of fashion and decorum, social convention, and so on. For Byrd, "It was all that simple. And it is something, I believe, that people beset by the complexities of modern life will understand instinctively. We are caught up in the winds that blow every which way. And in the hullabaloo the thinking man is driven to ponder where he is being blown and to long desperately for some quiet place where he can reason undisturbed and take inventory" (*Alone* 4).

Even the shelter utilized by Byrd—the simple, box-shaped, prefabricated hut that is sunk into the Barrier ice—is analogous to Thoreau's humble cabin. Both afford the comfort of solitude, the simplicity and coziness of close quarters, the economy of minimal accoutrements. Each place symbolizes an effort to counteract the ravages of contemporary society upon one's spiritual integrity. As Byrd says while contemplating the emptiness of the Barrier and the modest array of instruments atop his hut, "A man had no need of the world here— . . . half the confusion in the world comes from not knowing how little we need" (57).

Yet, there is a more than subtle difference between their respective shelters, a difference rooted in the relationship between an individual and his or her immediate environment. Thoreau's house exists as a part of a seamless connection between himself and the natural world. His home is not a defensive structure, but a mediating presence: "This frame, so slightly clad, was a sort of crystallization around me, and reacted on the builder. It was suggestive somewhat as a picture in outlines. I did not need to go out doors to take the air, for the atmosphere within had lost none of its freshness. It was not so much within doors as behind a door where I sat, even in the rainiest weather. . . . I found myself suddenly neighbor to the birds; not by having imprisoned one, but having caged myself near them" (Thoreau 168). By contrast, in Byrd's sealed, well-stocked, purposefully designed living space, the goal is not connection to the world but rather a life-sustaining isolation from it: "the means of a secure and profound existence were all handy, in a world I could span in four strides going one way and in three strides going the other. It was not a bright world" (*Alone* 53). Lurking beneath the security and efficient design of Advance Base is its all-important function of isolating and protecting Byrd from the dangerously inhospitable polar environment. Rather than allowing a creative interaction between Byrd and nature, Advance Base insulates Byrd from outside conditions. Byrd's sojourn becomes the ultimate "turning inward," eclipsing even the symbolic solitude of Thoreau, who rejects many of civilization's trappings but wholeheartedly embraces nature.[11] As a mere matter of survival, Byrd must construct a viable, self-contained world within his tiny shelter and, to a great extent, reject nature along with civilization. Thoreau strives to make his home a "natural" abode (witness his enthusiasm for the "advantages" of his dirt floor), but Byrd's Advance Base is a scientifically designed (and even pretested at Little America) artificial living environment, where all the resources needed to sustain life must be imported from the civilization Byrd is temporarily escaping. And unlike Thoreau, who can live off the land (and does, for the most part), Byrd can only live *within* and in spite of the land, drawing from his carefully hoarded stores in two supply tunnels adjacent to his hut.

Thus far, all this sounds much like a romantic investigation of the self, a spiritual looking inward. But Byrd is hardly a solipsist—he also seeks to gain empirical knowledge about the world outside his immediate surroundings. Indeed, an important connection between Byrd and Thoreau is the notion of an "experiment," an idea that is evoked by Thoreau in the Concord woods and carried to a far greater (i.e., more explicitly empirical) extreme by Byrd in the polar environment. Thoreau uses the word at least once, when he refers to his sojourn as "my own experiment" (Thoreau 135); I also detect an empirical tone within one of the more frequently quoted passages from *Walden:* "I went to the woods because I wished to live deliberately, to front only the essential facts of life, and see if I could not learn what it had to teach . . . . I wanted to live deep and suck out all the marrow of life . . . to drive life into a corner, and reduce it to its lowest terms, and, if it proved to be mean, why then to get the whole and genuine meanness of it, and publish its meanness to the world; or if it were sublime, to know it by experience" (172–73).

As Byrd says, Advance Base is a "quiet place where he can reason undisturbed" (*Alone* 4). Though the project carries spiritual overtones, the key principle of Byrd's endeavor is the rational application of scientific method: "Advance Base was no reckless whim. It was the outcome of four years of planning" (11). The product of purposeful design, Advance Base is also the means by which empirical observation will be brought to the as yet unexamined weather of the Antarctic interior. Thus Byrd's mission is an experiment in several important senses: it seeks to quantitatively measure climatic and astronomical phenomena, to test the quality and effectiveness of cold-survival techniques and gadgets, and to explore the psychological effects of extreme isolation. "Solitude," Byrd says, "is an excellent laboratory in which to observe the extent to which manners and habits are conditioned by others" (139). Method, consisting of observation and logical analysis, unifies both of these activities. Consequently, by reading *Alone* as a life experiment, we understand its connection between the personal and the scientific.

Out in the Cold: Byrd's Relationship with Nature

As suggested by the parallel with Thoreau, part of Byrd's project is to replenish his spiritual self not only by looking inward but also by experiencing and contemplating the rhythms of the natural environment, a goal ultimately at odds with his imperative to survive the Antarctic cold. Byrd is attracted to the prospect of quiet observation, the cold air against his skin, the clean, empty white of the Barrier thousands of miles away from an urban center, the utter silence of a landscape almost entirely devoid of life, human or otherwise. Just as minimal distractions, a definite routine, and a wealth of free time for reflection constitute the search for simplicity, the barren, ultra-simplified Barrier landscape itself highlights this process. A sparse natural environment implies a pure mode of existence and inspires a sense of personal connection with nature, an "exalted sense of identification—of oneness— with the outer world" (*Alone* 120). The clean austerity of the polar environment also strikes Byrd as aesthetically powerful:

> The night was spacious and fine. Numberless stars crowded the sky. I had never seen so many. You had only to reach up and fill your hands with the bright pebbles. . . . A sailor's sky, I thought, commanded by the Southern Cross and the wheeling constellations of Hydrus, Orion and Triangulum drifting ever so slowly. It was a lovely motion to watch. And all this was mine: the stars, the constellations, even the earth as it turned on its axis. If great inward peace and exhilaration can exist together, then this . . . was what should possess the senses. . . . The Barrier, austere as platinum, was world enough; and onto it I had trespassed but little. (57)

Byrd's language here is a nearly ecstatic celebration of infinite space and the sharp, clean aesthetics of stargazing. Yet while his description emphasizes the vastness of the night sky and the "numberless" quantity of stars, the controlling image is that of the empowered, all-encompassing self, which in the rapturous moment of observing nature has the potential to "reach up" and collect stars as if they were "bright pebbles." The act of quiet contemplation inspires Byrd to grand claims of symbolic ownership: "all this was mine . . . , even the earth as it turned on its axis." By planting himself at the southern hub of the globe, Byrd not only escapes the ravages and entrapments of modern Western society, but also declares instant possession of what he surveys. Just as the scientific outpost at Little America II—a microcosmic American society—stakes a symbolic claim upon the continent, so Byrd claims the firmament and the rotating earth in the process of connecting with nature.[12] Yet this claim is tempered by a respect for the special qualities of this "austere" world, as he notes that "onto it I had trespassed but little."

As in John Charles Frémont's nineteenth-century exploration reports, moments within Byrd's narrative reveal a connection between this claim of ownership and the feminization of nature. In language reminiscent of Frémont's erotic descriptions of the American West, Byrd describes the dramatic fluctuation of the southern aurora: "Where it [the auroral colors] had been only a moment before, the sky was once more clear; the stars showed as if they had never been dimmed. When I looked for the luminous patch in the eastern sky, it, too, was gone; and the curtain was lifting over the pole, as if parted by the wind which at that instant came throbbing over the Barrier. I was left with the tingling feeling that I had witnessed a scene denied to all other mortal men" (*Alone* 109). Here the observing, masculine subject revels in the contemplation of a "virgin" scene, one that has been "denied to all other mortal men" and that therefore carries an erotic charge. This somewhat voyeuristic scene portrays nature as a feminized object defined by and existing in opposition to the male explorer's gaze.

This brief moment in *Alone* connects with a key social aspect of Antarctic exploration: as Byrd notes in a mid-May journal entry, Antarctica "is the one continent where no woman has ever set foot," a fact that inspires him to wryly comment that "I can't say it is any better on that account" (142). The observation reminds us that Antarctic exploration science until the mid-twentieth century was a male-only enterprise. Little America and other expedition camps were places of masculine camaraderie (and rivalry); the southern continent, devoid of an indigenous human population, literally constituted a new and seemingly limitless arena for heroic exploits without the disturbing prospect of intercultural conflict. With the legacy of Scott, Amundsen, and

Shackleton's early-twentieth-century heroics as well as the implicit nationalistic impulses driving Byrd's explorations, it would seem that the relation between Byrd the explorer and the Antarctic landscape would be defined most appropriately by gender.[13] Indeed, upon first reading Byrd years ago, I fully expected his story to replicate and even exaggerate the romanticized and highly gendered metaphors of nineteenth-century exploration literature.

Yet Byrd's relationship to the Antarctic environment, surprisingly, bears little resemblance to Frémont's fantasies of conquest. Part of this stems from the character of the Antarctic environment itself. In contrast to the rich and arable North American landscape (Powell's arid regions notwithstanding), the Ross Ice Barrier upon which Byrd's station sits inspires no vision of fertility and agricultural bounty. For Frémont, conquering the land meant quantitatively assessing its resources, mapping its contours, and facilitating its settlement and cultivation. For Byrd, "conquering" is too strong and dramatic a word, for there is little to bring back—no timber, game, or native goods, no pathways to chart to distant towns, no trading routes to map and secure. The barren void of the Barrier landscape simply does not fit the gendered vocabulary of nineteenth-century landscape description. For this reason, I suspect, explicitly gendered rhetoric surfaces very infrequently in Byrd's account. Immediately after the above quoted passage, for example, Byrd states: "Even in my most exalted mood I never quite lost the feeling of being poised over an undermined footing, like a man negotiating a precipice who pauses to admire the sunset, but takes care where he places his feet. . . . Rime was forever choking the stovepipe, ventilators, even the exhaust duct . . . [a]nd, though walking had always been my principal relaxation, I almost never dared to get out of sight of the anemometer pole" (109–10). Byrd's persona quickly shifts from a confident admirer of nature to a trepidatious visitor within an inhospitable climate. As his simile suggests, the Antarctic explorer gazes upon nature from unsolid ground—Byrd has little time to leisurely observe his world and instead must focus his attention upon the mundane technological problems of maintaining proper ventilation and staying warm. Thus, rather than being linked with metaphoric desire (as in Frémont's case), technology becomes primarily a potential cause of difficulty and even unease. Byrd's claim of ownership and the potentially erotic response to nature thus give way to the stark realization of the extreme *limitations* of his position as a single human being within a vast, nearly featureless landscape.

Byrd's observations of the polar night sky and the Barrier weather also inspire his eloquent philosophy of "harmony," in which he views humanity serving an integral and purposeful role in the operation of the universe. Like William Paley, the theologian who over a hundred years before Byrd saw in the complexity and intricacy of the natural world profoundly powerful evidence of rational and divine design (God as universal architect—the divine "watchmaker"),[14] so Byrd (without explicitly evoking a higher consciousness) feels that the "rhythm [of the universe] was too orderly, too harmonious, too perfect to be a product of blind chance. . . . There must be purpose in the whole[;] . . . man was part of that whole and not an accidental offshoot. . . . The universe was a cosmos, not a chaos" (85). Byrd rather effortlessly combines a holistic, Thoreau-inspired transcendentalism with a view of a rationally designed, mechanistic universe. On one hand, human beings are purposeful subjects, whose control and observation of nature are legitimated by their status as integral parts of the (mechanical) system. At the same time, his language suggests a decidedly organic relationship: humans and nature seamlessly participate in a unified, universal consciousness, both elements part and parcel of the whole.

Such a combination suggests that Byrd's contact with nature is wholly positive, a model of ordered and benevolent interaction; "My whole life here," he notes, "in a sense is an experiment in harmony" (106). Yet an altogether different theme emerges from Byrd's account. Though aesthetic and spiritual nourishment seem to flow unidirectionally from the environment to human consciousness, the Barrier Ice ultimately saps Byrd's energy, acting as a physical, mental, and spiritual drain upon him. "The gloom, the cold, and the *evenness* of the Barrier are a drag on the spirits," he admits (238). Such an exchange process is, according to Stephen J. Pyne, a defining characteristic of the Antarctic environment:

> Antarctica is the Earth's great sink, not only for water and heat but for information. Between core and margin there exist powerful gradients of energy and information. These gradients measure the alienness of The Ice as a geographic and cultural entity. The Ice is profoundly passive: it does not give, it takes. The Ice is a study in reductionism. Toward the interior everything is simplified. The Ice absorbs and, an

imperfect mirror, its ineffable whiteness reflects back what remains.
. . . Cultural understanding and assimilation demand more than the
power to overcome the energy gradient that surrounds The Ice: they demand the capacity and desire to overcome the information gradient. (7)

The great "absorptive" character of Antarctica, Pyne argues, distinguishes it from all other landscapes, from any other place of human
habitation; humans are the "great anomaly" within the Antarctic
ecosystem (55). Unlike the indigenous emperor penguins or Weddell
seals, we are ill-adapted creatures who must bring all basic requirements for life along with us, creating a life-support shell in which to
enclose ourselves. To survive, to thrive, human beings must import the
devices of civilization as well as survival, for The Ice is an aesthetic as
well as an energy sink. In Pyne's view, blankness, obscurity, and noth-
ingness soon overcome all efforts of human understanding and artistic representation.

Byrd's experiment is a case study that dramatically verifies Pyne's
thesis. Once darkness completely shuts out the sustaining presence of
light, once the brutally cold temperatures have descended upon the
Barrier and penetrated the flimsy insulation of Byrd's hut, Byrd's relationship with nature undergoes a marked change. The profound lack
of aesthetic input from the surroundings, the overpowering silence of
the place excepting the howl of the winds and ticking of the instruments, the sluggish movements resulting from the cold—all begin to
wear upon Byrd's state of mind. Despite his doggedly positive outlook
on his daily existence, Byrd finds himself "craving change—a look at
trees, a handful of earth . . . anything belonging to the world of movement and living things" (142). But the Antarctic environment acts not
just as a blank slate or a harmless mask of neutrality—it swallows even
the effort at producing meaningful language: "Sometimes, while walking, I talk to myself and listen to the words, but they sound hollow and
unfamiliar" (140).

As Byrd's physical and mental health steadily deteriorates, the power
of the negative energy gradient becomes all too apparent. "Harmony,"
instead of signifying a positive, creative interaction between human
consciousness and outside environment, instead signals what a weakened and somewhat discouraged Byrd calls a "process . . . in the direction of uninterrupted disintegration" (197). Though he tries to take

comfort in his philosophy of humanistic affirmation, his disintegration is driven by climatic forces of extreme cold and darkness. The neat order of Advance Base as a life-support system collapses: "[A]ll around me was the evidence of my ruin. Cans of half-eaten, frozen food were scattered on the deck. The parts of the dismantled generator were heaped up in a corner, where I had scuffed them three weeks before. Books had tumbled out of the shelves, and I had let them lie where they fell. And now the film of ice covered the floor, four walls, and the ceiling. There was nothing left for it to conquer" (270). There is no order on The Ice—Byrd's imported framework of rational philosophy and scientific planning, a tiny pulse of concentrated physical and cultural energy, is pulled inexorably down the Barrier's energy gradient.

This entropic process, the dissipation of energy from Byrd to the vast environmental sink of heat, information, and aesthetics, is not merely a passive occurrence. Byrd actively resists the movement toward disintegration by attempting to impose reason and regularity upon his day-by-day existence. In order to retain his sense of daily structure as well as his mental integrity, Byrd doggedly applies various rational methods in the losing effort to exert control. Just as he once uses an improvised system of ordered trial and error to grope his way to his buried shelter (after having lost his bearings while on a walk in the darkness), so he hopes to prevent madness and death "by taking control of my thought. By extirpating all lugubrious ideas the instant they appeared and dwelling only on those conceptions which would make for peace. A discordant mind . . . would finish me off as thoroughly as the cold" (190). By husbanding his resources (food, fuel, and bodily energy) and disciplining his state of mind, Byrd hopes to control his destiny, to deny the environment his heat and information. He is so convinced of this strategy's efficacy (and desperate for it to succeed) that his language, paradoxically, takes on a tone of religious incantation: "But you must have *faith*—you must have faith in the outcome, I whispered to myself. . . . You must go on and on and on, trusting your instruments, the course you have plotted on the charts, the reasonableness of events. Whatever goes wrong will be mostly of your own making; if it is to be tragedy, then it will be the commonplace tragedy of human vulnerability" (174). Note that Byrd locates this potential failure squarely within a broad notion of "human vulnerability"; as he says, "whatever goes wrong will be of your own making." By placing the onus of responsibility on his individual will and endurance, he shifts the focus away from method—that is, the application of objective, rational thought. But because Byrd's life experiment is so deeply embedded within the discourse of control, observation, rational inquiry, and experimentation, his personal disintegration can also be read in terms of the inability of science, technology, and rational planning to master nature. His physical and mental deterioration in the face of a powerful, unrelenting, harsh environment mark a chilling counterpoint to Frémont's confident vision of science conquering the frontier West.

Byrd's gradual disintegration thus marks a dramatic change in his relationship to nature during his stay at Advance Base. Initially filled with a Thoreau-like wonder at the profound if minimalist beauty of the polar environment, Byrd soon realizes that any communion with the outdoors will be severely limited—if he is to briefly admire nature with the gaze of the explorer-hero, it will be through a frozen mask of ice and with numbing limbs and feet. His experiment in harmony becomes a brute effort at survival; his world a dark, dank, and cramped hut set in the midst of a vast ice field. The nineteenth-century imperative to conquer a feminized landscape simply does not apply, as the Barrier Ice suggests none of the possibilities for settlement and agriculture that so motivated Frémont and other explorers of the American West. The land-as-female metaphor gives way to the notion of The Ice as energy and information sink; the ice, wind, and total darkness of Byrd's world preclude anything but respect for the incredible power of nature and the imperative to survive.

Collecting Data: Technology and the Scientist-Hero

Byrd's stay at Advance Base is further complicated by the ironic reversal of power that occurs between him and the various weather instruments he tends. Instead of remaining passive tools controlled by a confident and knowledgeable scientist-hero, the meteorological instruments rule the day, dictating Byrd's daily schedule and reducing his energy to such a degree that he nearly becomes a slave to the objects under his watch. Such a relation between narrator and instrumental technology differs significantly from that in Frémont, for whom instruments are both the tools of quantitative analysis and a motif of masculinity. In this nineteenth-century "embodiment relation," the scientist-hero is clearly the site of authority: the scientific instruments, like nature itself, are passive. In *Alone*, however, technology becomes active and takes on a life of its own: instead of merely being used, the instruments exercise their "will" upon the hapless Byrd. In contrast to Frémont's romantic persona, Byrd becomes an increasingly powerless tragic hero as the narrative unfolds, his health and presence of mind nearly disintegrating before the workings of instrumental technology just as it does in the face of the Antarctic environment.

Unlike Frémont, who seldom indulges in self-analysis, Byrd reflects at length upon his status as a "scientific explorer." He freely admits that he is somewhat ill-fitted to the role of scientist: he possesses neither the in-depth knowledge of the professionally trained theorist nor the sophisticated tinkering skills of the accomplished technician. Ultimately, he is a liminal figure, occupying an ambiguous position along the spectrum of scientific know-how. While taking stock of his mental and physical state in the early stages of his incapacitation, he muses: "We men of action who serve science serve only a reflection in a mirror. The tasks are difficult, the objectives remote; but scholars sitting in bookish surroundings tell us where to go, what to look for, and even what we are apt to find. Likewise, they pass dispassionate judgment on whatever we bring back. We are nothing more than glamorous middlemen between theory and fact, materialists jobbing in the substance of universal truths" (179). Here Byrd makes an intriguing, if unsurprising, distinction: on one hand, trained "scholars sitting in bookish surroundings" possess theoretical expertise and thus represent the arbiters of scientific authority (or, as Byrd puts it, "dispassionate judgment"). These voices are defined by their passivity, their stasis, their residence within a comfortable shelter of authority—they constitute the nameless and faceless aspect of the institutionalized scientific community. Byrd almost seems to resent these invisible subjects, and the great geographical distance between them only augments their power. In contrast, Byrd views himself as a "man of action," part of the twentieth-century tradition of polar adventurers such as Robert Scott (for whom he expresses profound admiration) and, by implication, earlier American explorers such as Frémont and Powell (61). He embraces the persona of the rugged, independent explorer-hero who, in spite of possessing a lesser sum of knowledge, is the "active" agent that grants the "passive" theoreticians access to the material world; yet he also displays an ironic detachment from that persona by recognizing its "glamorous" trappings (a likely reference to both his fame and the fact that his highly visible public life is necessary to finance his expeditions). This dual perspective is evoked early in the narrative as Byrd describes his plans and preparations for the Advance Base mission: he takes pride that his "service as an explorer" had made him self-reliant even as he admits that he "was not nearly as handy as I had imagined" (32). Much later, in the midst of his despair, Byrd's profound failure to live up to such an impossible heroic standard moves him to recognize the very limitations of such a persona: "I was a fool, lost on a fool's errand" (179).[15]

One of the most compelling narrative threads of *Alone* is the story of how Byrd's personal autonomy is usurped over time by the very technology he supposedly maintains and controls. Byrd is responsible for a set of deceptively straightforward tasks, the reading and maintenance of assorted weather instruments—wind register, thermographs, barographs, hygrometer. In addition, he must maintain regular radio with Little America using a temperamental radio set and a Morse code transmitter. But as he wryly notes early on in his sojourn, "I was not long in discovering one thing: that, if anything was to eventually regularize the rhythm by which I should live at Advance Base, it would not be the weather so much as the weather instruments themselves" (62). The admission suggests not only Byrd's dependency upon the instruments' behavior and maintenance needs but also the profound degree to which he must insulate himself from the outside environment. Soon afterward, he tellingly reveals: "If I had any illusions as to being master in my own house, they were soon dispelled. The instruments were masters, not I; and the fact that I knew none too much about them only intensified my humility" (64). Rather than being an active authority (as he is back in the community of Little America, where he gives orders and supervises activities), Byrd is *acted upon* by his instruments, which mercilessly dictate his sleep patterns and his daily routine. This reversal of power also detrimentally affects Byrd's spiritual quest: he escapes the distractions and "complexities of modern life" (4) only to encounter a new and perhaps equally stifling set of responsibilities and baffling problems in his Antarctic outpost.

Byrd's personal disintegration with respect to technology is characterized best by his sometimes comical and nearly tragic misadventures with his radio. The communication between Advance Base and Little America is not fully reciprocal even from the relatively even-keeled start of Byrd's mission—the home encampment, using more sophisticated equipment, can transmit voice, but Byrd, using a more primitive apparatus, can only respond fumblingly in Morse Code (65). A full-fledged discussion on the Little America end is answered by a one- or two-sentence reply pecked out slowly by Byrd. To complicate matters even further, Byrd's battery-powered radio fails; he is forced to use his hand-cranked backup set, just as long-term exposure to fumes from the stove and generator makes him sick and reeling from dizziness and confusion. His ability to communicate is directly dependent upon his physical ability to provide power to the set, and in his weakened state, cranking is no easy task. It is all Byrd can manage to send out a word or two and to receive sporadic messages. Such is his frustration that his sense of rational cool-headedness gives way to paralyzing emotion: "From the beginning I had loathed the radio; now I hated it with a hate that transcended reason. Every day it left me helpless for hours" (268). When he does communicate, his transmissions are fictions, or "lies" as he puts it, for though he maintains a superficial optimism, the men at Little America read his silences as much as his sporadic codings as a warrant for a rescue mission. His ability to report data, to function efficiently as a scientific observer, slips further and further away as his physical deterioration increases.

Just as Byrd may access his fellow human beings at Little America only through the temperamental radio set, his experience of the outside environment is likewise dictated by the meteorological instruments. And while Byrd seems to draw strength from the hypnotic regularity of the instruments and the faithful accumulation of data, his relationship with technology is parasitic, with him as hapless host.

> I dare say that every ounce of egotism has been knocked out of me; and yet, today, when I looked at the small heap of data in the tunnel, I felt some stirrings of pride. But I wish that the instruments did not always make their demands, even though they require little actual strength. How pitilessly resolute and faithful they are. In the cold and darkness of this polar silence they steadfastly do their appointed jobs, clicking day and night, demanding a replenishment I cannot give myself. Sometimes, when my body is aching and fingers won't obey, they

appear utterly remorseless. Over and over they seem to say, "If we stop, you stop; if you stop, we stop." (202–3)

Though Byrd feels some "stirrings of pride," his sense of self-worth, the easy confidence he has formerly displayed, has been "knocked out." His "aching" body and disobedient fingers stand in stark contrast to the dependable, methodical operation of the weather instruments. Within such a setting, the power of technology contrasts with the vulnerability of the human subject. Byrd is the weak cog in the information-gathering apparatus that is Advance Base. What science that is done there—the gathering and recording of raw data—is handled almost entirely by the instruments themselves: environmental stimuli are detected, converted to electrical impulses, converted again to ink traces upon graph paper, and plotted against time. The process is almost self-perpetuating, as Byrd is needed merely to make sure the various detectors (for example, the anemometer cups) and electrical contacts are free, and that paper and ink are supplied. Though he tells himself that "without me they could not last a day," he is oppressed by the methodical action, the relentlessness of the instruments: "The clocks ticked on in the gloom, and a subdued whir came from the register at my feet. The confidence implicit in these unhurried sounds emphasized my own debasement. What right had they to be confident and unhurried?" (178). The weather instruments thus become the active agents of authority rather than the passive tools of an all-knowing scientist. In a parallel transformation, Byrd's personal deterioration reveals him to be a debased servant, rather than an omniscient controller, of the scientific process.

Rather than simply an inspirational story of human perseverance and self-affirmation, as the *Reader's Digest* version of Byrd's account would suggest, *Alone* dramatically depicts the breakdown of the explorer-hero in the face of oppressive environmental and technological conditions, as well as the inherent dependency of scientific inquiry upon human frailties and limitations. Byrd hoped to achieve a harmonious relation between himself and nature by applying reason and science to his state of mind as well as his physical environment. What results from his Thoreauvian experiment, however, is a profound lack of harmony. Byrd's attempts to impose order and regularity to his day-by-day existence cannot prevent him from being poisoned nearly to death by the toxic fumes of his generator. His self-described status as a "glamorous" scientist-explorer "jobbing in the substance of universal truths" does not save him from becoming a servant to the meteorological instruments he supposedly controls.

Alone poignantly dramatizes the dark side of exploration. Byrd's story is not a sanitized parable of conquest but a brutally revealing drama of human weakness and uncertainty, an anti-heroic account of tragic mishap and personal failure. Byrd's adventure is thus a fascinating counterpoint to the narratives of John Charles Frémont: for the Frémontian hero, not only does instrumental technology produce quantitative data about nature, but it also is a powerful and erotic extension of the self, enabling the explorer-scientist to symbolically conquer a feminized nature. Byrd's narrative, by contrast, depicts not a conquering scientist-hero but a vulnerable human subject seeking self-knowledge, spiritual replenishment, and communion with the natural world, goals that he never rejects even as he struggles to survive and maintain control over his claustrophobic surroundings. Instead of acting as passive extensions of the male self, the weather instruments that signify the scientific purpose of Byrd's mission take control, wresting authority from the human subject. Nevertheless, Byrd maintains great faith in the rational basis of science, a faith exemplified by his attempts to gather empirical knowledge about the Antarctic weather through the use of instrumental technology, maintain a comfortable living space within an inhospitable environment by careful planning and scientific management, and reverse the dangerous process of self-disintegration by the rational exercise of self-control. His failure in the last two objectives, though, combined with the tremendous cost of gathering the weather data, signifies the limits of scientific practice that were unacknowledged in Frémont's vision for the conquest and human occupation of the American West ninety years earlier.

Imagined Communities and
the Scientific Management
of Nature

■ THREE ■

"A Strange and Terrible Woman Land"

Charlotte Perkins Gilman's
Scientific Utopia

W hile the exploration narratives of Frémont and Byrd produce a complex portrait of the individual within nature—a perspective through which we gain insight into the relations among masculinity, heroism, science, and the environment—the writings of Charlotte Perkins Gilman shift the discussion from the role of the individual to the structure and function of the community within nature. A prolific author, outspoken feminist, and progressive intellectual, Gilman (1860–1935) published everything from philosophy to journalism to utopian fiction and was best known for critiquing the prevailing social conventions regarding the role of women in American society. This chapter focuses on one of her most widely read works, the utopian novel *Herland* (first published in serial form in 1915), a polemical critique of exploration science, gender roles, androcentric values, and social relations. Gilman's narrative not only challenges conventional biases against women but also comments upon the relationship humanity forges with nature; Herland society explores the possibility of reestablishing a vital connection between human society and the natural environment, even as it illustrates Gilman's abiding faith in the early-twentieth-century goals of progress and the control of nature.

The narrative framework of *Herland* addresses the practice and aims of exploration science in an insightful and humorous way and thus serves as an implicit commentary on the adventure narratives of

Frémont, Byrd, and other explorers. The novel exposes the gender biases of the Frémontian explorer-scientist and portrays him as less of a hero—and far less rational and objective in his assessment of women and nature—than he imagines. Gilman thus pokes fun at an American institution dating from the early frontier days, but more significantly she exposes the inherent weaknesses in any practice of science that casts itself in androcentric terms. The novel consequently suggests that scientific inquiry is not value-free after all, but rather a projection of male assumptions, interests, and biases upon the study of the natural world and human culture. Despite these views, though, Gilman also maintains an abiding faith in the scientific method and a steadfast dedication to progress, and she uncritically advocates the intensive technological management of nature. Her idealized, all-woman society lives in apparent harmony within the natural landscape, and certain aspects of this relationship demonstrate rather progressive ecological insights. However, the Herlanders exercise profound and systematic control of everything from the production of fruit and vegetables to the control of insects to the rearing of children. Gilman's early-twentieth-century utopia thus implicitly rejects the nineteenth-century explorer-scientist's goal of conquering nature, even as it depicts the seemingly benevolent but absolute scientific management of a local landscape. More generally, the novel's primary tension is emblematic of conflicting currents flowing through the broader American culture of the early twentieth century: the development of large-scale environmental management projects such as irrigation and forestry, which exemplify broad support for the scientific control of nature, and the advent of passionate arguments for wilderness preservation and resource conservation from naturalists, ecologists, and outdoors enthusiasts.

Bringing Exploration into Question

As a highly imaginative utopia as well as a well-argued piece of social criticism, *Herland* has been described as "an example of Gilman's playful best" (Jane v). Originally published in 1915 by Gilman in her ambitious one-woman periodical, the *Forerunner* (which ran from 1909 to 1916), the novel was written at approximately the midpoint of Gilman's distinguished career as a social activist, traveling lecturer, and writer.[1]

A dedicated feminist, she also espoused socialism, spurred on by her reading of Edward Bellamy's *Looking Backward* (1888). Respected during her lifetime for her literary efforts and intellectual skills, she remained largely neglected until the 1970s, when her work was reevaluated and reappreciated by feminists, literary critics, intellectual historians, and others.[2] Gilman is perhaps best known for her autobiographical short story "The Yellow Wallpaper" (1892), an exploration of personal insanity, and *Women and Economics* (1898), a social-historical critique that garnered her wide recognition in America and beyond (Jane viii). *Herland* is actually the second of a series of three utopian works by Gilman: the first, *Moving the Mountain*, appeared in 1911, and *With Her in Ourland*, the follow-up to *Herland*, was published in 1916. Her final authored work was her 1935 autobiography, *The Living of Charlotte Perkins Gilman*.

Herland, though in form somewhat different from most of Gilman's writing, nevertheless contains key themes important to her during her career—the questioning of gender roles, women's work, and social reform. The novel's basic plot is straightforward: three male explorers on a scientific expedition (most likely in the South American interior) learn of a "mythical" all-female society from the local natives and decide to mount a follow-up expedition on their own to investigate the rumor. While successful in finding the lost country of women, they are decidedly poor diplomats, and the Herland women suffer the explorers' excessive bravado and poor judgment only to a point. When the men panic after being surrounded and start firing their guns, the Herlanders subdue and detain them. An early escape attempt fails miserably, as the men are easily outsmarted by the patient, watchful Herlanders. They are well-treated prisoners, and their largely uneventful stay in Herland society is Gilman's vehicle for a series of spirited, back-and-forth discussions of such topics as sexuality, gender roles in society, the meaning of the "home," reproductive strategies, economic theories, Darwinism, social progress, the composition and function of the "community," religion, sports, and education. Without being mean-spirited, the novel thoroughly indicts the injustice, inequality, and fundamental illogic present in contemporary American society, as represented by the three male explorers. Gilman's narrative persistently challenges what it means to be female, as well as the values and interests behind the notion of the "feminine." For Gilman, "woman" is not a natural (biological) category, but rather a social construction subject to reevaluation and improvement. The women of Herland manage, often in humorous fashion, to undermine the male explorers' assumptions of what women are and should be like.

This summary suggests that the skeletal plot of male explorers captured by female society is necessarily subordinate to the "larger" concerns and issues dealt with in the dialogue between the American men and the Herlanders. Such a narrative device is *Herland*'s "MacGuffin," the term filmmaker Alfred Hitchcock gave to the scenario or gimmick that gives a story its excuse for being, but that is ultimately unimportant. With all due respect to Hitchcock, however, my analysis of Gilman's novel highlights the very process of exploration that gives *Herland* its push toward action.[3] Our three male scientist-adventurers —Terry Nicholson, Jeff Margrave, and Vandyck Jennings—proceed on a vaguely described "big scientific expedition" whose aim is to map unknown territory (2). They begin their endeavor in the classic fashion of explorer-heroes: full of confidence, spurred on by stories of local inhabitants (whom they recruit for bodily labor), they are attracted to the romantic danger of exploring a "strange and terrible Woman Land" (2). Despite assuming that an all-female society will be passive, the men travel armed: they expect to meet some degree of male resistance. Until they actually view Herland, they doubt (while fantasizing about) its existence: the implication is that only the colonizer's empirical inquiry can verify or disprove the nonscientific stories of the native population.

Like many Euro-American travelers and explorers of colonial America, the American West, South America, and Africa, *Herland*'s scientist-explorers are quick to consider the "new" ground they are covering as a potential economic resource and wellspring of personal profit. Upon hearing natives describe a river on a map as "red and blue," Terry (the most headstrong of the three) exclaims, "Let's go . . . Just us three. Maybe we can really find something. May be cinnabar in it" (3).[4] Gilman also establishes a strong connection between the desire to explore a feminized landscape and the desire to possess the human female. Both of these impulses are, from the very beginning of the novel, overtly sexualized. Danger, unknown territory, and sexual fantasy combine to initiate the male project of conquest:

We had our rest and lunch right there and pumped the man for further information. He could tell us only what the others had—a land of
women—no men—babies, but all girls. No place for men—dangerous.
Some had gone to see—none had come back.

I could see Terry's jaw set at that. No place for men? Dangerous?
He looked as if he might shin up the waterfall on the spot. . . .

"Look here, fellows," he said. "This is our find. Let's not tell those
cocky old professors. Let's go on home with 'em, and then come
back—just us—have a little expedition of our own."

We looked at him, much impressed. There was something attractive to a bunch of unattached young men in finding an undiscovered
country of a strictly Amazonian nature. (5)

The metaphor of land as female can also work in the other direction,
that is, female as land, suggesting the two terms are essentially inter-
changeable. The usual formula (as we see in exploration narratives such
as Frémont's) is to describe the land in sexualized terms. At points in
Herland, though, the opposite is true, as in Van's description of the
process of coming to know his wife, Ellador: "Suppose you come to a
strange land and find it pleasant enough—just a little more than ordi-
narily pleasant—and then you find rich farmland, and then gardens,
gorgeous gardens, and then palaces full of rare and curious treasures—
incalculable, inexhaustible, and then—mountains—like the Himalayas,
and then the sea" (89). In this rhapsodic passage, the growth of a relationship is likened to the process of exploration.

Furthermore, the scientist-explorers' views are based upon the familiar dichotomy of nature versus civilization, in which nature is coded
nonwhite and female while civilization denotes white and male. The
men assume that if the natives' belief in Herland is true, the community's culture will be ill-advanced: as Terry states, "we mustn't look for
inventions and progress; it'll be awfully primitive" (8). Soon, though,
they spot from the air "a land in a state of perfect cultivation, where
even the forests looked as if they were cared for"; the village displays
"clean, well-built roads . . . attractive architecture . . . ordered beauty"
(11). To our explorers, all these signify civilization and, by consequence, *men*. Their first interpretation is that the native mythos is simply false, that men (who are somewhere present) are ultimately responsible for these technological and architectural achievements. Even

after being captured by the Herlanders, and despite seeing no male in-habitants, the explorers are reluctant to admit that the well-planned architecture and technologies they encounter could have been de-signed and made by women. Later, while evaluating the building in which they are detained, Terry remarks, "This thing is a regular fortress—and no women built it, I can tell you that." Jeff concurs: "We saw some kind of swift-moving vehicles the first day . . . If they've got motors, they *are* civilized" (29).

We soon realize that Gilman is setting up the three scientist-explorers—and us—for a dramatic reversal of these assumed distinc-tions. Before long, Terry, Jeff, and Van discover that women, indeed, and *only* women are responsible for the technological and civil won-ders they experience. But Gilman does not merely prove wrong the male assumptions about "women's nature" and their capacity to pro-duce and use technology. *Herland* is a spoof as well as serious social criticism, and Gilman is skilled at turning events humorously upon themselves. The explorer-heroes prove to be far less than heroic: Terry's first blunder—taking an ill-advised shot at an unarmed group of women who initially surround the curious trio—is a rash act of cow-ardice. Later, when the fellows attempt an escape from the Herland confines, their flight ends unsuccessfully after a few days and in a de-cidedly unheroic manner: "They knew well we would make for our machine [plane], and also that there was no other way of getting down—alive. So our flight had troubled no one; all they did was to call the inhabitants to keep an eye on our movements all along the edge of the forest between the two points. It appeared that many of those nights we had been seen, by careful ladies sitting snugly in big trees by the riverbed, or up among the rocks" (44). Finally, the three explorers do not accomplish the logical end of their original mission, which is to open up the hitherto isolated Herland community to the outside world and thus pave the way for possible colonization. Terry, who would most strongly advocate such a strategy, is banished from the Herland society after attempting to rape his Herland wife, Alima. Van leaves with his wife, Ellador, to show her the outside world—both Terry and Van promise (rather conveniently) not to reveal the location of Herland. Jeff, married to Celis, stays on in the female society and rejects entirely his native country. The resolution, however improbable, is thus in favor of an uncolonized Herland.

Such a denouement suggests that *Herland* is a condemnation of colonialism, for not only does the exploration and colonization process go awry, but the Herland society is convincingly shown to be superior to that represented by the male explorers. However, as critic Thomas Galt Peyser has pointed out, "[s]uch a reading . . . [relies] too heavily on the assumption that a refusal to portray the existent [social structure] amounts to a rejection of social order, overlooking the possibility that even a vociferously adversarial ideal can underwrite dominant ideology" (1). In fact, our male adventurers are not the only (would-be) colonizers: the Herlanders themselves are of "Aryan stock," a people who were "once in contact with the best civilization of the old world." The original country, with a population consisting of both sexes, was a colonial power, one that utilized native slave labor (*Herland* 54–55). Thus, we find *Herland* complicit with what Peyser calls "an international theme: . . . the imperialist ventures of European powers" (Peyser 10). Gilman's critique of the exploration process should therefore be recognized as distinct from a wider and more profound condemnation of twentieth-century colonialism and racism.[5]

Critiquing Male Science

Underlying Gilman's satire of the male explorer-hero is an artfully constructed challenge to the status quo of scientific practice and the links between science and gender. Science was, at Gilman's time, a burgeoning and increasingly authoritative set of professional disciplines, and women were affected both positively and negatively by these changes. On one hand, women's educational and employment opportunities in science increased greatly during the second half of the nineteenth century. On the other hand, feminist historians of science argue that the process of professionalization was a reaction to what men identified as a "crisis of impending feminization" of science (Rossiter xvii). The formation of elite, all-male societies and professional groups comprised a strategy of "containment" and set limits to women's participation in science. The result was that women's considerable advancement in science by 1940 "occurred at the price of accepting a pattern of segregated employment and under-recognition" (xviii).[6] *Herland* challenges this state of affairs in at least two ways: by undermining the male explorer-scientists' claim to authority and objectivity, and by detailing the Herlanders' scientific activities and technical knowledge, which are not only extensive but also highly influential on how they manage their community and their relation to nature.

Gilman paints her three male explorers with different psychological and professional profiles, and they represent archetypal extremes. Terry, an independently wealthy playboy for whom exploration is a hobby, represents what are popularly known as the "hard" sciences: he is "great on mechanics and electricity" as well as an expert in vehicles and aviation (2).[7] Van, the novel's narrator, sums up Terry's abilities by noting that he is "strong on facts—geography and meteorology and those" (2). Not surprisingly, Terry is also the most aggressive and "masculine" of the trio: a certified womanizer at home, he is overconfident about his ability to seduce the Herland women and is greatly frustrated by his profound failures to do so. Gilman uses Terry as a foil for the other men—he is a classic male chauvinist, convinced of women's inherent inferiority and content to consider them merely as convenient sexual objects or nurturing, homebound mothers. He is also the only one of the three who resorts to violence as a means of resistance. In short, Terry's character embodies expertise in abstract, theoretical, quantitative science as well as overt masculine aggression and sexuality.

Jeff, by contrast, is a mild-mannered physician with proficiency in zoology and botany; his scientific knowledge is complemented by, according to his friend Van, the temperament of a poet (2). This combination connotes an almost "feminine" sensitivity (by American, and not Herland, standards), making Jeff's personality the polar opposite of Terry's. Even so, Jeff's attitude toward women is just as limiting. He consistently categorizes women in his own manner: "Jeff's ideas and Terry's were so far apart that sometimes it was all I could do to keep the peace between them. Jeff idealized women in the best Southern style. He was full of chivalry and sentiment, and all that. And he was a good boy; he lived up to his ideals" (9). While Terry strives to conquer and control women, defining them as sexual objects, Jeff objectifies women by placing them on a pedestal to be worshipped. In spite of his courtier attitudes, though, Jeff assimilates rather easily into the Herland social system. In Jeff's case, then, Gilman links the disciplines of botany and medicine—once the provinces of women's knowledge and expertise—with the character who is most sympathetic to the views of the Herlanders and who is most quickly "converted" to their beliefs and customs.[8]

Such descriptions place Terry and Jeff in extreme, nearly opposite positions, both psychosexually and scientifically, characterizations suggesting that both men view the world in a decidedly biased manner. As we might expect, their contrast leaves plenty of room in the middle ground, where we find Van. A sociologist by training, Van repeatedly describes himself as the most rational and even-headed of the three (2, 124). But though he is critical of both Terry's and Jeff's views toward women, Van seems to operate from within a peculiar sociobiological perspective, one with its own, less dramatic biases: "I held a middle ground, highly scientific, of course, and used to argue learnedly about the physiological limitations of the sex" (9). Van strives to be objective, to free himself from any emotional impulse, yet he is—at least early on—inflexible concerning the assumed inferiority of women. However, we know that Van narrates the story from a later perspective and that he views himself somewhat ironically. He admits to us, early on, that "with all my airs of sociological superiority I was no nearer than any of them" to predicting the basis of the Herland society. While the male chauvinist, Terry, is an easy target for Gilman's restrained ridicule, the sociologist's remarks are occasionally shown to be pedantic as well as absurdly wrong. After their first face-to-face meeting with three girls of Herland, whom the men find perched within a grove of trees, Van declares: "Inhabitants evidently arboreal . . . Civilized and still arboreal—peculiar people" (17). As she does throughout the novel, Gilman here pokes fun at the self-important scientist's tendency to formulate a quick overgeneralization. The statement exemplifies the men's general impulse to jump to conclusions concerning the Herland society—not to mention their inability to comprehend anything different from their own experiences. In the course of the novel, though, Van's story is one of gradual conversion—by degrees, his arrogance diminishes and he is persuaded of the superiority of the Herland culture to his own.

The psychological and scientific profiles of each of the male characters of *Herland* suggest that although the variety of scientific "types"—the aggressive, physical scientist; the sensitive, worshipful biologist; and the rational, detached social scientist—are exaggerated, they are connected with specific ways of treating women. But *Herland* does more than simply ridicule classic male stereotypes—the novel forces us to confront the issue of each man's status and profession as part and parcel of his psychological makeup. It is not just that *men* are sexist toward women, but privileged, well-educated, scientifically trained men in particular. Moreover, science itself reinforces and lends legitimacy to the male assumptions about women, not to mention those about the way the world operates in general. Gilman's trio of scientist-explorers are caricatures, but they are nevertheless effective archetypal characters who aptly represent the culture of the male scientific community.

Besides linking science with sexism, *Herland* also reveals other, disconcerting connections, such as the close relationship between science and violence. The novel makes no such explicit, general statement, but a few brief moments speak to such an association. One instance occurs when the three men, having been confined, awake from an anaesthetized sleep. They make a thorough search of the room to ascertain their situation, before Terry speaks up: "A council of war! . . . Now then, my scientific friend, let us consider our case dispassionately" (25). In this context, "dispassionate" simply means systematically considering—without prior prejudice—all possible "solutions" before choosing the most expedient toward a desired end (escape). Here, "science" and "objectivity" are conflated. Terry, the aggressor, is not calling for a literal war, of course—he does not intend to injure or kill his captors (to do so would wound his sense of gentlemanly chivalry, which he possesses in more modest quantities than Jeff). Yet, he is arguing for the assumption of the attitude of war—the need for approaching a situation with suitable urgency, for fighting relentlessly, if necessary. Behind a call for war is the specter of potential violence.

The linkage of the male scientists with violence is explored further by Gilman in the discussions of social progress (or lack thereof) among the men and the Herland women. When the men attempt to explain the presence of poverty in American society, they unwittingly draw stark differences between Herland and outside society. As Zava, a Herlander assigned to mentoring the men, says, "we don't know what poverty is" (62). Van, the sociologist, provides a to-the-letter social Darwinian explanation:

> I explained that the laws of nature require a struggle for existence, and that in the struggle the fittest survive, and the unfit perish. In our eco-

nomic struggle, I continued, there was always plenty of opportunity for the fittest to reach the top, which they did, in great numbers, particularly in our country; that where there was severe economic pressure the lowest classes of course felt it the worst, and that among the poorest of all the women were driven into the labor market by necessity.

They listened closely, with the usual note-taking. (63)

The Herlanders are grossly offended by this theory of social relations, in which economic theory and conservative politics are naturalized by the co-opting of the tenets of Darwin's natural selection. This misapplication of Darwin, of course, was prevalent in fin-de-siècle America and the subject of sociological debates in which Gilman actively participated. The following passage, from an anonymously published article entitled "Survival of the Fittest" (in an 1879 issue of the *Christian Advocate*), is an apt example:

All glory and honor and wisdom and power unto Him who selects, approves, rewards, conserves the best. What a blessing to let the unreformed drunkard and his children die, and not increase them above all others. How incalculable the pain in his billions of offspring, if vice and misery survive, and virtue and pleasure die. How wise to let those of weak digestion from gluttony die, and the temperate live. What benevolence to let the lawless perish, and the prudent survive. How charitable for the warlike to fall by violence, and the meek to inherit the earth. It is a great law of nature and of grace that he who obeys best, survives the fittest. One who obeys all the physical laws of nature lives longer, happier himself, gives to his children an improved constitution. So from the hour he begins to walk with God he obtains a better inheritance, and finds in his own soul the conservation of all his best energies, the survival of the fittest. (qtd. in Daniels, *Darwinism* 113)[9]

Gilman objects to social Darwinian rhetoric on several grounds: First of all, such a view is hypocritical concerning the issue of working women. The dominant (domestic) ideology is that women should not take part in the public sphere (e.g., in the workforce). As Terry says, "We do not allow our women to work. Women are loved—idolized—honored—kept in the home to care for the children" (61). Yet, such a view only applies in practice to the upper and middle classes; as Jeff subsequently admits, millions of poor women do, in fact, work. Secondly, social Darwinism forces upon our economic, social, and cultural relations a "struggle for existence" that Darwin claims takes place among living creatures as part of natural selection. As Gilman states in *The Man-Made World* (1911), "even in science, 'the struggle for existence' is, to the male mind, the dominant law, with the 'survival of the fittest' and the elimination of the unfit" (245). Such an emphasis on struggle, besides being a product of male-centered thinking, has disastrous social consequences. In economics and industry, Gilman continues, antagonism only serves to retard progress (251). In Herland, by contrast, no such struggle is imposed upon (or detected within) human social relations.[10]

The last part of the *Herland* passage quoted above—"They listened closely, with the usual note-taking"—raises still another important issue, namely that of science's purported objectivity. Throughout Gilman's novel the Herland women are characterized as calm, patient, dispassionate listeners, observers, and recorders: "They never expressed horror or disapproval, nor indeed much surprise—just a keen interest. And the notes they made!—miles of them!" (50). The men come to realize that "So far from being ignorant, they were deeply wise . . . and for clear reasoning, for real brain scope and power they were A No. 1. . . . They had the evenest tempers, the most perfect patience and good nature—one of the things most impressive about them all was the absence of irritability" (46).[11] In short, they represent the epitome of the methodical experimenter who proceeds to gather information and theorize inductively. Thus "objective" in Herland denotes both a method and an attitude: an elimination of subjective interference on the part of the observer, or the avoidance of personal and cultural bias. Although the men often claim to be objective, as in Terry's call for a "dispassionate" council of war (an oxymoron?) or Van's emphasis on his "scientific" or "moderate" or "rational" views, the general impulse of Gilman's novel is to demonstrate how utterly rooted the male explorers are in their cultural background, how, in fact, their views about women, heterosexuality, marriage, the family, the home, the workplace, and, by extension, the natural world (the focus of science) are socially constructed, arbitrary, and often illogical.[12] Thus we have something of a paradox. On one hand, Gilman punctures the confident authority of early-twentieth-century science. She questions the soundness of the scientific claims voiced by the men by placing them in an environment where such notions and theories hold no sway. It is as if the men were making statements of what they consider to be well-established scientific facts to a group of aliens. The Herlanders impassively record absolute statements made by the men, and in so doing, Gilman not so subtly emphasizes that such statements are, at base, conjectural rather than factual. When the Herlanders, in turn, describe how they have consciously improved their collective gene pool, the men voice their objections on scientific grounds:

> "But acquired traits are not transmissible," Terry declared. "Weissman has proved that."
> They never disputed our absolute statements, only made notes of them. (78)

But while *Herland* questions certain specific scientific claims, the text retains objectivity as a valid intellectual and methodological tool, as long as we define the term as the elimination of subjective bias and the maintenance of an "open" mind to alternative possibilities.[13] Rather than consider objectivity itself to be problematic, Gilman claims simply that the male scientists are failing to be truly objective.

A Different Kind of Science?

Gilman does more than take issue with the explorer-scientist and the male biases inherent in the scientific perspective. She also provides a fairly detailed portrait of what kinds of science an idealized, all-female society might practice, and what ends such scientific practice might serve. Here we begin to see how the novel links the practice of science to the central notion of community. Just as the men are surprised at finding skilled works of architecture (and other evidence of "civilization") within a society of women, they are quite impressed with the Herlanders' scientific accomplishments and knowledge. Van notes that the women "are marvelously keen on inference and deduction"; they practice astronomy, math, and physiology; "[t]hey had worked out a chemistry, a botany, a physics, with all the blends where a science touches an art, or merges into an industry, to suck fullness of knowledge as made us feel like schoolchildren" (64). This statement points to two important features of Herland science. First, the Herlanders are decidedly pragmatic—their technology is use-oriented, such as their electric-motored cars; even their clothing is "scientifically" designed to be functional and comfortable first, and attractive second (24–25).

The second point is that implied by the innocuous-looking deter-
miner "a"—note that Van says that the Herlanders have developed "*a*
chemistry, *a* botany, *a* physics" (my emphasis). Such a word choice by
Gilman might be an instance of imprecision; more likely, though, it
tells us that various sciences in Herland were independently developed
(which makes sense, since the society is effectively isolated geographically). Moreover, these scientific disciplines, though recognizable
enough, are somehow *different* from outside (i.e., androcentric) sciences. This more radical idea—that rather than one universal science,
there may be a male-centered science and a female-centered science,
which may or may not have similar foundational beliefs or methods—
is certainly consistent with Gilman's views on other topics, such as literature. On the latter point, Gilman argues that what we consider to
be "literature" is in fact the product of only half the human population,
namely men. She stresses that though men's literature has been considered to be universal and all-encompassing (because men equate
themselves with being people, while women occupy an inferior, less-
than-human position), in truth "men have given the world a mas-
culinized literature" (*Man-Made* 92). *Herland* suggests, albeit briefly,
a similar point about science: rather than only one possible path of development for a given discipline, there are at least two—male and female.[14] Science, as conceived by men, is not a universal or neutral
means of producing knowledge about the natural world or enabling
human beings to understand how nature works or how to utilize its resources. Rather, it is imbued with certain values, specific ways of thinking about humanity and nature. But once the *possibility* of a different
kind of science is raised, the question becomes how and to what extent
Herland science differs substantially from that represented by the
American explorers.

Here the novel does not quite realize its radical potential. On one
hand, the Herlanders' untempered emphasis on pragmatic science is
a key point of difference from science practiced (overwhelmingly by
men) in the late nineteenth and early twentieth centuries. The move
to professionalize science in America and Europe not only marginalized women from the coteries of scientific power and influence but also
reinforced the distinction between pure and applied scientific inquiry.
In this formulation, applied sciences such as engineering are viewed as
philosophically inferior to pure sciences such as physics, which seek,

as the saying goes, "knowledge for knowledge's sake." In late-nineteenth-century America, as historian Robert Bruce points out, scientists benefited greatly (in terms of prestige and funding) from scientific popularizers in the press and on the lecture circuit, who stressed the importance of practical applications of scientific research (354). Even so, many scientists "scorned the utilitarian argument . . . [and] [i]ncreasingly advocated science for the sake of science alone" (355). Moreover, the discourse of the papers presented within elite scientific groups, such as the American Association for the Advancement of Science, became increasingly specialized and complex. These factors created the perception of professional (i.e., masculine) science as a hermetic set of disciplines detached from daily concerns of the world (356). In *Herland*, by contrast, no such distinction between pure and applied science exists—the women instead "blend" the study of chemistry and physics with their applications in art and industry (*Herland* 64).

A more detailed analysis of Herland science, however, reveals an ambiguity within Gilman's utopian representation of scientific practice. Despite her satirical critique of the male explorers and, by extension, the scientific disciplines they represent, Gilman incorporates many of the basic tenets of early-twentieth-century natural science into the science of Herland—the objective, detached observer; the exercising of control over nature; the commitment to progress—ideas that resonate most strongly with those of John Wesley Powell, the subject of chapter 4. Moreover, as with Powell's vision for the American West, *Herland* dramatizes a unique and forward-looking relationship humans can forge with the environment. In Gilman's utopian society, science enables the whole community—human, plant, animal, mineral—to function in a self-sustaining, harmonious, and efficient way.

Control, Progress, and the Human-Nature Relation

In Herland society, control is everything. The relationship between humanity and nature is measured, nudged, pushed, pruned, and carefully attended to so that the community—consisting of both human and nonhuman elements—is maintained in a productive, viable state. Gilman believes that nature is in need of control by the rational human intellect, for it is fundamentally inefficient: "Nature's 'economy' is not in the least 'economical.' The waste of life, the waste of material, the waste of time and effort, are prodigious, yet she achieves her end as we see" (*Man-Made* 238). Here we detect a hint of the complex view of nature that Gilman holds: on one hand, natural processes—of evolution, of development, of growth—proceed inefficiently, slowly. On the other, the end *results* of these natural processes are often desirable. Instead of thwarting nature, then, we should strive to increase its efficiency, to speed its course toward an already known end. *Herland* gives us several concrete examples of how the human community may exert such control upon the natural world.

The Herland landscape, described by critic Polly Wynn Allen as a "nonurban, preindustrial paradise" (96), is so highly cared for and cultivated that the male explorers register great surprise at the society's horticultural and agricultural achievements. The Herlanders mold the landscape to optimize human occupation but also adapt their mode of habitation to the limits of the ecosystem. Such an approach combines a respect for the overall integrity of the land with a desire to change what may safely be modified and improved. As is customary, pragmatism guides any changes or modifications. Rather than let nature remain in a completely wild state, the Herlanders "deliberately replant . . . an entire forest area with different kinds of trees" so that every tree may produce edible fruit (79). Such concern for a species' practical value overrides the concern for aesthetics: only one particularly beautiful species is allowed to exist, and it is eventually "encouraged" to bear edible fruit after nine hundred years of experimental work. Animal populations are also scrupulously controlled; species that exact a heavy toll upon the land by grazing, such as cattle or sheep, are wholly eliminated (68). Any pest that is identified is quickly targeted for extinction—Ellador, we learn, comes to discover her life's work by accidentally finding, while in the forest as a child, a "female of the obernut moth," a pest that the Herland foresters had been trying to eliminate for hundreds of years (101). She is greatly praised by her elders and is inspired to work in forestry, perhaps the most control-intensive occupation in Herland society.

The scientific control of plant and animal life is a theme of other early-twentieth-century utopian works; H. G. Wells's *Men Like Gods* (first published in 1922) is a case in point. In Wells's novel, "the Utopian community had been given to the long-cherished idea of a systematic extermination of tiresome and mischievous species. . . . Ten thousand species, from disease-germ to rhinocerous and hyena, were put upon their trial. Every species found was given an advocate. Of each it was asked: What good is it? What harm does it do? How can it be extirpated? What else may go with it if it goes?" (92). The last question in the preceding quote signals a concern for the potentially negative effects of species extinction: often species that were "offensive in themselves were a necessary irreplaceable food to pleasant and desirable creatures" (93). Wells's Utopians mitigate this problem by retaining very small numbers of such undesirable yet valuable species. By contrast, this forward-looking recognition of the ecological "side effects" of landscape and species engineering does not surface in Gilman's *Herland*.

Herland's human citizenry is hardly exempt from the general emphasis on control. Since they recognize that people are as dependent upon available food resources as any other living creature, population is strictly—and scientifically—monitored and contained. At one point in their unusual history (and in characteristically unspectacular fashion), the Herland council leaders decided that rather than acquire more territory and natural resources to support a growing population, the people would practice disciplined population control. According to Van, they approached the problem as a matter of mere common sense: "They sat down in council together and thought it out. Very clear, strong thinkers they were. They said: 'With our best endeavors this country will support about so many people, with the standard of peace, comfort, health, beauty, and progress we demand. Very well. That is all the people we will make'" (68). Such population control, in contrast to the pest management practices cited above, is ecologically progressive in its concern for the limits of natural resources and its implicit critique of growth. However, it is hardly a simple affair, even in a society with only one biological sex (the Herlanders reproduce by parthenogenesis): the women implement a system of "negative eugenics," in which the majority voluntarily forego motherhood in order to stabilize the birth and death rate at a steady state (69). The Herland management of reproduction eventually develops into a highly ordered system of control that functions both on an individual and a social level. First and foremost, "a woman chose to be a mother, she allowed the child-longing to grow within her till it worked its natural miracle.

When she did not so choose she put the whole thing out of her mind" (71). The emphasis here is on the concept of *choice*—women, far from being forced into becoming pregnant, approach the decision rationally and, in the event that pregnancy and motherhood are not desirable, override what the men assume to be an overwhelming, "natural" impulse by an exertion of will, of unspectacular self-control. In *Herland*, Gilman portrays not women of "helpless involuntary fecundity" but "Conscious Makers of People" (68).

On the macro, or social, scale, the task of nurturing and educating children rests with a community of trained specialists rather than individual "biological" mothers. In one of the novel's most radical social critiques, the rearing of children is rationalized and streamlined by an efficient system of labor, one that dramatically challenges the notion of "family." For Gilman, the nuclear family unit of father-mother-children as a self-governing social entity—a concept rooted in nineteenth-century domestic ideology—is obsolete, inefficient, and fundamentally designed to subordinate women. Instead, in Herland the entire community—indeed, the nation—*is* the family. This system of bearing and raising of children exemplifies the Herland impulse to develop a specialized workforce, in which the distinction between public and private spheres is erased and all types of jobs and responsibilities are assigned to individuals specifically trained for such tasks. Gilman's envisioned approach is no less than the scientific management of all human labor, be it industrial, agricultural, or reproductive. Such ideas constitute a recurrent theme in Gilman's nonfiction work as well. In her 1904 essay "Domestic Economy," she outlines a detailed, quantitative proposal for a system of household management in which duties that were (and often still are) commonly left to the attentions of an inefficient, overwrought generalist, or housewife, are instead contracted out to specialized workforces (Ceplair 157–68).[15] And in her essay "The Labor Movement," published in 1892, Gilman succinctly describes the importance of individual specialization in labor: "The conception of society as an organism, with the individual man merely as a cell in the structure, is essential to the understanding of any human problem" (qtd. in Ceplair 62).

Another distinguishing feature of Herland science (and society in general) is an unflagging dedication to progress, specifically the continual betterment of the human condition, both physical and mental.

Gilman firmly believes in the inherent capability of the human race to improve itself—especially the lot of women—and to that end she views science, and rational thought more generally, as instrumental. As Van notes, "the most salient quality in all their institutions was reasonableness. When I dug into the records to follow out any line of development, that was the most astonishing thing—the conscious effort to make it better" (76). Perhaps nothing exemplifies this "conscious effort" of the Herland society to foster progress quite like their efforts to control and improve their own species development. Despite reproducing asexually and having a gene pool of only three million individuals, the Herland women exhibit a great amount of physical variability. Gilman's explanation combines the effects of natural processes with conscious human design: "they attributed it [variability in the human population] partly to the careful education, which followed each slight tendency to differ, and partly to the law of mutation. This they had found in their work with plants, and fully proven in their own case" (77).

Certainly this explanation's main function is narrative plausibility. More important, though, than the scientific accuracy of the Herlanders' history and development is the measure of control that characterizes the Herland dedication to social progress. Individuals, in this case, are like plants (but not in Hector St. John de Crèvecoeur's sense of being defined and shaped by their environment): the undesirable types can be "weeded out" by discouraging them from reproducing, while desired characteristics can be fostered by education and continued reproduction. Thus the Herlanders manipulate the human population in much the same way that they manage the forest flora and fauna, and all in the name of a rather hazily defined progress in which humans somehow become better. When Van, seeking out some example of "imperfection" in the Herland society, asks Ellador if her people exhibit any "faults," she replies: "When we began—even with the start of one particularly noble mother—we inherited the characteristics of a long race-record behind her. And they [faults] cropped out from time to time—alarmingly. But it is—yes, quite six hundred years since we have had what you call a 'criminal'" (82). Such statements are simultaneously incredible, impressive, and troubling, for underneath the cheerful dedication to social progress in *Herland* (and the overly optimistic and innocent-sounding declarations that human intelligence, for example, has "improved" steadily throughout the history of Her-land) are unpleasant currents of repressive reproductive policies. The impulse to control everything is taken to its fullest, and ugliest, end—that of fostering racial "purity" at the expense of certain "undesirable" social types. One issue that is never raised in *Herland* is who decides what is desirable and undesirable—such arbitrary qualities are taken for granted by both the women of Herland and the male explorers.[16]

The emphasis on control and the dedication to progress are, then, key features of Herland science and society. Gilman places much greater faith than did even John Wesley Powell in the capacity for ra-tional thought and scientific management to effect beneficial change upon the landscape and human community. Powell's *Report on the Arid Regions* advocated implementing a scientific approach to western land use and a doctrine of controlling nature; but this vision was set within a framework of *human adaptation* to an ecosystem's constraints (specif-ically, one characterized by a fundamental lack of water). Gilman, by contrast, describes in *Herland* an extraordinarily high degree of human impact upon the environment—just as the Herlanders eliminate "un-desirable" traits from within their gene pool, they excise unwanted quirks or irritations (such as pests) from the natural world.

Yet, as with the enforced cap on the Herland population, Gilman to some extent tempers the impulse to control nature in *Herland*. Gilman's forward-looking concern for environmental conservation echoes the views of progressive environmental advocates of the early twentieth century, such as John Muir and Theodore Roosevelt. As Van notes, "They had early decided that trees were the best food plants, re-quiring far less labor in tilling the soil, and bearing a larger amount of food for the same ground space; also doing much to preserve and en-rich the soil" (79). Thus conservation-minded agriculture benefits not only the people of Herland but also nature itself. Gilman even advo-cates the process of nutrient and waste recycling as another means of maintaining a stable human population and healthy natural resources. Instead of simply extracting food from the earth without considering long-term consequences, "[t]hese careful culturalists had worked out a perfect scheme of refeeding the soil with all that came out of it. All the scraps and leavings of their food, plant waste from lumber work or textile industry, all the solid matter from the sewage, properly treated and combined—everything which came from the earth went back to it" (80). Gilman's views on the importance of nutrient and re-source recycling are highly progressive, for they appear several decades before widespread air and water pollution, fossil fuel shortages, waste disposal problems, and excessive consumption of raw materials inspired heightened environmental awareness and, by extension, the recycling movement.[17]

These various aspects of Gilman's environmental perspective—the connections among humanity, science, and nature—coalesce in the notion of the community within nature as a functional unit. The communitarian impulse is very strong in Herland society: indeed, one of the problems Gilman sees in the dominant scientific explanations and theories of social relations is that they focus upon (and thus are limited to) the *individual*. Metaphors of Darwinian struggle bother Gilman precisely because they emphasize struggle among competing individuals rather than the collaborative, cooperative potential of the community. Such a view explicitly characterizes the way Herlanders conceive of the land they inhabit:

> Having improved their agriculture to the highest point, and carefully estimated the number of persons who could comfortably live on their square miles; having then limited their population to that number, one would think that was all there was to be done. But they had not thought so. To them the country was a unit—it was theirs. They themselves were a unit, a conscious group; they thought in terms of the community. As such, their time-sense was not limited to the hopes and ambitions of an individual life. Therefore, they habitually considered and carried out plans for improvement which might cover centuries. (79)

Gilman presents this scenario as an alternative to the system of private property and, more generally, as part of the critique of individualism. Nature—"the country"—serves as an integral part of the overall human community, and this integrated community becomes the basic unit of social relations. To maintain this community-based structure, Herlanders exert strong controls both on the human element (population control, elimination of private property) and the natural environment (improving agricultural methods, pest control, and conservation practices).

Thus another tension emerges from within the Herland social structure: on one hand the rationalist framework of progress and efficiency that permeates the Herland way of thinking mandates nature's control—nothing is left to chance in order to improve upon nature's perceived "inefficiency." Such a perspective resembles domination, a fundamentally antagonistic relationship between humanity and nature characteristic of the male explorer-scientist's worldview—one which, ironically, Gilman critiques. On the other hand, Gilman's description of the community unit that encompasses both humans and nature is anything but antagonistic; rather, it portrays the various components of the Herland managed ecosystem working in harmony, with human and nonhuman resources existing in a state of peaceful equilibrium.[18]

Charlotte Perkins Gilman's *Herland* is like a piece of glass with many facets. Held to the light one way, it appears as a utopia in the manner of Thomas More or Edward Bellamy, a product of imagination and fancy, a vision of an advanced, enlightened, efficient, and judicious society, a realm of hope and possibility for the lives of women. Read another way, it reveals a satire of the nineteenth-century epitome of American masculinity, the explorer-hero, a story that humorously exposes this detached yet romantic perspective as a rhetorical guise based upon gendered assumptions about nature and human culture. Held to a third angle, the colors and patterns reveal an innovative view of a productive, stable, and harmonious relation between nature and humanity. Like Susan Fenimore Cooper (chapter 5), who idealized the blending of forest, field, and town in her mid-nineteenth-century natural history of rural New York State, and John Wesley Powell (chapter 4), who proposed a new way of settling and governing the arid regions of the West in the 1870s, Gilman expands our notion of community by linking bird, tree, insect, water, earth, and human in close and apparently benevolent association. Yet this utopian vision is shaded and shaped by Gilman's abiding faith in the human control of nature, her commitment to the scientific management of everything from agricultural pests to human reproduction. Although ecologist and conservationist Aldo Leopold would later write in *A Sand County Almanac, and Sketches Here and There* (1949) of the need for humans to become "plain members" of the larger natural community (rather than domineering masters of it), Gilman advocates a rigorous program of control, each ingenious strategy a paean to progress. Thus *Herland* aptly reflects the fissures in American views of science and nature—as early-twentieth-century technology and scientific know-how created more and more opportunities for mastering the vicissitudes of nature and exploiting its resources, other voices sounded the need for cultivating a better, less wasteful, less domineering relationship with the environment through such practices as preserving land in national parks and replanting forests.

▪ FOUR ▪

"A Unit of Country Well Defined in Nature"

John Wesley Powell and
the Scientific Management
of the American West

C harlotte Perkins Gilman's fictional utopia illustrates the tension, on one hand, between an emerging ecological view of nature and the valuation of wilderness and, on the other, the ability of science and technology to control and even reshape the natural environment. This rift in American attitudes toward science and nature has intriguing historical antecedents in the late nineteenth century, a time of accelerated geographic expansion, the emergence of the United States as a world political and military power, the professionalization of scientific practice, and a burgeoning conservation movement. In this chapter, I leave the imaginative South American wilderness landscape of *Herland* and travel back a generation to the spaces of the American West, in order to focus upon the work of John Wesley Powell, one of the most important and influential scientists of his age. Though often praised and remembered on an individual level as a daring explorer and western icon, traits that closely associate him at first glance with men like John Charles Frémont and Clarence King, Powell shares with Gilman an intense interest in community—specifically, how the structure and potential of human communities depend upon a productive and responsible association with nature and the wise practice of science. But although representations of the environment and the exploration of scientific practice are secondary themes in Gilman's social critique, these issues take center stage in Powell's vision of the arid West.

Since the nineteenth century, Americans have associated the landscape of the West with freedom, adventure, and possibility—wide open spaces, immense skies, towering mountains, powerful untamed rivers, breathtaking landforms, and rough-and-tumble frontier communities have held an undeniable fascination and allure for us. Ironically, though, the American West has been a place where humans have sought to dominate and control nature on an unprecedented scale. Irrigation is one of the most dramatic examples of how the forces of science and technology have harnessed the vast natural resources of the western environment. As writer Wallace Stegner has observed, "if you are a nation of plenty and impatient of restrictions and led westward by pillars of fire and cloud . . . [y]ou may deny . . . [aridity] for awhile. Then you must either adapt to it or try to engineer it out of existence" (*American* 27). In the first part of the twentieth century, the United States Bureau of Reclamation constructed the vast systems of dams, canals, diversion ditches, and reservoirs that comprise what historian Donald Worster calls the "hydraulic west." Perhaps the best-known symbol of this society is the 726-foot-tall Hoover Dam, completed in 1935, an edifice universally touted as an engineering marvel and testament to human ingenuity and perseverance. Since then, virtually every major river or stream in the West has been dammed, and formerly barren lands of the arid and subhumid regions have been transformed into some of the most productive agricultural areas of the world.[1] The West's sprawling urban centers of Los Angeles, Phoenix, and Las Vegas have sustained themselves by tapping water from sources hundreds of miles distant. In answer to the dream articulated in lofty and prophetic terms by William Smythe, early-twentieth-century America's foremost proponent of irrigation, the rivers of the West have been tamed, and water has been contained and diverted for purposes of recreation, "free" power generation, agriculture, and flood control.[2]

We now realize that, despite the quantifiable success at increasing economic production and sustaining population growth, the triumphs of the hydraulic West have come at a great cost. Smythe's dream of a glorious irrigation society has proven to be a one-sided, overly optimistic vision. The Colorado River, dammed at several points along its channel, no longer reaches the sea in seasons of average precipitation. And along with many other rivers, the Colorado displays dangerously high salinity levels, the result of the artificial loading of salts from agricultural runoff. The large lakes created by Hoover, Glen Canyon, and other dams have fundamentally altered the ecology—and, some would argue, lessened the beauty—of the spectacular river canyons. Even the dream of efficient and dependable flood control has proved elusive, as rivers occasionally overflow their appointed channels and thus defy human efforts to mediate their flow (Limerick, *Legacy* 320–21).

In this rapid transformation of the West, one figure loomed particularly large—John Wesley Powell (1834–1902), explorer, geologist, ethnologist, philosopher, writer, and government leader. While Powell's daring explorations of the Colorado River in the late 1860s made him an admired public figure of the nineteenth century (a reputation that continues to this day), his role as a scientist, political reformer, and early advocate of irrigation practices has been debated among American historians from the early twentieth century onward. In 1905, William Smythe claimed Powell as the intellectual father of modern irrigation practices and cast him as an early champion for the construction of dams, canals, and irrigation systems (Smythe 261–63). In contrast, a contemporary historian, Mark Reisner, argues that Powell's message was fundamentally one of restraint and moderation in the control and use of natural resources, and that the "half-century of dam-building and irrigation development" that followed Powell's death in 1902 "went far beyond anything [he] . . . would have liked" (Reisner 53). Finally, Donald Worster, an environmental historian and thoughtful critic of the West's dependence upon large-scale irrigation, suggests that while Powell fully endorsed the process of controlling the western environment through the use of science and irrigation technology, he tempered his enthusiasm by advocating *local*, and not federal, control of resource management (*Unsettled* 22–23).

These changing historical interpretations suggest Powell should be examined carefully if we wish to understand the complex ways in which American scientists conceived of and represented the western environment after the business of initial exploration had been completed. Ultimately, pigeonholing Powell as either an environmental prophet or an early voice of exploitation oversimplifies his work and influence; as Worster eloquently states in his recent authoritative biography, Powell "called for building dams, for transforming the arid lands into an agricultural empire, though at the same time he extolled the wilderness and criticized ruthless corporations. To discover the man behind the celebrity, with all his ambivalence and contradiction, is to discover a more complicated America" (*River* xi). With Worster's observation in mind, I analyze Powell's work as a record of how someone with a great deal of firsthand knowledge of the western environment and a deep concern for how humans should live and work within this ecosystem used science to construct a representation of nature and suggest new strategies for reshaping the human community. In short, Powell made the practice of science central to our understanding of nature, the West, and ourselves.

This chapter focuses primarily upon Powell's landmark 1878 government publication, *Report on the Lands of the Arid Region*, in which he makes science serve several varied—and in some cases conflicting—functions. I argue that the text embodies two fundamental ironies concerning the relationships among science, nature, and humanity. These tensions account for both the complexity of the *Report's* structure and content and the ongoing debate concerning the historical significance of Powell's ideas for the American West. First, although Powell's rhetoric of science constructs nature as an active, self-regulating entity (an ordered system that can be understood and appreciated on its own terms), scientific know-how also provides the ideal means of controlling nature specifically for human use. In other words, though science gives us the tools to see nature on its own terms, it also conveniently inspires the vision of nature as it should be. This latter emphasis upon control encourages and justifies the use of natural resources and accommodates the ever-increasing demands (for water, arable land, etc.) of nineteenth-century white migration to the West.[3] Moreover, the doctrine of control is a logical extension of Frémont's project of conquering the landscape. Though Powell's rhetoric jettisons the gendered metaphors of both Frémont's narratives and conventional natural histories, science nevertheless exerts mastery over a mechanized nature. In place of the heroic masculine scientist investigating a feminized nature, the *Report* characterizes science as a detached, impersonal, authoritative process by which the machine-like workings of natural systems are analyzed, tweaked, and improved for human benefit.

Second, science for Powell is a means of articulating both doubt and hope about the human presence in the arid West. Powell's scientific representation of nature helps him to step back and clearly delineate the limits of human endeavor within the western environment. He expresses grave doubts that the present means of human occupation and use of the arid region's resources, by both the Native and emigrant populations, are prudent and efficient. Despite this inherent pessimism, though, the *Report on the Lands of the Arid Region* is ultimately a visionary document of hope for the future. For Powell, science is the ultimate problem solver, the means by which humans can control not only their natural environment but also themselves. In his hopeful vision of the West, the key to harnessing the power and wealth of nature lies in controlling and efficiently using water.

Just as important, however, is the scientific restructuring of the human presence in the arid regions. Powell fashions a scientific-agricultural utopia, a vision that embodies what many have recognized as the *Report*'s most radical proposal: the substitution of the community for the fundamentally flawed individual as the basic unit of social relations.[4] In a clever morality play that exposes both the misinformed good intentions of the yeoman farmer and the frightening greed of the venture capitalist, Powell concludes that the community, bound together by the scientific management of nature, can live most wisely and productively in the arid West. For Powell, the scientific method—not the explorer, cowboy, politician, or Native American, all of whom become effectively invisible in his narrative—serves as the symbolic savior of a troubled, constantly growing American West.

Exploring and Reimagining the West

Among American scientists of the nineteenth century, John Wesley Powell was one of the most versatile and influential. Son of a Methodist minister, largely a self-taught naturalist, and a Civil War hero who lost an arm at the Battle of Shiloh, Powell became a teacher, explorer, geologist, ethnologist, philosopher, and writer. He taught science briefly at Illinois Wesleyan University and then Illinois State Normal University in the mid-1860s. Then, his interest in the West stoked by reading the narratives of Frémont and others, Powell began his exploration career in 1867 by leading a group of students and amateur naturalists to investigate the White River in the Dakota Badlands, before heading south to the largely unexplored Colorado River country. Powell gained national attention when he directed subsequent parties on

Colorado River expeditions in 1869 and 1871. The first trip was a thrilling and dangerous boat voyage down to the as yet unexplored Grand Canyon, the second a more deliberate exploration of the Colorado Plateau that emphasized systematic topographical mapping and detailed study of resident Native American communities.

On the famous 1869 river expedition, Powell and his small party survived the destruction of one of their four wooden boats, the loss of most of their food, and the desertion (and eventual death) of three crew members to become the first white Americans to successfully navigate the wild Colorado and its many canyons. Powell's journalistic accounts of the trips, published serially and later in book form, fed a public imagination hungry for frontier adventure and established him as one of the key players in the ongoing exploration of the American West. That the stocky, bearded man with only one arm was able to lead such daring expeditions and scale rough, thousand-foot-high canyon walls impressed his colleagues and thrilled the public; in this sense, Powell is an important part of the tradition of scientist-heroes who traveled the nineteenth-century West. Powell subsequently became a key leader of government-sponsored exploration projects of the 1870s that strove to comprehensively map the vast western territories of the United States. Ferdinand Hayden, Clarence King, George Wheeler, and Powell conducted expeditions throughout the western states and territories, projects that provided geologist Clarence Dutton, painter Thomas Moran, photographer W. H. Jackson, and many others the opportunity to document and analyze the vast, varied, and sometimes surreal western landscape.[5] Powell also kept busy as a government bureaucrat (albeit a benevolent one)—at one time or another, he led various newly formed government agencies such as the United States Geological Survey and the Bureau of Ethnology.

As a writer, Powell's works include an expanded version of his Colorado River journals, published in popular form as *The Exploration of the Colorado River and Its Canyons* (1875); numerous scientific reports submitted to and published by the government in the 1870s and 1880s; and various articles written in the 1880s and 1890s for magazines such as *Century* and *Scribner's Monthly*, pieces designed to bolster political and popular support for land reform.[6] In contrast to the government reports of Frémont, Powell's writings were geared toward either a popular audience or a technical and professional readership. His widely read river exploration journals, though, share many characteristics with Frémont's narratives—the quantitative analysis of the landscape and the symbolic importance of instrumentation, the emphasis upon vision as the primary mode of experiencing nature, and the portrait of the masculine explorer-hero who confronts danger and overcomes monumental obstacles in the name of science. While these narratives have long been recognized as important examples of American nature writing, I find Powell's technical writings even more fascinating, for in them he fuses his scientific representation of the western environment with a groundbreaking vision of how it should be populated, used, and governed.

In August of 1878, Powell presented to the United States Congress his *Report on the Lands of the Arid Region of the United States, with a More Detailed Account of the Lands of Utah*. It contained the simple yet radical assertion that large portions of the West were technically desert regions and thus required more cautious, measured, and scientifically informed ways of living and farming than in the relatively humid and mild East.[7] Powell defined the contours of the arid region as beginning "about midway in the Great Plains and extend[ing] across the Rocky Mountains to the Pacific Ocean" (1), and he proclaimed that the "Arid Region of the United States is more than four-tenths of the area of the entire country excluding Alaska" (23), a statement that takes on great import when we realize that within this vast space of land "agriculture is dependent upon irrigation" (23). Herein lies the revolutionary aspect of Powell's text: these seemingly mundane ideas about the physical nature of the western environment were not widely held by land-hungry Americans moving west in the nineteenth century, nor were they greeted with enthusiasm in the halls of Congress. Clearly, Powell meant his *Report* to be nothing less than a revision of how Americans perceived the physical character of the western frontier.

Several years' worth of geological and hydrological research in the arid region had convinced Powell that this four-tenths of the nation was not a gardenlike agricultural paradise. It was instead a place where water, so abundant in the humid areas of the East, was scarce and therefore a precious resource to be conserved and managed wisely through careful irrigation practices. By his calculations, only 2.8 percent of Utah, for example, could "be cultivated by utilizing all the available streams during the irrigating season" (9). Powell's observations led him to present in his *Report* a direct challenge to the much-revered Homestead Act (1862), which granted 160 acres of new land per applicant. In a critique of the ecological assumptions underlying the act, Powell observed that 160 acres were too many for farming practices and far too few for purposes of grazing, and thus the act should be revised appropriately. Specifically, Powell recommended that the size of land meant for irrigated farming be 80 acres, while lands designated as grazing areas be sold in 2,560-acre units (*Report* 26–27). Perhaps most importantly, Powell recommended that "irrigation districts" be formed in the arid region, in which individual farmers would cooperate in constructing irrigation works and thus ensure judicious control and fair distribution of water, the limiting resource. In short, Powell asserted that the arid region was capable of sustaining *some* agriculture, logging, grazing, and mining, but not much. Above all, he believed that humans needed to adapt their ways of living and expectations to the limitations of the land.

As it turned out, the burgeoning political establishment of the West viewed Powell's *Report* with great distrust. His pragmatic, blunt message did not harmonize with the mid-nineteenth-century myth of the West as Garden propounded by the likes of Thomas Hart Benton (senator from Missouri and father-in-law of John Charles Frémont) and, later on, William Gilpin (the first governor of the Colorado Territory). Historian Henry Nash Smith argues that the "general optimism of the West, together with the economic interests of . . . [those] who stood to profit from continued settlement . . . was challenged by Powell's claim that the agricultural frontier was approaching a natural barrier" (198–99). Consequently, Powell's recommendations, as well as a report issued by the Public Lands Commission two years later, were outright ignored by Congress.[8] Powell continued to lobby for reform of the land system throughout the 1880s, but by the early 1890s, his survey funding had been significantly cut. With his political influence diminished and his monetary support gone, Powell finally resigned from the United States Geological Survey in 1894 to focus exclusively on his ethnological studies (Watkins xix). In the decades following Powell's death in 1902 (a year that, appropriately, saw the birth of the Bureau of Reclamation), some of his plans for land management came to pass in one form or another—the western topography was systematically and comprehensively mapped; rivers were dammed and diverted, and reservoirs created; water-control planning eventually took place within seven reclamation regions—while others never materialized. But although the political legacy of Powell's *Report* was decidedly mixed, his revisioning of science, the human community, and the arid environment undoubtedly influenced the character of western development.[9] From Powell's time onward, settlement and use of the land would revolve around the availability of water; debate would rage between those who wished to restrict access to and use of the land and those who strove to encourage it; and science would leave its mark, in projects such as Hoover Dam and Los Alamos, as a defining cultural force in the region.

Powell's Rhetoric of Science

Like Thomas Jefferson's *Notes on the State of Virginia* (1787), another text of both scientific and political import, Powell's *Report* is a complex, multilayered document. It takes as its foundation an empirical, systematic representation of nature; it is replete with figures, tables, and explanations of formulas; it is designed not to tell a story but to present an authentic, scientific account of a specific region of the country. The scientific method thus provides the rhetorical framework of Powell's *Report*, and two aspects of this rhetoric are particularly important: the emphasis upon quantitative data and the corresponding deemphasis upon the narrator's (i.e., the scientist's) individual subjectivity. In the *Report*, empiricism sharpened by argumentative precision meets the politically powerful myth of the West as Garden head on.

Powell's document inundates us with numbers, measurements, and quantitative analysis: the ten chapters and 195 pages of the *Report* contain four maps, one graph, twenty-six tables of data, and innumerable references to specific measurements and methods of analysis. One of the most central quantitative discussions in the *Report* occurs in chapter 4 and focuses upon the relation between land and water in the West. The key numerical ratio of this relation is the "second-foot" of water, or "the number of cubic feet [of water] which the stream will deliver per second" (81). By itself this number is an abstraction, until Powell informs us that "a continuous flow of one cubic foot of water per second . . . will, in most of the lands of Utah, serve about 100 acres for the general average of crops cultivated in that country" (84). Defining this numerical relationship has involved a long process of recognizing and evaluating variables in nature (for instance, the type of crop raised or the permeability of the soil), but Powell, in the end, relies on the direct observation of the experience of Utah farmers rather than inferring a number from the literature on the irrigation practices of other countries (83–84).[10] Such data are rooted in the experience of the western people and partake of the Baconian preference for direct observation and bias against a priori theory. "These are legitimate numbers!" he seems to be crying out, and because they are derived from the farming practices and experience of nonscientists, they are imbued with additional validity.

In addition to the *Report*'s emphasis upon quantitative data as a means of constructing arguments about climate and irrigation methods, Powell's rhetorical strategy de-emphasizes the narrator's subjectivity, a feature that was becoming standard practice in late-nineteenth-century scientific writing. Passive-voice sentence structures exemplify this approach. Consider the first paragraph of chapter 1, which is a summary of the physical aspects of the arid ecosystem and contains little quantitative data as such. There is no "I" voice, no narrative personality discernable here—the human subject is effaced from the sentences:

> It will be convenient to designate this humid area as the Lower Columbia Region. Rain gauge records have not been made to such an extent as to enable us to define its eastern and southern boundaries, but as they are chiefly along high mountains, definite boundary lines are unimportant in the consideration of agricultural resources and the questions relating thereto. In like manner on the east the rain gauge records, though more full, do not give all the facts necessary to a thorough discussion of the subject. . . . Experience teaches that it is not wise to depend upon rainfall where the amount is less than 20 inches annually. (1–2)

The largely passive construction of this passage is common throughout the *Report* as well as formal scientific rhetoric today. But even when active voice is used, Powell makes it clear that it is not he who is coming up with this information; these conclusions and inferences are not personally derived, but *method* based. The rain gauge, not Powell or any of his survey team, provides information. *Experience*, not Powell, not the "I" narrator present in varying degrees in an exploration adventure, teaches us certain things about the natural world. Thus, the whims of the individual scientist are assumed to be negated by an impersonal scientific narrative.

The *Report*'s claim to scientific authority is strengthened further by the circumstances of its composition. Although up to this point I have been referring (mostly for the sake of convenience) to Powell as the author of the *Report*, in fact the text is a collaborative document, with various chapters contributed by key participants in Powell's surveys throughout the 1870s. Although Powell is the primary author (he wrote five of the *Report*'s ten chapters and approved the content and format of the other five), the text is clearly the product of a group effort—Powell's collaborators included G. K. Gilbert (chapters 4 and 7), C. E. Dutton (8), A. H. Thompson (9), and Willis Drummond Jr. (10). The *Report*'s collaborative authorship strengthens its claim of scientific rigor and also de-emphasizes the work and voice of each individual scientist, including Powell. This de-emphasis is important, for it fosters the impression that the work of science has been carried out by a team. As readers, we view the scientists working together in an idealized process of communal assent, a democratic ritual of hashing out an idea and trying it against other valid possibilities. Within this scenario the potential for correction (noticeably absent from a subjective "I" statement) is there in force. The names of the scientist-authors do pop up now and then in the *Report*, but mostly in a spirit of collaboration and mutual reinforcement (xi, 84, 110).

Finally, the tone of caution exhibited by each contributing author of the *Report* is another way the rhetoric rests upon the scientific method rather than the power of individual authority. An apt example comes from Gilbert's "Water Supply" chapter: "On the whole, it may be most wise to hold the question an open one whether the water supply of the lake has been increased by a climatic change or by human agency. So far as we now know, neither theory is inconsistent with the facts, and it is possible that the truth includes both" (76). This statement, at first glance, simply may appear to be a tentative hedge, an effort to avoid a firm conclusion. Ironically, though, this feature is a key strength of this work of scientific rhetoric. For the purposes of Powell's *Report*, an admission of uncertainty or ignorance can be effective in driving home a crucial point: we do not know enough about this area; we can say only so much with a high degree of confidence; therefore, we must proceed cautiously and not pretend that we do know exactly what is occurring. Such uncertainty may be rooted in the lack of adequate data or, more significantly, in the complexity of nature itself; as Gilbert remarks,

> The weather of the globe is a complex whole, each part of which reacts on every other, and each part of which depends on every other. The weather of Utah is an interdependent part of the whole, and cannot be referred to its causes until the entire subject is mastered. The simpler and more immediate meteoric [weather] reactions have been so far analyzed that their results are daily predicted; but the remote sources of our daily changes, as well as the causes of the greater cycles of change, are still beyond our reach. Although withdrawn from the domain of the unknowable, they remain within that of the unknown. (70–71)

Part of the myth that Powell and his associates are trying to debunk, after all, is the belief that we know all we need to know about the West. Such a cautionary and measured perspective does not mean, however, that the methods of science are futile, for Gilbert's comments imply that even the complex interdependencies of nature will reveal themselves to empirical description and analysis.

The Report's language of science thus displays two primary features: the emphasis upon quantitative, empirical data and a corresponding de-emphasis upon individual subjectivity.[11] This move toward the impersonal voice of science and away from the individual's view facilitates two of Powell's explicit goals: to construct a representation of the arid environment on its own terms (and not those of the humid eastern portion of the United States) and to critique the role of the human individual in the arid ecosystem.

Representing Nature: From Contradiction to Control

Powell's rhetoric of science serves a variety of purposes in the 1878 *Report*, and chief among these is a detailed and accurate representation of the "Physical Characteristics of the Arid Region" (Powell's title for chapter 1); his representation of nature, however, is anything but straightforward. On one hand, the language of science permits him to view nature on its own terms, apart from human assumptions and expectations. The quantitative analysis of the environment as an entity measured by numbers, seasonal fluctuations, and cause-and-effect processes portrays nature as an active, self-governing system. Such a representation of the arid ecosystem in some respects resembles the ecocentric views of wilderness advocates such as Henry David Thoreau, John Muir, Mary Austin, and Aldo Leopold. On the other hand, Powell's vision of nature is also fundamentally mechanistic, a view that facilitates the belief that nature can and should be controlled. By ascertaining the physical characteristics and fundamental processes of a mechanical system, the scientist presumably has the tools to alter that system or push it in a specific direction. Thus Powell's *Report* exhibits an unacknowledged tension between the recognition of nature's self-governance and the perceived need for control, between nature responded to and nature dominated. Powell's view of the western landscape as an independent, self-regulating system ironically gives way to the assumption that the machinery of nature can be directed and modified by human action. The latter impulse closely aligns the *Report* with land management practices in the early twentieth century advocated by forester Gifford Pinchot, who in his 1910 book *The Fight for Conservation* claimed that "The first duty of the human race is to control the earth it lives upon" (45), and organizations such as the Bureau of Reclamation. Thus, the starkly contrasting environmental sensibilities of Muir and Pinchot exist side by side in Powell's portrait of the West.[12] For the spokesman of the arid region, a quasi-ecocentric representation of nature and the belief that the environment can and should be controlled are mutually reinforcing ideas.[13] Consequently, Powell's ideas do not align neatly on one side or another of the conservation debate simmering in America in the late 1800s and early 1900s. As Donald Worster observes, though Powell found much "to respect or emulate in nature," he maintained "a greater faith in human interventions in nature than others in the conservation movement had" (*River* 489).

Powell sees nature as an active space, one that has been wrongly assumed to be a static tableau simply waiting to be acted upon by human agriculture, logging, settlement, and so on. Such a characterization sets his version of nature apart from Frémont's vision of a passive landscape. When Powell makes apparently innocuous statements such as "divisional surveys should conform to the topography" (22) or "the natural timber lands of the Arid Region . . . [are] an upper region *set apart by nature* for the growth of timber necessary to the mining, manufacturing, and agricultural industries" (6, emphasis mine), he is instead making the important point that nature has agency. The spaces of the arid region determine how the settlement plots should be set up—the long used and arbitrary methods of government surveyors are obsolete because they do not take into account the changed relation of water and the land. This concept of nature's inherent ability to organize its own space is echoed in one of Powell's later essays, "Institutions for the Arid Lands": "In a group of mountains a small river has its source. A dozen or a score of creeks unite to form the trunk. The creeks higher up divide into brooks. All these streams combined form the drainage system of a hydrographic basin, a *unit of country well defined in nature*, for it is bounded above and on each side by heights of land that rise as crests to part the waters" (*Selected* 46, emphasis mine). Here, natural formations, not survey officials in Washington offices, create the boundaries of the region.

The above passage cites one of the key self-regulating natural systems Powell analyzes in the *Report:* the hydrographic basin, a relatively low area of land into which water drains from higher areas. An example is the closed system of the Great Salt Lake, which, "having no outlet, has its level determined by the relation of evaporation to inflow" (58). As Powell represents it, the hydrographic basin is an area of land that has functional integrity: in other words, the fluctuations in the level of the lake are one aspect of a system that encompasses the lake, the adjacent lowlands, the mountain streams that drain into the lake, and the mountain slopes that isolate the basin from the surrounding area. Powell's method of analyzing this system endows the Salt Lake drainage basin with the power of self-regulation:

> As the water falls it retires from its shore, and the slopes being exceedingly gentle the area of the lake is rapidly contracted. The surface for evaporation diminishes and its ratio to the inflow becomes less. As the water rises the surface of the lake rapidly increases, and the ratio of evaporation to inflow becomes greater. In this way a limit is set to the oscillation of the lake as dependent on the ordinary fluctuations of climate, and the cumulation of results is prevented. Whenever the variation of the water level from its mean position becomes great, the

resistance to its further advance in that direction becomes proportionally great. For the convenience of a name, I shall speak of this oscillation of the lake as the *limited oscillation.* (58–59)

This is a detailed description of self-control, a narrative of stability in which Powell emphasizes undramatic qualities such as "limits." The lake's behavior is nonlinear—"oscillation" denotes a quasi-circular movement, back and forth, that eventually seeks a balance, much as a moving pendulum is slowly drawn to a stable position by the combined forces of gravity and friction. Even more important, who or what sets the limit? Not the observing scientist, but the system itself, self-acting and self-perpetuating in a predictable cycle.

Powell's intention, however, is not merely to describe the drainage system and other natural features; ultimately, his goal is to control the landscape through the power of science. Thus the *Report* exhibits a tension between nature as it is and nature as it should be. This process of control suggested in the *Report*, seen broadly, has two facets: the quantitative description of a system's behavior and the suggested artificial means of altering and improving this behavior with an end to human benefit. This emphasis upon control differs from the "heroic" scientific exploration of Frémont and King; in their narratives, it matters mainly that space is mapped, that territory is legitimized by making it known. Powell's analysis, in contrast, is much more future-directed: scientific data not only describe the landscape's contours but also guide the development of land policy and the use of natural resources.

Powell looks at the hydrographic basin, a system he has characterized as active and self-regulating, and sees opportunities for the scientific irrigator to exert control over the arid environment. He concludes that an unmodified nature is simply inadequate to support human endeavors such as farming: "the water cannot be used for irrigation on the lands immediately contiguous to the streams. . . . The waters must be taken to a greater or less extent on the bench lands to be used in irrigation. All the waters of all the arid lands will eventually be taken from their natural channels, and they can be utilized only to the extent to which they are thus removed, and water rights must of necessity be severed from the natural channels" (42). In this context, nature does not dictate use. As Powell sees it, building irrigation systems (consisting of canals for redirection and reservoirs for storage) is a way to assert human independence of natural conditions. While we must react intelligently to the limitations of a given space, ultimately we can escape the constraints of the self-regulating system. Such faith in the potential of irrigation leads to the supremely confident statement that "Crops thus cultivated are not subject to the vicissitudes of rainfall; the farmer fears no droughts; his labors are seldom interrupted and his crops rarely injured by storms" (10). Moreover, irrigation practices are tied to the necessity for profitable farming: control means bringing nature "into line" in order that humans may participate in the economic sphere.

How can we account for this apparently ironic shift in Powell's descriptions of nature? How can he transform the arid ecosystem from a self-governing entity with powerful agency into a system that requires human control? Note, of course, that nature's so-called inadequacy is not a fault *within* the system, a built-in imperfection. Rather, Powell recognizes that any such limitations are human-determined: in the absence of people necessarily forced to operate within a profit-driven economic system, nature would do marvelously by itself. Science is the only means, however, by which the human presence and economic stability may be reconciled within the system. Thus, in some sense, Powell's shift to a control-centered view of nature (ideas that served as a transition into Gifford Pinchot's early-twentieth-century practices of resource management) is driven by, in his view, the decidedly unnatural forces of economic and political necessity.

A deeper, epistemological basis exists for this shift as well: rooted within Powell's representation of nature as a self-regulating system (e.g., the hydrographic basin) is a fundamentally mechanistic viewpoint, a metaphor for nature that emerged during the Scientific Revolution in Europe during the sixteenth and seventeenth centuries, the time of Bacon, Descartes, Hobbes, and Newton. As historian Carolyn Merchant argues,

> The removal of animistic, organic assumptions about the cosmos constituted the death of nature—the most far-reaching effect of the Scientific Revolution. Because nature was now viewed as a system of dead, inert particles moved by external, rather than inherent forces, the mechanical framework itself could legitimate the manipulation of nature. Moreover, as a conceptual framework, the mechanical order had associated with it a framework of values based on power, fully compatible with the directions taken by commercial capitalism. (*Death* 193)

Even as Powell acknowledges that nature is an independent entity with agency, he interprets it as a machine that operates predictably and systematically rather than as an organism endowed with self-consciousness. Just as the water level of the Great Salt Lake drainage basin oscillates from high to low (an apt example of a machine, indeed), Powell's view of nature as a system swings back and forth between an ecocentric conception of an independent, self-governing nature and a mechanistic representation that responds to outside (human) control. Built into the concept of the machine is the assumption that we can fix it if it breaks down, re-engineer it to perform to our specifications, and control its performance according to the rational goal of efficiency.[14]

Absent from the *Report*'s descriptions of nature are the gendered (or, more generally, organic) metaphors common in nineteenth-century nature writing (see chapter 5) as well as in the exploration narratives of Frémont and King. In this sense the *Report*'s rhetoric bears closer resemblance to twentieth-century ecosystem analyses than to the literary conventions of nineteenth-century nature writing. Yet Powell's mechanistic portrait of nature is congruent with the gendered opposition of a passive, objectified nature and an active, rational, and masculine scientist-explorer; consequently, the impulse to manage the arid ecosystem is a logical extension of the Frémontian impulse to conquer the feminine wilderness. Without coloring his text with sexual metaphors, Powell nonetheless sets up a relation in which a rather impersonal science (rather than a romantic scientist-hero) masters the workings of a great machine, modifying its contours and behavior to produce a desired end. As with Frémont's rhetoric of conquest, Powell's science is a means of exerting power over nature.

Science: The Expression of Doubt, the Language of Hope

For Powell, the tools of science provide not only the means to represent and control nature but also a method by which to direct the rational settlement of the West. The latter purpose is better understood by recognizing that science is paradoxically cautious in the interpretation of data, while confident about its basic method. To this day, scientific discourse is often characterized by both a pragmatic sense of doubt (as embodied in questions such as "What's wrong with this theory? What are its weaknesses or gaps?") and a profound undercurrent of hope (most evident in the widespread belief that science is the ultimate means of learning about nature and fostering human progress). Along these lines, Powell's *Report* ironically proffers science as a means of articulating both doubt and hope about two contentious issues concerning the development of human communities in the arid regions of the American West in the 1870s. How does this scientific appraisal of the western environment deal with the Native peoples of the area, who have evolved very different ways of living within the arid region and adapting to its limitations? Second, how does science serve to critique and redefine the structure of the white communities that are forming and developing at a rapid pace in the arid West?

As a document expressing scientific doubt, the *Report* bluntly defines the profound limits of human endeavor with respect to nature as a whole. Such a belief grows out of Powell's contention that the arid region is not the agricultural paradise the "boosters" of the West would have white Americans believe—rain will simply not follow the plow. In addition, Powell articulates skepticism that the region's present human population is living prudently and efficiently. Powell critiques the living practices of both the Native American and Euro-American populations and contends that the former group destroys natural resources while the latter will abuse those resources without a clear vision of future use and development.

Powell's scientific appraisal of the arid region and its human element eventually comes to terms with the Native peoples of the area, who have developed their own ways of living within and adapting to the dry environment, and who have existed there for many hundreds of years. This particular issue in the *Report* is, however, very easy for readers to miss, since Powell mentions Native Americans only twice in the entire document. There is, moreover, not a single reference to "Indians" in the *Report*'s comprehensive index. Such a near-omission seems odd, especially in light of the fact that he was intensely interested in the culture, beliefs, languages, and arts of various western tribes. Powell, in fact, spent a great deal of time studying the Native peoples during his explorations of Utah, Colorado, and Arizona; he also served as the first director of the Smithsonian's Bureau of Ethnology, which strove to understand and document the languages and customs of Native Americans.

Nevertheless, within the scope of Powell's *Report*, the only destructive human activity mentioned as a significant problem is that caused by the Native Americans, who, he states, "systematically set fire to forests for the purpose of driving game" (17). Though Powell gives the tribes the benefit of the doubt by reminding us that their acts are borne of necessity and not of "a wanton desire . . . to destroy that which is of value to the white man" (17–18), he rather bluntly suggests a harsh solution to the "problem": "The fires can, then, be very greatly curtailed by the removal of the Indians" (18). Such statements make it very clear that when he talks about this destruction, it is not an ecocentric regard for nature or even aesthetics that concerns him, but rather the potential loss of natural resources available to the white population. Second, Powell tacitly assumes that the negative effects of a certain group of people (Natives) can be offset by the appropriate measures of control exercised by another group (white settlers). In this view, Native Americans are not fellow citizens, but merely an ecological problem to be overcome. In effect, the *Report* takes the issue of destructive human activity and places it squarely upon the shoulders of the Native peoples. As a so-called primitive culture, they cannot access the scientific perspective available to the white explorer-scientist; the only space left for them within Powell's discourse is literally *within* the natural system, as an integral though problematic part of it. As part of nature, rather than objective observers or controllers of it, they can be modified (i.e., physically removed) with no further compunction or difficulty than in diverting a stream of water.

I should stress Powell's attitudes toward the Native Americans he befriended, depended upon, studied, and ultimately helped to displace are quite complex. His journals are evidence of his general compassion and sympathy for the various southwestern tribes he encountered in his scientific travels. On a person-to-person level, Powell displayed considerable respect for the detailed knowledge systems and cultural practices of each tribe, and as an ethnologist he was instrumental in emphasizing the differences among Native cultures (rather than projecting blanket generalizations onto them). Yet, his professional position ultimately led him to consider the Native peoples as objects of scientific study and anthropological preservation, rather than autonomous individuals and cultures. Powell's philosophical framework consisted of an "evolutionary" view of human cultures, in which white Euro-Americans were assumed to be "civilized" and thus evolutionarily advanced, while Native Americans, being "savage," were seen to be culturally unevolved.[15]

Powell's objectification of the arid region's Native peoples is indeed deeply disturbing, especially when we consider that he was one of the more enlightened members of his culture about the inherent value and importance of Native societies. But as it turns out, Powell's advocacy of the scientific management of human beings does not merely refer to his views on Native Americans and his recommendation that they be removed from the natural system. His scientific sensibility leads him to conclude that the Euro-Americans in the arid region are just as badly in need of carefully managed control as are the scattered Native tribes and the environment itself. In short, Powell sees that fundamental changes are needed in white social relations in order to foster "a system of governance to achieve environmental conservation, democratic decision making, and community stability" (Worster, *Unsettled* 15). Consequently, the *Report* contains a strong critique of individualism and argues that the social unit of the local *community* is better adapted to living wisely and productively within the western environment.

Within the first two chapters of the *Report*, Powell bolsters his scientific program by constructing what I loosely identify as a mythic drama—in the process, he attempts to integrate science seamlessly into the fabric of western settlement. This drama he presents is a Manichean morality play, a struggle between potential good and impending evil, and the story amounts to a critique of the autonomous individual, that staple ingredient of American political thought. In presenting such a critique, Powell runs up against one of the most powerful myths of the American West, "a story about a simple, rural people coming into a western country . . . and creating there a peaceful, productive life" (Worster, *Under* 6). This is the vision of the independent, hard-working, land-owning farmer—the yeoman of Jefferson and Crèvecoeur.

Despite his attachment to the yeoman farmer, his sensitivity to the "want of all persons desiring to become . . . settlers . . . in the great Rocky Mountain Region" (*Report* 29), Powell has a fundamental problem with the notion of spirited American individualism in the arid West. To begin with, the archetypal westering pioneer built up in the American consciousness by exploration narratives, western histories, and dime novels may be appealing—but this supposedly virtuous individual is short-sighted. As Powell states, "The pioneer is fully engaged in the *present* with its hopes of immediate remuneration for labor. The *present* development of the country fully occupies him" (41, emphasis mine). Such a state of affairs directly conflicts with Powell's future-oriented scientific approach. Science, in contrast, provides the tools with which to plan for the future and go beyond single-minded fixation on survival in the here and now in order to maximize production from an environment relatively limited in agricultural resources.

While the "good" individual is flawed, though perhaps not irreparably so, Powell also identifies an "evil" character in his drama of opposites: the venture capitalist, who ruthlessly speculates on land and attempts to monopolize the most precious of the region's resources, water. This version of individualism gone sour is not merely short-sighted but is also selfish, as Powell tells us:

> [I]t is believed that it is best to permit the people to divide their lands for themselves—not in a way by which each man may take what he pleases for himself, but by providing methods by which these settlers may organize and mutually protect each other from the rapacity of individuals. . . . [A]ll values inhere in the water, and an equitable division of the waters can be made only by a wise system of parceling the lands; and the people in organized bodies can well be trusted with this right, while individuals could not thus be trusted. (38)

This is a powerful statement, the core of Powell's argument for the restructuring of the relation between human beings and nature in the available space of the arid region. While he draws a distinction between the yeoman settlers and the rapacious speculators—and thus points out the limitations of each—he also argues that the protagonist in this western struggle is not so much the individual per se as the dynamic *community* of individuals (the "people in organized bodies"), working collectively, "mutually protecting each other." Interestingly, Powell evokes a moral precept to underlie his critique of the frontier individual—only the community can be trusted with handling the region's vital resources. Thus, Powell argues that just as nature needs to be controlled (i.e., irrigated), so does *human* nature require regulation, in order that the control of nature does not escalate into abuse.

Powell's scientific understanding of the arid environment undergirds his critique of individualism and emphasis upon communitarianism. Like the arid ecosystem, individuals might function at a sustainable level if left to their own devices, but their happiness and capability of production are augmented by scientific "improvements." In sum, the process of scientific management can control the political relations between humans and the ecosystem just as effectively as it can exercise control upon nature.

In the end, Powell's 1878 *Report*—ostensibly a dry scientific description of the arid lands of the American West—is a sophisticated reformulation of the relationships among nature, science, and human society. Once quietly ignored by Congress for its challenges to the political forces of American western expansion, the *Report*'s emphasis on the scientific control of a mechanical nature anticipated the massive technological transformations of the region during the twentieth century—changes largely responsible for the widespread development of and explosive population growth in the hydraulic West. At the same time, Powell's recognition of nature's self-regulating properties and his belief that agriculture and apportionment of property must conform to the landscape display elements of an ecocentric perspective that would emerge in the writings of preservationists such as John Muir and, later on, ecologists such as Aldo Leopold, Rachel Carson, and Loren Eiseley. For Powell, science itself (not the explorer-hero) becomes the ultimate problem solver, giving us the tools to construct a detailed empirical representation of the arid region and to reconfigure how human communities should be organized with the western ecosystem.

· Part 3 ·

Nature's Identity and
the Critique of Science

FIVE

"The Earth Is the Common Home of All"

Susan Fenimore Cooper's
Investigations of
a Settled Landscape

F rom within the forests of central New York State in the mid-1800s, a land of expansive woodlands, rolling hills, quiet lakes, and small but growing communities, writer and naturalist Susan Fenimore Cooper published a book entitled *Rural Hours* (1850), which described the local environment and rural customs of her home village, Cooperstown. Cooper's text, like that of fellow diarist and enthusiastic observer of nature Henry David Thoreau's *Walden* (1854), is organized as a daily journal and covers the span of one year, season by season. Within this deceptively simple structure, however, is a complex, multilayered narrative that integrates natural history, cultural analysis, and personal stories—together, these elements form an environmental and social snapshot of Cooperstown in the mid-nineteenth century.

As one of the earliest works of nature writing by women in America and an important part of the nineteenth-century natural history tradition, Cooper's *Rural Hours* is an intriguing and instructive counterpoint to both the adventurous exploration narratives of Frémont and Byrd as well as the scientific management of nature espoused by Gilman and Powell. While the Frémontian explorer mapped unknown territory, viewed nature as an obstacle to be withstood and conquered, and shaped the romantic persona of the scientist as frontier hero, the ideas and perspectives of naturalist-writers such as Cooper offered alternative readings of the human-nature relation and the function of science.[1] *Rural Hours* draws upon the tradition of American and European natural history writing in the qualitative description of the environment and its inhabitants. Though Cooper occasionally characterizes the land as female, a common convention in nature writing, she does not make nature a passive object of scientific conquest and in the process reproduce the separation between the human and natural communities. In addition, Cooper's local natural history paints a complex and multidimensional portrait of an established rural society within its natural setting, in the process suggesting that humans are merely one part of a given ecological community and need to see themselves within that broad context in order to improve their own social relationships. In this sense, Cooper finds a degree of kinship with the writings of Gilman and Powell, both of whom envisioned idealized communities in which stability is fostered by a harmonious relation between nature and science.

In this chapter I closely examine Cooper's scientific, literary, and environmental approach as a naturalist and writer to her local community—one where humans, animals, plants, and inorganic materials interact and affect one another. Cooper explores various rhetorical strategies and conventions of natural history, such as anthropomorphism, to underscore the fundamental connections between humanity and nature as well as to communicate spiritual, moral, and social lessons. *Rural Hours* also articulates a rather forward-looking, if limited, conservation ethic in which wild areas as well as developed and cultivated lands are valued, thus presenting science as a means of connecting with rather than controlling nature—in this sense, her work can be characterized as proto-ecological. However, by addressing but not fully resolving our conflicting desires to preserve or exploit nature, as well as the role of science in mediating this conflict, Cooper exemplifies mid-nineteenth-century tensions between romanticizing the cultivated landscape and becoming alarmed at the ever-accelerating loss of wild areas. *Rural Hours* thus anticipates some of the challenges faced by late-nineteenth-century environmental advocates such as John Muir as well as twentieth-century ecologists such as Aldo Leopold, Rachel Carson, and Loren Eiseley.

Literary and Cultural Contexts: Ways of Reading Rural Hours

At least three nineteenth-century literary and cultural currents provide a historical context for Cooper's *Rural Hours:* her own family's tradition in letters and regional history, the writings and scientific work of American women, and the developing and predominately male tradition of natural history writing. These multiple contextual strands suggest many possible readings of Cooper's *Rural Hours,* options that are further extended by the text's artful fusing of several literary subgenres—the local ramble, the seasonal journal, the natural history essay, autobiography, and rural history. To begin with, Cooper's book can be considered the third part of a family trilogy about the Cooperstown locale, and consequently it is rooted in the prior exploration and settlement of the land.[2] Cooper's grandfather, William Cooper, published *A Guide to the Wilderness* in 1810, a book that outlined his role in the settlement of the area and served as a source of practical advice to would-be settlers in central New York State. James Fenimore Cooper, Susan's well-known father, who enjoyed a lengthy literary career, depicted the Cooperstown landscape in *The Pioneers* (1823), the first installment of what would become the "Leatherstocking Tales." Critic Lucy Maddox considers the multigenerational interest in the Cooperstown locale to be significant to our understanding of *Rural Hours;* the book, she claims, "completes a pattern, providing final documentation of the moral and cultural significance of the great undertaking that begins with the grandfather's confrontation of the wilderness and ends with the daughter's inheritance of a place that is no longer wild but comfortably rural" (141). This literary and familial heritage not only signifies Cooper's significant investment in and attachment to the area but also ensures that her reading of the Cooperstown landscape would resonate with the human stories and environmental changes resulting from past exploration and settlement.

Rural Hours is also a notable example of the work and writings of other nineteenth-century women who practiced natural history (particularly botany) or scientific popularization in America. Before the widespread professionalization of the sciences as male-dominated disciplines in the latter half of the nineteenth century, women scientist-writers like Cooper contributed greatly to the scientific education of a broad range of readers.[3] Women's interest and participation in the study and practice of natural history were fostered by naturalist organizations that cropped up in American cities in the 1800s, and that made themselves readily available to female participants. These "lyceums" for science even existed in more sparsely populated rural regions, and the instruction in and inspiration for science that they provided was reinforced by scientific texts written by and for women (Rossiter 3–5; Norwood 3).

One of the most famous of these is Almira Hart Lincoln Phelps's *Familiar Lectures on Botany*, which was first published in 1829 and eventually sold around 275,000 copies.[4] Impressive in both detail and scope, the text introduces readers to the purpose of methods of botany within the larger context of natural science, outlines the anatomy and physiology of plants, discusses and even critiques the various classification schema used by botanists (with an emphasis on Linnaean descriptive taxonomy), covers principles of biogeography and economic botany, and finally includes a practical flora designed to help readers identify species in the field. Phelps urged American women to make and study their own botanical collections, and she popularized science for women as a positive supplement to family and religious life. In line with popular conceptions about the role of women in society, she did not encourage women to become "professional" scientists per se; for her, the "study of science was . . . not to threaten the established social order by taking women out of the home but to enrich and elevate their domestic life" (Rossiter 7). Other scientific instructional texts written in the United States include Sarah Hale's *Flora's Interpreter; or, The American Book of Flowers and Sentiments* (1832) and Lucy Hooper's *The Lady's Book of Flowers and Poetry* (1848). These texts differed radically from Phelps's in their structure and purpose: Hale, for example, seeks to "stimulate curiosity respecting the subject of botany, than to impart instruction in the science" (ix). After a brief introductory section explaining botanical basics, the bulk of the book consists of an alphabetical list of flowering plants—each one classified, succinctly described, and juxtaposed with two or three snippets of poetry from English and American authors. Such texts artfully mixed science and sentiment and rested upon the assumption that botanical study was conducive to moral improvement in young women (Norwood, *Made* 16–17).

Cooper's emergence as a naturalist-writer in 1850 heralded the arrival of a second and third generation of American women scientists who pursued botany, ornithology, and entomology from the latter part of the nineteenth century through the early twentieth century. In her landmark study of American women's literary and scientific engagement with nature, Vera Norwood contends that Cooper "found a space in which to write a classic naturalist's essay . . . [and] framed the context in which many American women have produced such works from her day to the present" (*Made* 28).[5] Most of these women were amateur rather than professional scientists, often lacked access to museum collections and academic libraries, and carried out their work in relative isolation and obscurity; yet some forged productive working relationships with well-known scientists, often by active correspondence, and published their observations in articles and books. One notable example is Graceanna Lewis (1821–1912), a versatile naturalist with particular skills in ornithology and illustration, who published several natural history articles in the late nineteenth century, including an essay entitled "Truth and the Teachers of Truth" in which she argued for the reconciliation of Darwinian theory with the notion of God as creator. Mary Treat (1830–1923) was a highly respected naturalist who counted Asa Gray and Charles Darwin among her friends and correspondents. Treat made several original contributions to botany and entomology, such as her observations of how the carnivorous pitcher plants and bladderworts capture insects; she published a range of articles in magazines such as *Harper's* and *American Naturalist* as well as the book *Home Studies in Nature* (1885), which describes her detailed observations of a one-acre backyard plot. Olive Thorne Miller (1831–1918) wrote about a variety of habitats from Maine to southern California and specialized in writing about nature for children; her books include *Little Folks in Feathers and Fur* (1875) and *A Bird Lover in the West* (1894). Lastly, Florence Merriam (1863–1948), who also published under her married name of Bailey, was a formidable intellect and a prolific writer, producing five books (four before she was forty years old) and numerous articles on birds. Merriam was the first female member of the American Ornithologists' Union and a contributor to *Audubon Magazine, Condor, Auk*, and *Bird-Lore*; her books include *A-Birding on a Bronco* (1896), *Birds of Village and Field* (1898), and *Among the Birds in the Grand Canyon Country* (1939).[6]

To a greater extent than any of these works by her fellow women scientist-writers, Cooper's *Rural Hours* recently has become a recognized part of the established tradition of American natural history writing, whose major contributors include Thomas Jefferson, William Bartram, Alexander Wilson, and John James Audubon in the late eighteenth and early nineteenth centuries; Henry David Thoreau (particularly his later writings) in the middle part of the nineteenth century; and John Burroughs, John Muir, and Mary Austin in the late nineteenth and early twentieth centuries. These writers exemplified the practice of literary natural history—the close and careful observation of plants, animals, and birds within a given environment—as expressed in descriptive, analytic, and quite often autobiographical essays.[7] Such texts introduced generations of American readers to the life and physical character of rural and wild landscapes, communicated scientific knowledge about nature accessibly and eloquently, defined and celebrated the beauty and power of nature, and reflected upon the relationship humans had forged and might yet construct with their environment. As ecocritic Michael Branch suggests, our natural history literature not only turned "American attention toward the cultural possibilities of the land and . . . [spoke] for the divinity of wilderness, [but also] valorized the dual urge to document wild nature and to express concern regarding its critical endangerment by human development" (1059). Finally, the ecological science that developed in the twentieth century—and that had popular expression in the works of ecologist-writers such as Aldo Leopold, Rachel Carson, and Loren Eiseley—has many of its roots in the natural history tradition of the nineteenth century.[8]

Lawrence Buell, whose book *The Environmental Imagination: Thoreau, Nature Writing, and the Formation of American Culture* (1995) was a major contribution to the burgeoning field of ecological literary criticism, lauds Cooper's *Rural Hours* as the first major American example of "literary bioregionalism" and as an essential part of the literary and environmental context for Thoreau's *Walden*, perhaps the most revered work of American nature writing. Buell suggests that "as a reinterpretation of place, Cooper's essay is a *tour de force* of the same sort [as *Walden*]: the ecological transformation of a somewhat stolid Yankee community by seeing it from the woods, seeing it indeed as if it were properly part of the woods, rather than seeing the woods as ancillary to itself" (265–66). Another of Cooper's most perceptive critics,

Rochelle Johnson concurs with Buell and others that Cooper's view of nature "deepens our understanding of the environmental imagination" (Johnson, "Placing" 65); however, she further argues we should resist reading *Rural Hours* primarily in terms of Thoreau or (like Norwood) through the lens of nineteenth-century literary domesticity and separate spheres ideology. For Johnson, both perspectives may "overemphasize the degree to which an author is concerned with the cultural as opposed to the natural" (81); instead, she views Cooper as making "a conscious entry into American natural history writing—a male-dominated genre" (79). Besides contributing to the discourse of natural history, *Rural Hours* advances a kind of cultural critique about the nature of rural landscapes and communities: Johnson suggests that Cooper integrates a consideration for wilderness into the relationships among "morality, virtue, and the design of landscape and architecture," for *Rural Hours* promotes not only conservation and preservation of rural landscapes but also the study of natural history as part of a cultivated person's education ("Susan" 49).

These various interpretations, I believe, are ultimately complementary rather than contradictory. Although Cooper most certainly stands as an early figure in women's nature writing, her literary techniques and scientific sensibility also link her with the mostly male natural history tradition in the nineteenth century; in this sense, her work shows the difficulty of drawing clear lines between natural history practiced by men and women (Buell 44). Even as she addresses themes and subjects typically ascribed to women writers—home, community, social customs, moral standards—she learns from and contributes to the scientific discourse of natural history, as evidenced by the works of other naturalists she cites throughout *Rural Hours*. Consequently, though a strong contrast is evident between Cooper's local natural history and the frontier adventures and exploration narratives of male explorers such as John Charles Frémont, John Wesley Powell, and Clarence King—both in terms of rhetorical structure and the persona of the scientist-narrator—much less radical distinctions exist between Cooper and the work of, say, John Burroughs, whose nature essays centered upon his home of Riverby in New York's Hudson River valley and greatly appealed to women readers.

In the end, *Rural Hours* is fascinating not only because it combines multiple strands of the nature writing tradition but also because it provides a complex and fairly substantial critique of the relation between nature and the human community. Cooper's analysis is all the more impressive given the conventions and strictures of natural history discourse, particularly in the era before Darwin and the advent of ecology proper. While pre-Darwinian natural history assumed a static version of nature in which species were unchanging, discrete entities and humanity resided at the center of a divinely ordered universe, evolutionary theory transformed nature into a dynamic arena of change, displaced human beings from their privileged position of authority, and questioned the necessity of a divine Creator. Over a similar timeframe, the development of ecology as a scientific discipline stressed the interconnections and interactive processes among all components of a given environment—soil, air, water, energy, and organisms—rather than simply the naming, describing, and classifying of species. Cooper's book appears in the fuzzy transitional zone of the mid-nineteenth century and thus provides a sense of past assumptions about science and nature as well as glimpses of ideas to come. More specifically, Cooper explores and implicitly challenges the limits of natural history, for even as she employs rhetorical conventions such as gendering the landscape, reading evidence of divinity within the natural order, or anthropomorphizing animals, she constructs a proto-ecological view of the Cooperstown community in which the human presence is read within the context of the whole environment. Cooper's delight in the pastoral landscape and emphasis on description do not prevent her from interpreting the land in the context of process and change and advocating a rather forward-looking conservation ethic.

Cooper's Integrative Natural History

The fact that the first edition of *Rural Hours* in 1850 was anonymously credited to "a lady," and that Cooper characterized the book as a series of "many trifling observations on rustic matters" that "make no claim whatever to scientific knowledge" (3) both signify her adherence to standards of feminine modesty. But her admission that the book contained nothing of scientific note is humility taken too far. Though *Rural Hours* does not report on original scientific findings or chart new territory, the text includes close and detailed observations of plant and animal species, comparative taxonomy, habitat characterization, and discussion of behavioral patterns and adaptations. Cooper also refers to and comments upon the work of naturalists such as John James Audubon, Alexander Wilson, Thomas Nutall, and James Ellsworth DeKay, references that at times go well beyond mere acknowledgment and are often witty critiques of older theories.[9] While meditating on the subject of migration behavior in swallows, for example, Cooper states that "It is amusing to look back to the discussions of naturalists during the last century"; past observers of birds had surmised that swallows spent the winter months either "torpid . . . in caves and hollow trees" or "under water . . . in the mud, at the bottom of rivers and pools!" (166). She finds it strange, from her mid-nineteenth-century vantage point (in which swallows have been confirmed and classified as a migrating species), that "men, both learned and unlearned, often show a sort of antipathy to simple truths" (167).

Although close and detailed description of natural phenomena as well as occasional commentaries upon the writings of other naturalists comprise the foundations of Cooper's scientific approach to nature, other aspects of her rhetoric—the relationship between gender and the landscape, the emphasis upon unity and interconnectedness, and the anthropomorphization of living creatures—provide special insight into what I call her integrative natural history. Cooper's passion for observing nature and representations of the landscape are shaped in part by prevailing cultural associations of women with nature and her own rather conservative notions about gender and women's role in society; at times, however, *Rural Hours* also shows Cooper's ability to step outside these conventions and even critique the assumptions behind them.[10]

In line with the beliefs and writings of influential women such as Catherine Beecher, Cooper in many respects considered herself a woman rooted in the domestic sphere. For many years she faithfully attended to her father and served as his secretary, to some degree subordinating her interests and writing career to his own.[11] Her interest in botany and ornithology, fostered by her grandfather De Lancey and her grandmother Cooper as well as her reading of contemporary naturalists, was an acceptable activity for genteel, middle-class women in nineteenth-century America, and Cooper, like many others, did not see her avocation as a potential profession. In the sections of *Rural Hours* in which she comments upon village life and domestic arrangements, Cooper remarks that a woman's activities should be centered upon the home. During a visit to a nearby farmstead and after seeing the results of the farmwife's spinning and weaving work, she remarks that "it is certainly pleasant to see the women busy in this way, beneath the family roof, and one is much disposed to believe that the home system is healthier and safer for the individual, in every way. Home, we may rest assured, will always be, as a rule, the best place for a woman; her labors, pleasures, and interests, should all centre there, whatever be her sphere of life" (99–100).[12] A bit further on, she criticizes the hairstyles of a few visitors to the farm: "a number of women in that neighborhood had their hair cropped short like men, a custom which seems all but unnatural" (100). In another context, Cooper praises American society by noting that "in no [other] country is the protection given to women's helplessness more full and free—in no country is the assistance she receives from the stronger arm so general—and nowhere does her weakness meet with more forbearance and consideration" (106). Cooper apparently had clear views on what constituted proper work, behavior, and appearance for the two sexes, and her ideas on gender closely align with the separate spheres ideology that held sway in the mid-nineteenth century. In this sense, Cooper's life and activities "mirrored the picture of proper womanhood touted in ladies magazines and sentimental novels of the time" (Norwood, *Made* 26).

These values and beliefs are to some extent reflected in her representations of nature in *Rural Hours*. Echoing the rhetoric of Frémont and other naturalists of the nineteenth century, Cooper occasionally identifies the land as female, referring to the earth as a mother and once discussing nearby Otsego Lake in maternal terms (10, 104), though the infrequency of such explicit evocations may indicate merely an unconscious nod to rhetorical convention. When assessing the relative merits of wild and cultivated roses, she favors the "peculiar modesty about the wild rose which that of the gardens does not always possess" (75). This contrast leads her into an extended analogy between roses and womanhood: "it reminds one of the painful difference between the gentle, healthy-hearted daughter of home, the light of the house, and the meretricious dancer, tricked out upon the stage to dazzle and bewilder, and be stared at by the mob. The rose has so long been an emblem of womanly loveliness, that we do not like to see her shorn of one feminine attribute; and modesty in every true-hearted woman is, like affection, a growth of her very nature, whose roots are fed with her life's blood" (75). The analogy says as much about women's social position and what constitutes proper behavior as it does about nature itself. Together, these passages suggest that Cooper places some stock in the traditional association of women and the natural world during her era—the casting of the environment as either a nurturing mother, an innocent virgin, or a wild and potentially dangerous seductress.[13]

However, such characterizations undeniably can serve different purposes depending upon their context and the overall objective of the writer. Frémont's vision of the land as virginal and seductive, for example, facilitated his project of conquest by mapping and settlement. Fifty years later, wilderness advocate John Muir would evoke similar images in his descriptions of the parks and forest reservations of the West. In essays written to educate the public about the beauty and grandeur of the West's wild spaces, and to spur tourists' interest in visiting these places of solitude and quiet and advocating their protection, Muir portrays a scene in which "it seems as if Nature, glad to make an open space between woods so dense and ice so deep, were economizing the precious ground, and trying to see how many of her darlings [flowers] she can get together in one mountain wreath" (*Our* 23). Later on, he describes Yosemite in rapturous, celebratory tones: "its marvelous beauty, displayed in striking and alluring forms, woos the admiring wanderer on and on, higher and higher, charmed and enchanted" (57). Nearly identical in expression to Frémont but written in the spirit of the nascent conservation movement at the beginning of the twentieth century, Muir's evocations of a female nature serve not the conquering impulse but the desire to preserve and experience wilderness.

In one of the few places in which Cooper explicitly evokes a female nature, she goes beyond mere description to explore the very conventions by which we characterize the land. She devotes one of the longest single entries in *Rural Hours* to philosophical reflection on the character of autumn and suggests that our gendered metaphors for nature (in this case, for each of the seasons) are rooted in linguistic conventions and cultural experiences, not in any inherent quality of the land or season. While some readers may be tempted to skip Cooper's long review of poetic portraits of the fall, the section in fact displays a remarkable degree of critical awareness. Cooper begins her musings by noting that "Autumn would appear to have received generally a dull character from the poets of the Old World" (202), a recognition that both disturbs and amazes her, given the splendor of autumnal colors in central New York. She further notes how these representations are related to how the word *autumn* is gendered (masculine, usually) in various European languages, and how such gendering is usually linked to cultural values peculiar to a given nation (204). English provides a special case, since nouns are not linked to gender, and thus "poets are allowed to do as they choose in this matter" (205)—namely, to personify autumn as feminine rather than masculine.

Overall, her literary analysis reveals that there is no single given way to represent a season (and, by extension, nature itself); rather, she finds heterogeneity in European and American literary characterizations. And while she feels that literature on the whole has given autumn short shrift by misrepresenting it as a dull, colorless, depressing season, she notes that the last half-century has witnessed a rediscovery of autumn in English literature, one marked by what she terms a "much more definite and accurate" approach to natural description. This change she attributes to the rising fashion of landscape painting, the emphasis upon a natural style of gardening, and, most importantly, the trend toward realism and concrete experience in representation: writers have "learned at length to look at nature by the light of the sun, and not by the glimmerings of the poet's lamp" (208). Curiously, she mentions nothing of science as a direct influence upon these representations; yet, her emphasis upon realism and observing "by the light of the sun" suggest that the eye of the naturalist produces a much different portrait of nature than that of the poet. Moreover, her extended literary analysis hints that while Cooper, on one hand, indulged in conventional tropes in her representations of nature, she also was greatly aware of and sensitive to how such metaphors are strongly determined by a wide range of cultural forces.

This complexity of Cooper's use of gendered language in *Rural Hours*—in one sense typical of her time, in another sense exploratory and questioning—illustrates how her representation of the human-nature relation differs substantially from the gendered images found in male-authored exploration texts of the mid-nineteenth century, in which the scientist-hero defines himself apart from nature. Cooper's local explorations of the countryside find her establishing close connections among the plants, animals, and humans she observes, connections that bear little resemblance to the Frémontian impulse to conquer or control. Notwithstanding her modest claims about her book's significance, Cooper in fact suggests an alternative way for human society to flourish within the natural world, one based on connection, integration, and conservation. Such an approach was taken up in various ways by subsequent nature writers such as Thoreau, Burroughs, Muir, Austin, Leopold, and others—knowledge of nature's interconnections brings humans into closer contact with the world around them, establishes familiarity and intimacy rather than distance. But while a dominant theme of these writers' work was the individual's relationship with the environment—the classic self-in-nature paradigm so central to much of our national literature, and nowhere more evident that in Thoreau's *Walden*—Cooper's insistent focus on the community in nature also links her with the visionary works of John Wesley Powell and Charlotte Perkins Gilman.

Part of this shift from the questing self to the community is evident in Cooper's self-effacing narrative perspective and grounded in her religious view of humankind as subordinate to God in the visible world.

> At hours like these, immeasurable goodness, the infinite wisdom of our Heavenly Father, are displayed in so great a degree of condescending tenderness to unworthy, sinful man, as must appear quite incomprehensible—entirely incredible to reason alone—were it not for the recollection of the mercies of past years. . . . What have the best of us done to merit one such day in a lifetime of follies and failings and sins? The air we breathe so pure and balmy, the mottled heavens above so mild and kindly, the young herb beneath our feet so delicately fresh, every plant of the field decked in beauty, every tree of the forest clothed in dignity, all unite to remind us, that, despite our own unworthiness, "God's mercies are new every day." (45)

For Cooper, the proper human posture within the divinely created universe is one of profound humility and respect. What is stunning in this passage is Cooper's evocation of the *particulars* of nature—air, heavens, herbs, trees—as literal gifts to humans to use wisely. The fragility of these elements is underscored: the herbs might well be carelessly trampled, the air could be made impure, and so on. She impresses the reader with both the delicacy as well as the significance of these connections between human and nonhuman elements. Such mundane things as the act of breathing deserve our thanks, for we enjoy and benefit from such acts "despite our own unworthiness."

Another aspect of Cooper's vision of nature is her recognition, through the scientific observation of plant, animal, and human communities, of the common links among all living species, not only in one particular place but in widely separated regions as well. She enjoys following "these links, connecting lands and races so far apart, reminding us, as they do, that the earth is the common home of all" (56). Such a passage is typical of Cooper, who often dispenses nuggets of commentary or insight within the specific context of communicating the details of a plant, bird, or mammal. Something as simple and humble as a "common showy plant"—the May apple, for instance—is in fact an indicator of something more important, namely, a connection between otherwise divergent "lands and races" (for the plant is found in both North America and Central Asia). The actual foundation for this connection is Cooper's strong belief that "the earth is the common home for all," a phrase that anticipates more recent ecological thinking on the fundamental interdependence of organisms and their environment.

Embedded within this idea of home is the notion of community, one of Cooper's major themes. Her faith in the virtues of domesticity and concern for matters of the home translate into an interest in how plant and animal communities function and a concern for their preservation. In *Rural Hours*, she highlights activities that link human and nonhuman elements within a larger, ever-changing whole. Cooper's emphasis on the community entails a substantial shift away from the paradigm of scientific mastery over nature; the human element is instead considered to be a *part*, rather than simply the final purpose or the prime architect, of the natural world. An appropriate example of this perspective is Cooper's eloquent tribute to the area's forests, a place where "[e]very object . . . has a deeper merit than our wonder can fathom; each has a beauty beyond our full perception" (125–26). For Cooper, the woods are dignified, linked with the past, permanent and unchanging compared to human works. Though the forest is a "noble gift to man" in terms of its "utility and their beauty" (125), it is also a place where humans may retreat for spiritual reflection and the appreciation of God's handiwork. The woods hold this power not just because of their inherent beauty, but also because of "the peculiar nature of the forest, that life and death may ever be found within its bounds, in immediate presence of each other" (126). Cooper feels that the forests are as vital a part of the human community as the town square or an individual's home—the woods provide "a sweet quiet, a noble harmony, a calm repose, which we seek in vain elsewhere, in so full a measure" (127). In her appreciation of the forest as a thing of beauty, evidence of God's creative powers, and place for calm reflection and spiritual renewal, Cooper anticipates John Muir's passionate celebration of western forests several decades later. Within the majestic coniferous forests of the Sierra, Muir wrote, "we find a new world, and stand beside the majestic pines and firs and sequoias silent and awestricken, as if in the presence of superior beings new arrived from some other star, so calm and bright and godlike they are" (*Our* 74).

A third important aspect of Cooper's rhetoric is her use of anthropomorphic description, a textual feature that *Rural Hours* shares with other works of natural history. At face value anthropomorphization seems highly problematic: the projection of distinctly human characteristics, desires, or behaviors onto nonhuman entities strikes most of today's scientists as inappropriate—to anthropomorphize is to infuse subjectivity into ostensibly objective scientific discourse, to indulge in potentially misleading rhetoric rather than straightforward empirical description. Although popular scientific writing might make use of such metaphors, they have no place in formal technical description. But since little distinction existed between popular and technical scientific writing in the eighteenth and nineteenth centuries, natural historians freely used anthropomorphic metaphors as one way to reach beyond mere physical description and thus communicate with a broad readership. Like that of fellow naturalist-writers William Bartram, John James Audubon, John Muir, and John Burroughs, Cooper's manner of reading animal behavior is part ecological analysis and part social commentary; anthropomorphism is a process by which her social, religious, and philosophical values are projected onto her descriptions of nature. Yet this rhetorical strategy, though it treads uncertain ground between scientific (i.e., realistic) description and literary expression, does more than liven up the text or mirror the author's ideological biases. For Cooper, in particular, anthropomorphism is one pathway toward an integrative natural history in which human characters, interactions, and customs are inseparable from the broader natural community.

A key parallel between *Rural Hours* and Bartram's *Travels* (1791), a cornerstone of early American travel literature and natural history, is the anthropomorphic description of bird behavior, though the trope occurs far more frequently in *Rural Hours* than in Bartram's widely read narrative. In his book's introduction, Bartram states that "Birds are in general social and benevolent creatures; intelligent, ingenious, volatile, active beings; and this order of animal creation consists of various nations, bands, or tribes, as may be observed from their different structure, manners, and languages" (25). He implies that bird societies not only mirror ours but also potentially serve as a positive model for human interaction. Bartram also stresses the intrinsic value of various organisms when he, for example, endows birds with traditionally human emotions: "With what peace, love and joy, do they end the last moments of their existence!" (88). Certainly, such characterizations serve to narrow the distinction between humans and other creatures; Bartram says that the "parental and filial affections seem to be as ardent, their sensibility and attachment as active and faithful, as those observed in human nature" (21). Notice here that the standard of comparison rests in humans, not in nonhuman creatures. Such comparisons reinforce his belief that the (perfect and good) work of God is manifest in all living things, and not limited to us. Bartram's rhetoric thus tends more toward an abstract appreciation of divine handiwork rather than an explicit claim that nature provides us with specific social and moral models.

The essays from John James Audubon's *Ornithological Biography* (1831–39) complement his lavish and anatomically precise illustrations, and though the famous artist-naturalist never considered himself a writer as such, his prose stands as a compelling example of American natural history writing in the first half of the nineteenth century. Like Bartram, Audubon recognizes a connection between the beauty of nature and God's creative facilities—he describes the song of the white-crowned sparrow as a sound "so sweet, so refreshing, so soothing, so hope inspiring . . . [that] you experience a pure delight, produced by the invitation thus made to offer your humblest and most sincere thanks to that all-wonderous Being . . . [and] his mighty power" (132). Elsewhere, Audubon draws freely from the annals of human behavior to recount the habits of the birds he illustrates; an apt example is his discussion of the Canada Goose courtship rituals, which feature elaborate dances and motions between males and females, as well as violent encounters among competing males. Indeed, Audubon pushes the knights-in-battle analogy as far as he can when he notes, "Were the weapons more deadly, feats of chivalry would now be performed; as it is, thrust and blow succeed each other like the strokes of hammers driven by sturdy forgers" (153). Perhaps his most dramatic description is saved for the White-Headed (Bald) Eagle, which Audubon characterizes as an efficient and beautifully designed killing machine, one possessing a "ferocious, overbearing, and tyrannical temper" (103). His descriptions of the eagle alternate between detailed accounts of its anatomy and behavior and passionate commentary on the bird's perceived bad character. The essay is framed ironically, since it begins with a rhapsodic tribute to the eagle's status as our national symbol, only to end by echoing Benjamin Franklin's opinion that the bird does not deserve such a position, as its character is besmirched by its greed, lust for violence, and essential cowardice. For Audubon, the bird that steals fish from the smaller osprey—and even pilfers rotting carcasses from vultures—is a flawed symbol indeed. Although Audubon clearly admires the eagle's power and physical gifts, his prose projects highly negative human characteristics onto the bird; it is only in the context of judging human behavior—a highly anthropocentric position—that he can evaluate the habits of the eagle so harshly. For Audubon, then, anthropomorphic description is a conceptual device that allows him to make sense of the behavior of bird species—the moral codes he recognizes form a filter through which to interpret the design of nature.

Although Bartram, Audubon, and others—including Cooper—did not question the appropriateness of such rhetorical projections, naturalist John Burroughs took up the issue of anthropomorphism in nature writing in his 1905 book *Ways of Nature*, and his critique of the practice provides an instructive slant on Cooper's approach fifty years earlier. One of America's most respected nature writers and author of over two dozen books, most of which centered upon the natural history of his farmstead in the Hudson River valley, Burroughs became consternated over what he considered to be the "false natural history" contained in some popular stories about nature. His criticisms in what came to be called the nature-fakers controversy centered upon the writings of Ernest Thompson Seton and William Long, who Burroughs felt improperly anthropomorphized animal behavior without explicitly identifying their work as fiction (Black 130–31).[14] In *Ways of Nature*, he admits that "This sentimental view of animal life has its good side and its bad side. Its good side is its result in making us more considerate and merciful toward our brute neighbors; its bad side is seen in the degree to which it leads to a false interpretation of their lives" (60–61). Furthermore, Burroughs recognizes that the "tendency to sentimentalize nature has . . . largely taken the place of the old tendency to demonize and spiritize it. It is anthropomorphism in another form, less fraught with evil to us, but equally in the way of a clear understanding of the life about us" (108). Thus Burroughs puts the personification of nonhuman life in a broad context of humanity's misconceptions about nature, even as he acknowledges that such a misguided perspective can foster empathy between us and our animal kin. Ironically, Burroughs's own views of nature and the relation between humanity and other animals were greatly influenced by his sympathetic reading of Darwin; it cannot have escaped him that Darwin's notion of evolution via natural selection implies a much closer connection between humans and other animals than that posited by the prevailing Christian worldview, which creates a fundamental distinction between humans (who are made in God's image) and the rest of nature (over which humanity is granted dominion).[15] Moreover, as critic Ralph Black notes, Burroughs himself occasionally personified birds in his early work (136–37)—in *Wake-Robin*, his first book of nature essays, the cow bunting is passingly described as "quite a polygamist, and usually has two or three demure little ladies in faded black beside him" (18).

His early rhetorical indulgences notwithstanding, Burroughs's critique rests upon three fundamental concerns: the definition and limits of animal intelligence; the goals of accuracy and realism in natural description; and the distinction between the literary and scientific interpretation of nature. Though he notes that natural selection works to hone intelligence just as it has "developed and sharpened the claws of the cat and the scent of the fox" (81–82), Burroughs argues that human intelligence is fundamentally different from the quasi-intelligent "instinct" displayed by many animals. Animal intelligence—hard-wired instinct—is acquired genetically and cannot be improved over time (80–81); and although animals do indeed display emotions, curiosity, and even altruism (64–65), they lack the property of self-awareness and critical reflection, hallmarks of human intelligence. Second, Burroughs values realistic representations of animal behavior, especially in the context of nonfictional natural history; the goal here, he states, is "unadulterated, unsweetened observations" (15). As he says in the introduction to *Wake-Robin*, "what I offer . . . is a careful and conscientious record of actual observations and experiences," a nod to realism in his effort to give the reader "a live bird,—a bird in the woods or the fields,—with the atmosphere and associations of the place, and not merely a stuffed and labeled specimen" (v–vi). This last statement evokes Burroughs's third concern: the differences between, on one hand, straightforward scientific description of natural entities and phenomena and, on the other hand, literary naturalism, the rhetorical process by which a writer can connect the human to the natural, reflect on those connections, and awaken sympathies toward nature on the part of readers (*Ways* 192–93). As it turns out, the subtle personification of animals—imaginative assessments of their characters, for example—can pass Burroughs's muster, provided it does not falsely ascribe singularly human intelligence to other creatures, for they serve an important rhetorical function.

Burroughs turns to his friend and fellow naturalist-writer, John Muir, as one who knows where to draw the line between scientific accuracy and artistic license—in the former's view, Muir humanizes the animal world without straining readers' credulity (*Ways* 193).[16] A quick look at several passages in *Our National Parks* illustrates both the range and purpose of Muir's anthropomorphic description. Sometimes Muir attempts to gauge an animal's state of mind, without indulging in obvious personification, as when he describes an "anxious doe" who seems to him "a fine picture of vivid, eager alertness" (143). In other passages, he uses human analogies to describe the sound of a sage cock, whose voice is as "clear in tone as a boy's small willow whistle" (161–62); or he subtly humanizes the actions of a blue grouse hen, who will feign lameness to distract a potential predator from her young. The bird exhorts her young "to run and hide and lie still, no matter how closely approached, while . . . [she] goes on with her loving, lying acting" (163). More frequently, though, Muir will, almost with tongue in cheek, briefly cast an animal or even a plant in human guise, a strategy clearly meant to draw an emotional response rather than substitute as scientific description: a woodchuck is "bulky, fat, aldermanic"

(149); bears are "effective forest police" (141); humble insects "go mountaineering" (174); even Arctic flowers are "plant people" who "speak Nature's love as plainly as their big relatives of the South" (6). The contrast of these passages with Muir's more distant and analytical descriptive approach elsewhere in the text is obvious, yet the effect is not one of ascribing a "higher" intelligence to plants and animals, but rather to underscore the fundamental connections between the humans and their wilderness neighbors. For Muir, who derives spiritual sustenance from nature as if his very life depends upon it, these brief portrayals of other creatures as people are not meant to humanize them so much as expand the notion of "people" itself—in other words, to endow environmental citizenship upon all living things. In that sense, Muir's literary technique parallels his ecological worldview of the forest as an interlinked community of neighbors, bound up in a web of relationships they may not detect but cannot escape.

These variations on the anthropomorphization of nature provide a useful context for understanding Cooper's use of the trope at midcentury. Unlike the "nature-fakers" at whom Burroughs takes umbrage, she does not ascribe self-conscious intelligence to her subjects; rather, like Bartram and Audubon, she makes certain ethical and moral connections between animal behavior and human relations. But while Bartram's anthropomorphization primarily celebrates the divine perfection of nature, on one hand, and Audubon's approach reads human foibles into animals' behavioral patterns, on the other, Cooper endows nonhuman species with human characteristics in order to convey constructive ethical messages to the humans in the larger community. A good example of such a lesson is Cooper's evaluation of the "very remarkable instinct . . . of a sitting bird" (23). She observes that this usually highly active creature

> will patiently sit, for hour after hour, day after day, upon her unhatched brood. . . . [S]he will rather suffer hunger herself than leave them long exposed. . . . The male among some tribes occasionally relieves his mate by taking her place awhile, and among all varieties he exerts himself to bring her food, and to sing for her amusement. But altogether, this voluntary imprisonment of those busy, lively creatures is a striking instance of that generous, enduring patience which is a noble attribute of parental affection. (23)

Here Cooper attributes certain human domestic characteristics to the avian pair: both the male and female engage in a "voluntary imprisonment" in order to efficiently perform the duties of incubating the eggs, an activity that implies a generous spirit of self-sacrifice on the part of each bird. Apparently, the birds give up a measure of personal freedom in order that domestic order and familial happiness may be achieved. Cooper's sketch also suggests that the birds have developed a teamwork approach to family duties. Male and female work together and even perform, in some cases, the same tasks (for example, incubating the eggs). This passage presents the bird family unit as a representation of the very best in human "parental affection." Rare personal qualities of "generous, enduring patience" are displayed as a matter of course in the animal kingdom, if we only take the time to look. Certainly, though, Cooper's representation of the bird family is also a projection of her implicit beliefs concerning gender roles within the American domestic sphere. Though the bird pair shares some duties, Cooper depicts the male as the main provider who "exerts himself to bring . . . food, and to sing for . . . the amusement" of the nest-bound female, a depiction that mirrors the arrangement of patriarchal households.

Another example involves barn swallows, who "are very busy, cheerful, happy tempered creatures, remarkably peaceful in their disposition, friendly to each other, and to man also. Though living so many together, it is remarkable that they do not quarrel, showing what may be done in this way by sensible birds, though very sensible men and women seem, too often, to feel no scruples about quarrelling themselves, or helping their neighbors to do so" (35). The swallow community functions here as an ideal standard of behavior and temperament, beside which human failings are only magnified. Cooper, in a good example of gentle humor, plays on the word "sensible" to nail down her object lesson. The swallows are sensible because they show good judgment—their relationships, even in close quarters, are wisely maintained in harmony rather than conflict. It would seem, though, that the attribute of sensibility is not enough to guarantee harmonious human relations in similar situations, for Cooper recognizes that people (even the sensible variety) constantly bicker with and oppose one another. Thus the swallows put the supposedly human characteristic of being sensible to effective use, whereas people cannot seem to achieve such a level of interaction. Perhaps it is a sort of "bird sensibility" that Cooper is speaking of, in the end, for it is the human community that consistently fails to do what the rest of the natural world finds so simple and easy.

Thus Cooper anthropomorphizes natural creatures to stress their commonality with human culture as well as to instruct readers in matters of religious and social import. Both purposes underscore the idea that the human community is part and parcel of the wider community of nature, and that the improvement of our relationships and moral qualities requires seeing ourselves in that larger context. Like those of John Muir, Cooper's personifications foster a strong sense of connection and even identification between people and their nonhuman neighbors. The net result is that we can read *Rural Hours* as much more than a chronological record of natural observations, on one hand, and a random assortment of local history, anecdotes, and civic "lessons," on the other. Rather, passages in Cooper's journal interweave these features, exploring the human and nonhuman elements together with the aim of characterizing their specific interaction.

An extended example along these lines is Cooper's discussion of the ecology of the "church-yard." Cooper's winding relation of the history and fate of the New England cemetery is a multilayered discussion of ecology, human history, and personal narrative. She begins on a nostalgic note, observing that "Church-yards are much less common in this country than one might suppose, and . . . it seems probable this pious, simple custom of burying about our churches, will soon become obsolete" (179). The yards symbolize a time when the human population was less dense, the pace of life less frenetic, the rage for building and town development less marked. For Cooper, the humble congregation of graves becomes a powerful cultural marker, a vivid link to the past embedded within and threatened by the present. "The stillness," she says, "the uselessness . . . of the old church-yard in the heart of the bustling city, renders it a more striking and impressive *memento mori* than the skull in the cell of a hermit" (180). The real reason for her nostalgia, we soon learn, is that these historical artifacts, links to the recent human past, are threatened by the urge for civic growth. Cooper objects to such changes—proposed only, she feels, "that a little more coin may jingle in our own pockets"—on the grounds that removing the graves would not only cut us off from a vital sense of human history but also violate the memory of the "dead . . . [who are] entrusted to the honor of the living" (180). Cooper's final appeal, in her defense of the traditional churchyard, is to our religious and moral sensibility: "a just consideration of Death is one of the highest lessons that every man needs to learn" (181).

At this point in her entry, the role nature plays in the life of a churchyard is still unclear. But her general protest at the waning of the churchyard and the social forces responsible for this change are a prelude to her discussion of the specific natural history of a particular site, the Episcopal churchyard, whose oldest grave is dated 1792. Cooper details the site's past in terms of the deceased human occupants and the surrounding plants and trees—both are part of the evolution of a local space. In the beginning, she says, "at the time these graves were dug, the spot was in a wild condition, upon the border of the forest, the wood having been only partially cut away" (181–82). As a result, "the spot soon lost its forest character" (182). Cooper narrates the human transformation of the land, one that thus far seems to be following the customary procedure of human development at the expense of wild nature.

As it turns out, though, this transformation is rather complex: human industry claims more and more of the land's resources, but nature is flexible and responds to human intrusion not so much in terms of battle but rather of adaptation and cooperation. The "older trees [that] were all felled," for example, "may have been used as timber in building the little church"; thus, rather than being shipped off to another locale, or burned for fuel, they are recycled, in a sense, back into the local scene (182). Cooper notes how the character of the surrounding forest has changed since the original cutting.

> Happily, at the time of clearing the ground, a few young bushes were spared from the axe, and these having been left to grow at will, during the course of half a century, have become fine flourishing trees. The greater number are pines, and a more fitting tree for a Christian church-yard . . . could scarcely be named. . . . [T]heir growth is noble, and more than any other variety of their tribe, they hold murmuring communion with the mysterious winds, waving in tones of subdued melancholy over the humble graves at their feet. A few maples and elms . . . appear among them, relieving their monotonous characters. Some of these have been planted for that purpose, but the pines

themselves are all the spontaneous growth of the soil. Judging from their size, and what we know of their history, they must have sprung up from the seed about the time when the first colonists arrived—contemporaries of the little town whose graves they overshadow. (182)

Much is packed into this brief passage, as Cooper evokes the natural as well as the human history of a place. Such histories, more importantly, are not divergent, nor even parallel, but intertwined. They adapt to, reflect, and amplify one another in the consciousness of the present observer who is attuned to such historical development. Pine trees, having grown from small understory bushes when the canopy species were cut down, become nature's response to the clearing of the land. This opportunistic response, rather than becoming a disturbance or problem, is appropriate, even "noble," as the trees "hold murmuring communion" in the churchyard. The next stage of human intervention is not destructive, but rather complementary to the response executed by nature: settlers plant maples and elms as a gesture toward restoring the variety and vibrancy of the earlier, varied forest. The newer, harder woods not only "relieve the monotony" of the pines (and thus function aesthetically) but also serve as a direct connection to the *human* history of the locale, for their age and development, their concreteness, are a visible indicator of the time of original settlement, a tangible link to the past.

Nearly one hundred years later, ecologist and land steward Aldo Leopold would write about "a certain country graveyard that I pass in driving to and from my farm" in his landmark seasonal journal and ecological autobiography, *A Sand County Almanac* (44). Like Cooper, who senses that the identity of a place is defined not just by the marks of human culture but also by the presence and preservation of its natural inhabitants, Leopold reads significance in the small and simple rural cemetery, which "is extraordinary only in being triangular instead of square, and harboring, within the sharp angle of its fence, a pinpoint remnant of the native prairie on which the graveyard was established in the 1840's" (45). For Leopold, a mid-twentieth-century witness to the industrialization of agriculture and the reshaping of the Midwest's rural landscape—transformations of nature and threats to wilderness that people of Cooper's generation could scarcely imagine—much resides in "this yard-square relic of original Wisconsin [which] gives birth, each July, to a man-high stalk of compass plant or cutleaf Silphium" (45). Leopold watches for the plant's flowery emergence each year—waits for it and notes the very date, year by year—until the long-ignored patch is eventually cut by a roadside mowing crew, which had removed the fence from the graveyard. The compass plant, even in its precarious corner-of-the-graveyard existence, is a window into the past, as much a part of the living history of the Wisconsin landscape as the human record of sod breaking, logging, and settlement. Though the isolated fragment cannot begin to replace the vast expanses of original prairie, and thus the seasonal blooming of the lonely compass plant is tinged with melancholy, the thoughtless and unremarkable loss of even that forgotten bit disconnects the human observer from the land's real history, its deeper meaning and relevance.

Striving toward Conservation

While Leopold's mown-over cemetery is a humble symbol of the fast-disappearing native landscape as well as society's pervasive disconnection from its ecological history, Cooper's churchyard is a setting where humanity and nature creatively and positively interact, a place where the human-nature relation works. Yet Cooper, too, recognizes that such places are endangered (or at least increasingly rare), an example of another key theme of *Rural Hours*—conservation. Just as she champions the churchyard environment, Cooper voices concern about environmental changes and sounds a lament for nature's abuse, a viewpoint decidedly at odds with mainstream mid-nineteenth-century American views of forests and prairie soils as vast resources to be tapped at will. In this respect, Cooper's natural history is surprisingly forward-looking, anticipating better-known works of wilderness philosophy and conservation such as George Perkins Marsh's *Man and Nature* (1864) and *The Earth as Modified by Human Action* (1874) as well as the later writings of Muir and Leopold.[17]

Though the word *ecology* had yet to be defined at the time of the first publication of *Rural Hours*, Cooper's recognition that populations of certain plants and animals were declining not only demonstrate a proto-ecological viewpoint but also emphasize the need for effective conservation.[18] In various entries, she rues the decline of the quail, the pigeon, the whippoorwill, and other birds—in some cases she attributes the decreases to direct human intervention (e.g., hunting), while in others she reserves judgment as to the cause. With respect to plants, she notes the decline in numbers and diversity of native wildflowers, which elder inhabitants claim had been much more numerous in previous generations, but she fails to explicitly connect the shift to the area's settlement and development. In contrast, her analysis of nonnative species—plants purposefully or unwittingly introduced to the locale—demonstrates great sensitivity to the complexities of a given ecosystem and the widespread shifts in plant diversity that may result from the introduction of an "alien" (64–65). Nevertheless, while Cooper recognizes that some of the transplanted Old World species are mere weeds that "chok[e] . . . up all our way-sides" (65), others are beneficial in terms of their cooking or medicinal value. Accordingly, her view of what constitutes a "weed" is ecological rather than emotional, for she recognizes that the designation of a given plant as harmful or useful, beautiful or ugly, is made according to human tastes and values, not inherently "good" or "bad" properties of the species (66).

Cooper's passionate discussion of trees gives us the best insight into her conservation ethic. During an early spring hike, Cooper relates an experience familiar to present-day Americans who have come across clear-cut areas in an otherwise expansive forest: "A disappointment awaited us—several noble pines, old friends and favorites, had been felled unknown to us during the winter; unsightly stumps and piles of chips were all that remained. . . . Their fall seemed to have quite changed the character of the neighboring fields; for it often lies within the power of a single group of trees to alter the whole aspect of acres of surrounding lands" (6). Cooper expresses the impact of the harvested trees on two levels. The cutting first represents a void in the previously healthy human-nature relation: kinship between the human and nonhuman elements once existed but was violated. What Cooper and her comrades feel is a profound loss of connection and familiarity—theirs is not an abstract loss, but the missing of a good friend. Such familiarity is a key theme throughout *Rural Hours*—later in the spring, for example, Cooper exclaims, "How pleasant it is to meet the same flowers year after year!" (29). Human abuse of nature, for Cooper, disrupts the year-by-year, season-by-season process of renewing one's acquaintance with the natural world. Second, she registers the loss of the trees within the context of the natural community, a reaction that carries an emotional jolt. Though this lament is made in terms of the visual impact of the scene, and thus partly appeals to an anthropocentric natural aesthetic, nevertheless Cooper expresses consideration for the overall integrity of a given area. In other words, though abuse of nature might be technically limited to a given space, that area is not isolated and, in fact, affects the spaces adjacent to or surrounding it.

Cooper's conservation ethic is best expressed in her detailed and multilayered argument for sensible forestry. She notes with concern that "another half century may find the country bleak and bare; but as yet the woods have not all been felled" (128). Her guarded optimism is tempered further by the realization that "few among the younger generation now springing up will ever attain to the dignity of the old forest trees. Very large portions of these woods are already of a second growth" (131). While Cooper takes heart in the vastness of the eastern forests at midcentury, she recognizes that agriculture and, especially, excessive logging threaten the remaining wooded areas and have in some cases changed their very character. What is seriously lacking, she feels, is a conservative approach to using the forest—although she never doubts the economic necessity of cutting trees, she criticizes the lack of foresight among those "whose chief object in life is to make money" (132). Arguing for business prudence, she points out that at the rate of consumption, the state's pines will be gone by 1870; moreover, she calculates that New York State's forest-based economic production surprisingly outstrips that of agriculture (133). Given these realities, she advocates the preservation of tree stands and selected old-growth areas, as well as planting new trees to replace logged forests. But beyond providing monetary incentives for conservation, Cooper stresses that trees "are connected in many ways with the civilization of a country; they have their importance in an intellectual and in a moral sense" (133). Conserving trees is not only practical; it avoids unnecessary waste—an economic, moral, and ecological virtue: "There is something in the care of trees which rises above the common labors of husbandry, and speaks of a generous mind. . . . [I]n planting a young wood, in preserving a fine grove, a noble tree, we look beyond ourselves to the band of household friends, to our neighbors" (134).

Such a sensitivity for the integrity of Cooperstown's forests registers strongly throughout Cooper's natural history and leads, for a third-generation observer of the central New York community, to the

inevitable issue of development versus preservation (one that dominated much of James Fenimore Cooper's work as well, particularly his
1823 novel *The Pioneers*). Which option, given a historical appreciation
of the land and the naturalist's acute eye toward the various interactions between humans and nature, is preferable? In one illuminating
passage, Cooper remarks: "Of all the works of the creation which know
the changes of life and death, the trees of the forest have the longest
existence. . . . [T]he woods preserve unchanged, throughout the greatest reach of time, their native character: the works of man are ever
varying their aspect; his towns and his fields alike reflect the unstable
opinions, the fickle wills and fancies of each passing generation; but
the forests on his borders remain today the same they were ages of
years since" (126). Here Cooper celebrates the apparent permanence
of nature, the awe-inspiring age of the forests, and the breadth of nonhuman history they suggest. Such rhetoric ironically portrays human
endeavor as slight in comparison with the activities and processes of
the natural world and seems somewhat out-of-phase with Cooper's
recognition of wasteful and destructive logging practices.

At other moments she approaches this theme from a different direction and exults in the scenic (or aesthetic) virtues of cultivated land
maintained in a careful and appropriate balance with forested tracts. In
commenting upon the general outlay and topography of the area, she
notes that "[t]he whole surface of the country is arable. . . . This general fertility, this blending of the fields of man and his tillage with the
woods, the great husbandry of Providence, gives a fine character to the
country, which it could not claim when the lonely savage roamed
through wooded valleys, and which it must lose if ever cupidity and the
haste to grow rich shall destroy the forest entirely. . . . No perfection
of tillage, no luxuriance of produce can make up to a country for the
loss of its forests" (139). In this instance, Cooper admires the aesthetics of the classic pastoral landscape, but this celebration of "fertility" is
mitigated by her insistence on the "blending" being the crucial factor.
That cultivated land be in *balance* with wild forest is most significant:
human "tillage" complements "the great husbandry of Nature," a relation superior to the effect of either state alone. What Cooper identifies in the simple pastoral is an effectively realized—and, unfortunately, all too easily disturbed—equilibrium in the relationship
between humans and nature, an integration of culture and nature.[19]

Moreover, Cooper feels that it is Euro-American culture that is responsible for this balance—the "lonely savage," by merely "roaming," is unable, in her view, to achieve a similar state of aesthetic harmony in the environment. Perhaps this is because Cooper, like most of her contemporaries, assumes not only that white culture is superior to Native customs, but also that Native Americans are little more than one small *part* of the larger panorama of nature, an idea later echoed in John Wesley Powell's *Report on the Lands of the Arid Region*. In her appreciation of the aesthetic benefits of Euro-American agriculture and her denial of agency to the Native population to effect such a "fine" transformation of the landscape, Cooper evokes her forebears' racist associations of Native Americans with a vast, desolate, terrifying, and potentially evil "wilderness."[20]

Cooper's local natural history celebrates the divine order of nature, advocates the conservation of vital resources such as forests, and portrays a human community living in reasonable (though hardly perfect) balance with the larger environment. For Cooper, science is neither a means of objectifying nor of controlling nature, but rather a system of study meant to foster moral and intellectual connections between the observer and the outside world. As such, her explorations of "familiar" ground provide a fascinating counterpoint to the nineteenth-century exploration narratives portraying a frontier hero of science seeking to map and conquer a passive, feminized environment. While recognizing nature's interdependencies leads her to stress conservation practices for both ethical and economic reasons, Cooper's aesthetic appreciation of the pastoral landscape and devotion to the rural community suggest a tempered, rather than a radical, view toward the potential restructuring of the human-nature relation. Thus, while Cooper ultimately accepts and even celebrates human development and agricultural stewardship as a staple of the American landscape, her proto-ecological perspective as well as her humble approach to understanding her environment anticipates the vision and ethos of Rachel Carson and Loren Eiseley, two of the twentieth century's most important critical voices on the relation between science and nature.

SIX

"The Relentless Drive of Life"

Rachel Carson's and
Loren Eiseley's Reformulation
of Science and Nature

Though Susan Fenimore Cooper witnessed significant changes to the landscape of her home county during the nineteenth century—the loss of old-growth forests, the decline in numbers of certain wildlife species, the increase in both cultivated land and human population—the genteel naturalist scarcely could have imagined the scale of transformation that occurred throughout the twentieth century, in terms of not only the land but also scientific practice itself. Two such developments provide the context for this chapter: the tremendous growth and diversification of science and the ever-accelerating development and degradation of the natural environment.

The explosion of scientific knowledge has been both impressive and bewildering, resulting in a wide array of specialized fields—biogeochemistry, molecular biology, neurophysiology, astrophysics, and population ecology, to name but a few. In contrast to the previous century, when science was only beginning to diverge into a complex latticework of disciplines and subspecialties, the vast majority of today's scientists communicate mainly to others in their narrowly defined field. Organic chemists and comparative anatomists, for example, struggle to understand or ignore altogether each other's work, and to the layperson the technical jargon of either field is incomprehensible. Such a situation places a premium on scientists who can communicate complex ideas to general readers and nonspecialists, not merely for the necessary (if somewhat self-serving) reason of maintaining public support for scientific funding, but also to educate the public about the history of science as well as the significance of current research. During the twentieth century, many articulate scientist-writers in Europe and the United States—including Albert Einstein, Julian Huxley, Jacques Monod, Jane Goodall, Stephen Jay Gould, Richard Dawkins, Carl Sagan, Louise Young, and others—have taken up this task.[1] They have been joined by the growing ranks of science journalists, who produce books, essays, and newspaper articles reporting upon research across the sciences and paint compelling portraits of scientists at work.

Occurring alongside this impressive expansion of knowledge within the sciences and among the public is the ongoing worldwide environmental crisis, a situation characterized by industrialized and chemically intensive agricultural practices; rampant development of urban, suburban, and even rural areas; deforestation and loss of wetlands; pollution of air and water resources; increased rates of species extinction and endangerment; rising levels of greenhouse gases as well as substantial depletion of the protective ozone layer in the atmosphere; exponential growth in the human population; and lack of effective hazardous waste disposal.[2] The relationship between the growth of science and these environmental problems is both complex and uneasy. On one hand, the synthesis of science and technology with global capitalism has created an array of problems, from the terrifying threat of nuclear winter to the mundane presence of caustic chemicals in the household. On the other hand, environmental scientists in fields as diverse as ecology, ornithology, and anthropology have worked diligently to study the processes and causes of environmental degradation, to suggest ways our technology-based society can ameliorate its impact upon our surroundings, and to inspire interest in and respect for resource conservation and wilderness preservation among the public.

In America, a select few individuals have played key roles in both the communication of scientific knowledge to a general audience and the shaping of our environmental attitudes; their efforts represent one path toward a reconciliation between scientific and technological innovation and environmental consciousness-raising. Among them are Rachel Carson and Loren Eiseley, two important and widely read scientist-writers whose work exemplifies the best of popular scientific writing in the mid-twentieth century and eloquently communicates the spirit and ideas of that era's environmental movement. This chapter depicts Carson and Eiseley as modern-day naturalist-writers who offer artistically sophisticated environmental critiques of science and suggest how the empathetic exploration of nature can transform the way science regards the natural world. By bridging the gap between popular and specialized writing and emphasizing an ethical approach to the environment, Carson and Eiseley hearken back to the rhetoric of nineteenth-century naturalists such as Susan Cooper; at the same time, they develop innovative strategies of literary representation. Their emphasis upon ecological relationships and evolutionary processes revises the strongly gendered and mechanistic representations of nature prevalent in the nineteenth century. In a broader sense, Carson and Eiseley study nature with respect and care, and proffer science not as the ultimate instrument of human domination of nature but as the means to achieving a new environmental ethic.

Genesis of Two Scientist-Writers

Rachel Carson and Loren Eiseley stand out in my survey of scientist-writers for two reasons: in contrast to their predecessors in this book, Carson and Eiseley were formally trained as scientists in graduate programs, and they each cultivated early ambitions toward literary careers. Carson (1907–64) was born in Pennsylvania and from an early age displayed interests in nature, science, and writing. A superb student, she studied English while majoring in zoology at Pennsylvania College for Women, where she was mentored by Mary Scott Skinker, an accomplished and energetic biology professor. Skinker encouraged her to pursue science as a career and was instrumental in securing a summer research post for Carson at the prestigious Marine Biological Laboratory in Woods Hole, Massachusetts, in 1929. Carson's summer of research in the vibrant scientific community at Woods Hole not only was her first direct experience of the sea but also served as her introduction to graduate-level research in marine zoology, which she would continue that fall at Johns Hopkins University. After earning her degree with honors, spending several more summers conducting research in Woods Hole and teaching at Hopkins and the University of Maryland to support herself—all the while surmounting the considerable challenges faced by women striving to carve out a successful career in science—Carson began a long and productive career as a writer, editor, and researcher with the Fish and Wildlife Service. Though the work in her government post was demanding and sometimes monotonous, it afforded her security and, more importantly, gave her travel opportunities to research natural resource publications (such as a series of informative brochures for the newly established national wildlife refuges), access to a wide variety of scientists and writers, and inside knowledge of government procedures, both good and bad.[3]

Carson spent her own time exploring the eastern seacoast at every opportunity, spending long hours in quiet observation and often collecting specimens of marine animals and plants to examine under her dissecting microscope. She also wrote, and though her first book, *Under the Sea-Wind* (1941), did not sell well (owing in great measure to the almost simultaneous attack on Pearl Harbor and despite kudos from critics), her second, published ten years later, was a best-seller. *The Sea around Us* (1951) ranks as one of the finest examples of twentieth-century nonfiction; it won both the National Book Award and the Burroughs Medal for excellence in nature writing and established Carson as a science writer of major rank. Carson's subsequent financial independence enabled her to purchase a home on the Maine coast and quit her job with the government, thus providing her with more time for explorations, research, and writing. Before her untimely death in 1964 from breast cancer, Carson published two more landmark books: *The Edge of the Sea* (1955), which completed her sea trilogy by focusing on the ecology of the marine habitats of the eastern coastal region, and *Silent Spring* (1962), her groundbreaking indictment of the indiscriminate use of chemical pesticides that would galvanize the environmental movement of the 1960s and 1970s.

Loren Eiseley, born in Nebraska in 1907, the same year as Carson, also combined an early interest in the natural world with a fascination for the flow of language. Just as Carson expressed an early ambition to be a professional writer, Eiseley in high school declared he wanted to be a "nature writer," a rather impressive prediction considering the long and meandering path he would take to that vocation. In essence, Eiseley started out as a writer, shifted to being a scientist, then eventually combined the two disciplines by authoring a unique series of essay collections that would establish him as one of America's foremost interpreters of nature and science. By 1933, Eiseley had finished his undergraduate degree at the University of Nebraska (after numerous interruptions during the early years of the Great Depression when he wandered the West hobo-style by jumping railroad cars), published several poems in small magazines such as *Prairie Schooner*, and began graduate study in anthropology at the University of Pennsylvania. After receiving his Ph.D. in 1937, Eiseley taught at the University of Kansas and then at Oberlin College, all the while conducting field research in the plains states where he collected data on the evolution and cultural diffusion of the people of the American Plains. In 1947 he accepted the chair of the anthropology department at the University of Pennsylvania; by that time, he had begun to develop the style of the "concealed essay," the rhetorical technique he would develop for the next decade and use in his first and most widely read book, *The Immense Journey* (1957).[4] That book, combined with 1958's critically lauded history of evolutionary thought, *Darwin's Century*, cemented Eiseley's reputation as a gifted writer, scholar, and science critic. Though his scientific output would slow considerably after the late 1950s, Eiseley remained a productive and esteemed writer and lecturer until his death in 1977, publishing several volumes of essays (including two collections I examine in detail here, *The Unexpected Universe* and *The Invisible Pyramid*), three volumes of poetry, an autobiography, and other works of nonfiction.

Symbols of the Naturalist's Ethos

In contrast to Frémont, Powell, Byrd, and other explorers discussed in previous chapters, Carson and Eiseley did not investigate new, uncharted territory. Both, however, were anything but "bench scientists" bound to the laboratory (despite the countless hours each spent indoors writing and reading), for Carson and Eiseley practiced their science in the naturalist tradition, out in the field making observations and collecting specimens of interest. The voices and sensibilities of their books thus are shaped not by the abstract musings of a theoretical scientist but by concrete experiences within nature. In this section, I discuss Carson and Eiseley's thoughts on exploration, as both literal act and symbolic attitude, as a way to introduce and characterize their narrative self-presentations, particularly with respect to the posture one strikes in relation to the natural world. While hardly exhaustive, these observations lend insight into each writer's characterization of nature and critique of science.

Carson tramped the variegated shorelines of Maryland, Massachusetts, and Maine, spent long hours in quiet observation of mudflat or rocky cove, regularly inspected organisms under her microscopes (which she usually returned to the point of collection), and wrote notes about her findings that she later revised for her books about marine ecology. Carson also was greatly interested in the history of maritime exploration—she avidly read classic works such as Matthew Fontaine Maury's *The Physical Geography of the Sea* (1855) and included a survey of navigational and exploration history in the last chapter of *The Sea around Us*. The chapter explains how "through many voyages undertaken over many centuries, the fog and the frightening obscurity of the unknown were lifted from all the surface of the Sea of Darkness" (211), and briefly recounts, for example, the discovery of the Antarctic continent and the failure to find the elusive Northwest Passage. And while Carson characterizes the history of exploration and navigation as a steady march toward an as yet unattained complete knowledge of the sea's surface features, she also pays tribute to the ingenious methods of ancient navigators such as the Polynesians, who used the stars as navigation tools and sometimes released birds while out on open water to guide their ships back to land (212). Her admiration for and survey of past exploration highlights certain qualities Carson viewed as essential to effective scientific inquiry: innate curiosity, the willingness to take risks (whether geographic or literary), perseverance in the face of ignorance or physical challenge, and the creativity to solve problems and devise innovative solutions.

The Edge of the Sea, Carson's third book, introduces its readers to marine ecology and biology and serves as a field guide for those interested in deepening their knowledge of the rocky shorelines, sandy beaches, salt marshes, and coral reefs of the eastern coast. Although Carson rarely refers directly to herself in her major works, in *The Edge of the Sea* she provides brief glimpses of her naturalist persona. Here she defines what she means by the exploration of nature, though the information here is less a concrete method than a general ethos—a way of approaching the environment with the intellectual tools of science and the values of someone who feels a part of a natural order and beauty. Exploration becomes the ideal means to acquire an ecological education, not only for the reader but also for Carson's narrator, who expresses a nostalgic wish to be able to view the land as Audubon saw it more than a hundred years earlier. In an understated fashion, Carson informs us that "One of my favorite approaches to a rocky seacoast is by a rough path through an evergreen forest that has its own peculiar enchantment" (41), a narrative technique that invites the reader to identify with Carson's personal perspective. Later, she describes a walk along the sandy beach in which she was "always aware that I was treading on the thin rooftops of an underground city" (140); namely, the burrows of the ghost shrimps scattered throughout the tidal flat. In another telling moment, she resists taking a specimen of the fragile-looking West Indian Basket Star, for "to disturb such a thing would have seemed a desecration" (225). Carson's narrator is thus a benevolent presence in the landscape, a citizen of the earth, one whose purpose is merely to observe and teach rather than catalog, map, and conquer. As critic Vera Norwood observes, Carson's "voice in the sea books was that of a tantalized watcher . . . [whose] discoveries were not couched in heroic battles of confrontation, but in surprises attendant on one who waits" (*Made* 152).

Eiseley is much more forthcoming in his self-presentation, as most of his writings incorporate a strong autobiographical element. He frames his first and most widely read work, *The Immense Journey*, as "a somewhat unconventional record of the prowlings of one mind which has sought to explore, to understand, and to enjoy the miracles of this world, both in and out of science" (12). This process begins with Eiseley's forays into the fossil-rich territory of the American Plains, where he did much of his early fieldwork as a physical anthropologist. Eiseley's narrative persona is part philosopher, part scientist, part poet, and part wanderer—a complex blend of roles that shift and combine imaginatively throughout his essays. Moreover, Eiseley is a master at leading us down an unexpected path after setting up a commonplace scene or ordinary encounter, thus changing his perspective on a particular problem or finding new ways of asking questions. In *The Immense Journey*'s lead essay, "The Slit," Eiseley initially portrays himself as a romantic, lone explorer of the desolate American Plains, a wanderer on horseback: "Some lands are flat and grass-covered, and smile so evenly up at the sun that they seem forever youthful, untouched by man or

time. Some are torn, ravaged and convulsed like the features of pro-
fane old age. . . . It was to such a land I rode, but I rode to it across a
sunlit, timeless prairie over which nothing passed but antelope or a
wandering bird" (3). Such a description would not be out of place in
the mid-nineteenth-century narratives of Frémont, but Eiseley is not
interested in sketching a portrait of the heroic scientist. Instead, he dis-
mounts from his horse and shimmies down into a deep, narrow crack
in the ground, a slit that (in contrast to the "timeless prairie" above)
is a "perfect cross section through perhaps ten million years of time"
(4). Here he finds a fossil skull, a remnant of a primitive mammalian
ancestor, which inspires him to reflect upon the long journey represented by evolutionary change. The reflective moment is typical of
Eiseley: scientific investigation for him is essentially a process of discovery and close observation, of looking for evidence of life's development and complexity in unusual landscapes or familiar scenes. Eiseley can transform nearly any experience into a creative exploration,
whether floating on his back in the Platte River, watching birds fly
around his suburban backyard near Philadelphia, or walking the night
streets of Manhattan. Exploration thus becomes an intensely personal
process of introspection and reflection, as much as a disciplined
strategy of scientific analysis.

Another key aspect of Eiseley's naturalist persona is his insistence
upon the personal, subjective, and therefore limited nature of his engagement with nature. When he evokes the nautical explorers of the
sixteenth century, for example, it is to stress not their heroism or access to truth, but that they were "confused by strange beasts or mon-
strous thoughts" (14). Like these men of the past, Eiseley offers up
merely "a bit of my personal universe, the universe traversed in a long
and uncompleted journey" (13). Often the goal of his rambles is rather
humble, as when he ventures out of his suburban home near Philadelphia and, "over the protests of my wife that I will catch cold," looks for
the first signs of impending autumn (195). Yet no matter the occasion
for his wanderings, Eiseley's narrator is a careful, deliberate observer,
one who pauses to examine small aspects of nature and whose temperament is characterized not by the brave gallantry of Frémont or
even the stoicism of Powell, but by longing and an almost melancholy
loneliness:

As the long months passed, I began to live on the slower planes and to observe more readily what passed for life there. I sauntered, I passed more and more slowly up and down the canyons in the dry baking heat of midsummer. . . . Now and then I found a skull in the canyons, and these justified my remaining there. I took a serene cold interest in these discoveries. I had come, like many a naturalist before me, to view life with a wary and subdued attention. I had grown to take pleasure in the divested bone. (183)[5]

Yet another connection to the idea of exploration is one of Eiseley's central motifs, the journey, which dominates his first book and recurs in various guises in his subsequent essay collections. *The Immense Journey* is thus a series of many interlocking journeys—a walk in the woods, an anthropological expedition to the Plains, the course of one's lifetime, the evolutionary development of diverse species, and the process of scientific inquiry itself. Eiseley layers and connects these multiple senses of the word most artfully, and consequently he expands our notion of what it means to explore nature through the tools and methods of science. Beyond scientific knowledge and the desire to observe and learn from nature, what is most vital to the process of exploration is the imagination, which can take us to places, such as the depths of the abyssal ocean, that instruments and life-support systems cannot access (34). Nevertheless, Eiseley cautions us against looking for inherent meaning, for transcendent truth, in such investigations: the evolutionary journey that led to humanity's presence on earth "has altered with the chances of life, and the chances brought us here; but it was a good journey—long, perhaps—but a good journey under a pleasant sun. Do not look for the purpose" (6–7).

Perhaps Eiseley's most explicit discussion of the possibilities and limits of scientific exploration is his 1969 work *The Unexpected Universe*, a book published near the culmination of the most ambitious, costly, and technologically driven exploration program in American history: the *Apollo* lunar missions. In his opening essay, "The Ghost Continent," Eiseley contrasts himself to heroic explorers of myth (Odysseus) and recent history (James Cook) by insisting that "I claim no discoveries, . . . [but] claim only the events of a life in science as they were transformed inwardly" (3). Odysseus is a literary emblem of the exploration impulse within humans—the achievement of impressive deeds, the lonely journey into unknown territory, the confrontation with danger and ignorance, and the desire to return home. At the same time, he notes that scientists such as Cook and Darwin were as heroic as Odysseus in their travels and search for knowledge; Cook, in particular, he lauds as the "genuine Ahab of the ghost continent" (17). But Eiseley's tribute to the heroic is tempered by the recognition of Odysseus's imperfections—his many deceptions, his resort to senseless violence in the execution of his servants. He notes finally that "the Odyssean voyage stands as a symbol of both man's homelessness and his power, a power more unregenerate than that which drove Odysseus to string the great bow before the suitors" (24). Eiseley sees that human exploration ultimately is a flawed though necessary process, one in which the impulse to conquer and control the natural environment is a false goal. The challenges posed by the exploration of space in the late 1960s powerfully illustrate our "simplistic conception of the word *frontier* as something conquerable in its totality"—though this may hold true for the forests we have cut for timber, the hubris of the Odyssean explorer runs into trouble in "the wilderness beyond the stars or concealed in the infinitesimal world beneath the atom" (42).

For Eiseley and Carson, then, exploration is not merely an arena for ambitious individuals bent on "discovering" new lands, mapping unknown territory, and bringing wilderness areas under the control of science and capitalism. Instead, their investigations are opportunities to apply the observational and analytical methods of science to understand natural processes: the interactions in a coastal marine ecosystem, the diversity of plant life, the evolutionary relationships between humans and bacteria. Explicitly for Eiseley and implicitly for Carson, exploration is best understood as a state of mind, an imaginative engagement with the larger world, a thought process that allows the twentieth-century scientist to escape the confines of laboratory and bureaucratic protocol and connect the larger public to the insights of science through the tools of literary expression. In this formulation, their scientist personae reject the hubris, ambition, and guise of objectivity characteristic of the explorer-hero in favor of the benevolent naturalist represented by William Bartram, Susan Cooper, Henry Thoreau, and John Burroughs. Carson and Eiseley redefine science as a process of engaging nature creatively, hesitantly, and with respect; this approach contributes in no small way to both the appeal of their prose and the fact that their representations of nature are founded upon both ethical and ecological principles.

Experiments in Metaphor and Perspective

As scientists, Carson and Eiseley were products of the ecology age: while their narrative personae partake of the naturalist tradition, their representations of nature show how far science had come since the early nineteenth century, when descriptive natural history predominated and the biology of functions, processes, and interrelationships was still in its infancy. If nature is mysterious, unpredictable, and forever changing for Eiseley, the student of evolution and anthropology, it is a harmonious, ebbing and flowing whole for Carson, immense yet intimate, secret yet approachable. Carson's sea books, long admired as definitive works of American nature writing and scientific popularization, integrate evocative descriptions of marine life and environments with an ecological sensibility rooted in cutting-edge marine science. In the sea trilogy, which I focus upon here, Carson emphasizes the complex, interconnected cycles of nature, stresses the importance of identifying with and understanding the point of view of other organisms, and questions our faith in the technological domination of nature.

At the heart of Carson's ecological perspective are the natural cycles of the sea. The death of one organism becomes the sustaining life force for another, as illustrated in this passage from *Under the Sea-Wind*; prey becomes predator becomes prey again, in a never-ending recycling of nutrients, rendered here without the least trace of sentiment: "The ghost crab, still at his hunting of beach fleas, was alarmed by the turmoil of birds overhead, by the many racing shadows that sped over the sand. . . . [H]e dashed into the surf, preferring this refuge to flight. But a large channel bass was lurking near by, and in a twinkling the crab was seized and eaten. Later in the same day, the bass was attacked by sharks and what was left of it was cast up by the tide onto the sand. There the beach fleas, scavengers of the shore, swarmed over it and devoured it" (35). Carson also depicts the interconnections among organisms in smaller, seemingly self-contained environments. In one passage she describes an osprey's nest as an ecological hub, supporting several other birds that cohabitate peacefully (84–85). In others she depicts the variety of life found on a floating sea buoy (93) or the close proximity of highly specialized creatures living in a coastal pond (219). As critic Rebecca Raglon has noted, "What fascinated her most in nature were intertwined processes, long sweeps of time, the way lives of various creatures developed and intersected, and the continuity of life that persisted through all change" (200). The cycle of life is thus the emblematic metaphor within Carson's writing.

More generally, Carson's use of metaphor not only demonstrates her skill as a writer but also provides insight into her perspective on nature and the relation among science, the study of the environment, and the use of literature. The challenge any science writer faces in choosing and using metaphors is considerable, for the risks are great. Apt comparisons and artful figures of speech are necessary to persuade, to grip and hold an audience, to draw readers into the often-dry regions of technical information or scientific theory, even to articulate an idea that cannot be otherwise expressed. Contemporary scholars of science and literature convincingly assert that metaphor cannot be separated from scientific knowledge, whether we are considering the mundane act of writing a journal article or the abstract realm of sophisticated theory construction.[6] Metaphor is thus part and parcel of doing science: the big bang is as much an effective analogy as it is a working description of the universe's earliest moments. Much of the time, scientists use metaphoric expressions and concepts freely but half-unconsciously; their understanding of the power and the limits of such metaphors is tacit, perhaps in some cases even unacknowledged. For science writers communicating to the general public, though, the use of figurative expressions, comparisons, and analogies is (to a great extent) a conscious, deliberate, carefully controlled activity geared toward conveying accurate information and engaging the reader.

It was not necessary for Carson to look far when it came to devising analogies for the natural processes she observed and described: other natural phenomena proved a rich resource of rhetorical ideas. She appeals to her readers' general knowledge of nature and uses this to describe unusual marine organisms, habitats, or behaviors. In *Under the Sea-Wind* she describes, for instance, "hoardes of crustaceans . . . diatom meadows [and] . . . goblin-headed young" (107). Later in the book, while discussing the life cycle and migration patterns of the eel, she notes that "[u]pward passage through space in the sea was like passage through time in the Arctic world in spring, with the hours of sunlight increasing day by day" (262–63). Here, one natural event becomes the explanatory tool for conveying another, less familiar occurrence. But this technique has an implicit effect as well: by such metaphors Carson reinforces her view that all of nature is interconnected and unified, that rhythms and processes in one part of nature correspond in form or function to other cycles and patterns. As Carson's readers, we are struck not only by the diversity but also the frequent reoccurrence of pattern in nature.

In the context of geologic time, metaphors reveal fundamental truths about nature's workings. In a passage from *The Sea around Us,* Carson explains how the "continental shelf is of the sea, yet of all regions of the ocean it is most like the land"; in particular, the "Dogger Bank of the North Sea shelf was once a forested land inhabited by prehistoric beasts; now its 'forests' are seaweeds and its 'beasts' are fishes" (58). What superficially appears to be two completely different ecosystems, widely separated by space, are in fact analogous—provided we view them from a long-range perspective that embraces the passage of time and global climate change. This metaphor thus stresses the similarity and continuity between land and sea and highlights the process of change as central to our understanding of the evolution and ecology of marine environments.

This notion of time and gradual change is evident in one of my favorite passages from *The Sea around Us*—the chapter entitled "The Long Snowfall," in which Carson describes the long-term accumulation of sediments upon the ocean floor. For Carson, a defining image of the sea is the "steady, unremitting, downward drift of materials from above, flake upon flake, layer upon layer—a drift that has continued for hundreds of millions of years, that will go on as long as there are seas and continents" (74). She first compares this process of sedimentation to a familiar process, snow—an apt metaphor, for a snowfall is gradual, silent, surprising in its potential for accumulation. The example also underscores the difference between the short duration of a single human lifetime versus the vast stretches of geologic time. Carson's metaphor shifts, though, when she states that "sediments are a sort of epic poem of the earth. When we are wise enough, perhaps we can read in them all of past history" (75). Literature becomes the key to understanding the significance of the accumulated sediments: by taking core samples from the floor of the sea, we can "read" various bits of information about that part of the ocean—how thick the sediments are, what kinds of marine organisms comprise its layers, whether major variations in climate occurred over the eons.

In a rhetorical strategy similar to Susan Cooper's nearly a century before, Carson employs tightly controlled anthropomorphic description in *Under the Sea-Wind* as she characterizes the life cycles of various marine animals: Rynchops, the black skimmer (a migratory gull-like bird); Blackfoot, the sanderling (a common shore bird); Scomber, the mackerel; and Anguilla, the eel, among others. Carson felt a close connection to the organisms she studied and wrote about, and she tried to represent this empathy carefully in order to engage the general reader's imagination and interest in science without compromising the scientific integrity of her account. As she once wrote in her 1937 *Atlantic Monthly* essay "Undersea": "To get the feeling of what it is like to be a creature of the sea requires the active exercise of the imagination and the temporary abandonment of many human concepts and human yardsticks. . . . On the other hand . . . we must not depart too far from the analogy with human conduct if a fish, shrimp comb jelly, or bird is to seem real to us—as real a living creature as he actually is" (qtd. in Brooks, *Speaking* 278).

Carson thus presents animals as characters, a narrative technique she learned from reading the books of Henry Williamson, one of her favorite nature writers; the essays in *Under the Sea-Wind* are both ecological primers and life-cycle narratives of particular creatures. Within this context, she occasionally attributes human emotions to animals, as in this description of Rynchops, who "swept far over the salt marshes, taking joy in flight and soaring motion" (8). Or she notes, in a carefully qualified way, the special sense by which a fish may develop a familiarity with its habitat: "By the younger shad the river was only dimly remembered, if by the word 'memory' we may call the heightened response of the senses as the delicate gills and the sensitive lateral lines perceived the lessening saltiness of the water and the changing rhythms and vibrations of the inshore waters" (16). Note here how she interprets memory strictly as a physiochemical process and not as an aspect of humanlike consciousness, thus preventing the description from slipping into pathetic fallacy. In contrast to Cooper, who anthropomorphized birds and other creatures primarily to extract social lessons from their observed behavior, instruction that could be put to use in the home and community, Carson personifies animals in order to foster the reader's intellectual and emotional connection with that creature. For Cooper, then, the point is for humans to mimic or adapt the positive behaviors of birds; for Carson, the object is simply to see from the bird's point of view, to grasp that creature's existence by a shift in perspective. As she remarks in a letter to a reader of *Under the Sea-Wind*, "As far as possible, I wanted my readers to feel that they were, for a time, actually living the lives of sea creatures. To bring this about I had first, of course, to think myself into the role of an animal that lives in the sea. I had to forget a lot of human conceptions" (Carson, *Lost* 56).

This technique of Carson's also can be seen in her description of a swordfish preying on a school of herring, narrated from the visual perspective of gulls in flight:

> The gulls saw the two black fins sink beneath the surface; saw the outlines of the swordfish blur as the large fish dropped deeper into the water and moved beneath the herring. What happened next was partly hidden from the gulls by the seething water and spurting spray; but as they dropped closer and hovered with short wing beats—drawn by awareness of a kill—they could see a great dark shadow that whirled and darted and lunged in a frenzy of attack in the midst of the closely packed ranks of herring. And when the water that foamed to whiteness had grown calmer, more than a score of herring floated at the surface with broken backs and many others swam feebly and listed dizzily, as though they had been injured by glancing blows from the sword. (*Under* 162–63)

Rather than teaching a behavioral or social lesson, this passage depicts the battle between predator and prey from the overhead yet somewhat limited view of the gull, who ultimately enters the picture as a scavenger of the herring that escape the swordfish's pursuit. Carson thus places us directly in nature's scene, letting us observe events through the gull's eyes. What sympathy we may feel for the humble herring in this red-in-tooth-and-claw passage is tempered by our identification with a scavenger species and our expanded knowledge of this complex food chain. Consequently, despite her enthusiasm for exploring nature and her willingness to express wonder and celebrate beauty in nature, Carson does not romanticize the natural environment, nor does she draw explicit moral lessons from natural events, such as predator-prey relationships. Her use of metaphor is thus a carefully controlled compromise between literary expression and scientific accuracy. As critic Lawrence Buell concurs, Carson's evocations of kinship between the human and animal worlds "must be adumbrated within the bounds of documentary" (207).

Eiseley, too, uses metaphor in innovative and sometimes risky ways, and his literary techniques to a great extent determine the structure and texture of his representation of nature. For him, nature is an "interlinked and evolving web of life" (*Unexpected* 83); a place where "the dance of contingency . . . outwits us all" (77); an arena of adaptation, change, and process. Sometimes Eiseley's analogies border on the outrageous, as when he describes humans as "myriad little detached ponds with their own swarming corpuscular life, . . . a way that water has of going about beyond the reach of rivers" (*Immense* 20). Such a characterization recognizes our physiology as dynamic and complex, connects our fluids to the lakes and rivers we take for granted as sources of fresh water and recreation, and deflates our sense of importance as a species (since we are, in one sense, mere transport systems for water, the universal solvent of life).

Like Carson in her use of anthropomorphic description, Eiseley experiments with the use of varying perspectives, different vantage points that illuminate physical laws or natural phenomena. Such shifts in perspective characterize his intriguing essay "The Judgment of the Birds," in which he describes "what only the solitary approach can give—a natural revelation" (*Immense* 164). The essay explores a transformative experience of the narrator while in New York City—an unlikely place for an epiphany about nature, Eiseley concedes; but then again, the root of his method is to be open, at any place and time, to learning from the nonhuman world. In this case, observing a flock of pigeons circling high in the predawn sky above Manhattan, he realizes poignantly that the universe is not the sole province of humanity but rather is the home of many diverse creatures—even the sprawling city, "man's greatest creation [seen] from a strange inverted angle, . . . was not really his at all" (167). But this altered perception, a heightened awareness enabled by Eiseley's empathy with the commonplace urban birds, "is not a gift allotted merely to the human imagination. I have come to suspect that within their degree it is sensed by animals, though perhaps as rarely as among men. The time has to be right; one has to be, by chance to intention, upon the border of two worlds. And sometimes these two borders may shift or interpenetrate and one sees the miraculous" (167).

The moment is typical of Eiseley's writing: a simple occurrence, a common setting, or an everyday observation forms the occasion for viewing the world through different eyes, an alternative vision that both transcends human perception and expands consciousness. Another such moment occurs in the essay "The Flow of the River," in which Eiseley meditates upon the universality of water and the intimate connection between the human body and the outer environment. Such a realization, he notes, may only happen "[o]nce in a lifetime, if one is lucky, [when] one so merges with sunlight and air and running water that whole eons, the eons that mountains and deserts know, might pass in a single afternoon without discomfort" (*Immense* 16). While wandering along the streambed of the wide, shallow Platte River of Nebraska, over ground that he had explored many times before on scientific expeditions, Eiseley's narrator decides to lie down and float along with the current—perhaps against his better judgment, for he is not a good swimmer, and the Platte is a tricky river rife with unexpected dangers such as quicksand pockets. What happens next in his account, though, is quite extraordinary:

> For an instant, as I bobbed into the main channel, I had the sensation of sliding down the vast tilted face of the continent. . . . Moving with me, leaving its taste upon my mouth and spouting under me in dancing springs of sand, was the immense body of the continent itself, flowing like the river was flowing, grain by grain, mountain by mountain, down to the sea. . . . I touched my margins with the delicacy of a crayfish's antennae, and felt great fishes glide about their work. . . . I *was* water and the unspeakable alchemies that gestate and take shape in water, the slimy jellies that under the enormous magnification of the sun writhe and whip upward as great barbeled fish mouths, or sink indistinctly back into the murk out of which they arose. (19–20)

Eiseley's consciousness, indeed his very physical self, merges with the river, the diverse life forms it supports, and the geologic formations that comprise its origin and path.

The moment also is emblematic of a key difference between Carson's and Eiseley's narrative approaches: Carson alters our perception of the natural world by transforming our vision and experience to that of an animal, but she herself maintains a comfortable distance from the scene. Eiseley reveals himself, making his consciousness fluid and open to the reader and leading to his evocation of the "unspeakable al-chemies" that occur in the turbulent flow of water, a vague allusion to the origins of life and an unsettling way to connect us with natural processes. But this unsettling, I think, is one of Eiseley's chief methods of introducing an idea—here, the dependence of human life upon the flow of water, the connection of our species to all other life forms; the realization that a given moment in time is connected by geologic and hydrologic cycles to past ages. For Eiseley, such moments are much more than idylls of "nature appreciation"—they are visions of process, commonality, and evolution, a profound shift away from our limited human perspective.

Beyond Gendered Nature and the Myths of Conquest and Control

Previous chapters discuss two major representations of nature in the nineteenth century—the first, nature as female, is an explicitly gen-dered view of the environment (as articulated in Frémont's exploration narratives); the other, nature as machine or self-regulating system, ul-timately portrays the environment as a passive space receptive to the control and manipulations of masculine science (as rendered in Pow-ell's vision of the arid West). The first view is a myth of dramatic con-quest, the second a myth of systematic control. On the surface they could not seem more different, as one is rooted in an organic world-view and the other in a mechanistic notion of nature. Moreover, the mechanistic model achieved dominance within scientific thinking by the eighteenth century (an authority that continues to the present day), while the nature-as-female and other organic metaphors have persisted mainly in the nonscientific margins of popular culture.[7] Both, however, are shaped by the cultural values associating men with science and women with nature, and in that sense they complement one another, as opposites often do.

Other texts examined in this study, from Cooper's natural history to Gilman's feminist utopia to Byrd's Antarctic memoir, implicitly draw from or challenge these myths in various ways from the point of view of the explorer-scientist or amateur naturalist. None of these authors, however, fully reject either conceptual model or manage a resolution between the two views. In contrast, Carson and Eiseley not only replace the bravado of the explorer-hero with the understated approach of the naturalist, but they also loosen the tenacious hold of the female and machine metaphors for nature upon the scientific imagination. In an era when important branches of environmental science, population ecology and systems ecology, strove to develop sophisticated mechanistic models of predator-prey relationships and energy flows, Carson's and Eiseley's environmental perspective stresses nonmechanistic factors such as interconnection, chance, and evolution. Moreover, though Carson's and Eiseley's culture was characterized by contrasting gender roles and expectations in postwar America, their representations of nature transcend narrowly defined categories,[8] in much the same way that their ethos of scientific investigation revises the hero-persona of Frémont, the faceless method of Powell, or the tragic figure of Byrd. Their explicit repudiation of the mechanistic worldview and implicit defeminization of nature add up to an intriguing shift in how gender functions within the scientific investigation of nature.

The nature of Carson is active, complex, multifaceted, ever changing. No mere machine—devoid of life, mystery, or unpredictability— nature instead is a powerful unifying force, a constantly evolving arena where we witness, in Carson's words, "The Relentless Drive of Life" (*Edge* 2). Unlike Eiseley, who directly examines the nature-as-machine metaphor in his essays as a philosophical problem, Carson does not address the issue explicitly. Her views emerge indirectly from her perspective as a working biologist—someone focused on life's complexities, adaptations, and paradoxes. Although machines are built for efficiency and respond to human tinkering, life is often anything but efficient—a fact she highlights in a discussion of sea anemones, some of which take up residence in the abandoned wood crevices bored by another creature, since gone. "Seeing anemones in such an improbable place," she writes, "one wonders how the larvae happened to be there, ready to seize the chance opportunity presented by that timber with its neatly excavated apartments; and one is struck anew by the enormous waste of life, remembering that for each of these anemones that succeeded in finding a home, many thousands must have failed" (187–88). Here two decidedly nonmechanistic elements—chance and waste—combine in the sea anemone's successful struggle for existence.

Even more tellingly, Carson's depiction of nature makes little distinction between living and nonliving elements, for both participate in the complex cycles of life; in her view, all of nature is alive and full of potential. In another passage from *The Edge of the Sea*, she notes how life's power to shape rock rivals that of geophysical forces: "In a tide pool observed for sixteen years by a California biologist, periwinkles lowered the floor about three-eighths of an inch. Rain, frost, and floods—the earth's major forces of erosion—operate on approximately such a scale" (50). An earthy example of this view of nature within Carson's work, though, is the chapter entitled "Realms of the Soil" from *Silent Spring*, which begins with a multiple-page discussion of soil structure and ecology. This chapter is a brief but eloquent manifesto on the centrality of life and living processes to the foundation of nature itself: the earth under our feet. "Life not only formed the soil, but other living things of incredible abundance and diversity now exist within it; if this were not so the soil would be a dead and sterile thing," Carson states (53). Soil, like the rest of nature, cannot be divided easily into living and nonliving components—rather, it is a product of life's constant and ever-changing interaction with inorganic elements such as water, air, and minerals. Seen in this light, soil is not a static, predictable entity, but something that "exists in a state of constant change, taking part in cycles that have no beginning and no end" (53).

While Carson's perspective on nature seems incompatible with the mechanistic metaphors of the nineteenth century, it also has few of the qualities of the goddess or virgin characteristic of nineteenth-century views of nature as female. Carson's writing largely eschews gendered metaphors or images, but one notable exception to this generalization occurs in *The Sea around Us*, in which Carson entitles the first major section "Mother Sea." Paradoxically, though, rather than merely feminizing the ocean as a nurturing, benevolent entity (and thereby limiting and objectifying it), Carson explores the possibilities of the maternal metaphor as a heuristic device in several ways. In doing so, she uses the age-old associations of nature and woman not to simplify or objectify nature but to illustrate its complexity and power. First, she notes that "within the warm saltiness of the primeval sea . . . molecules . . . somehow acquired the ability to reproduce themselves and begin the endless stream of life" (7). Though knowledge of life's origins in the early 1950s was largely speculative, most scientists agreed that the nutrient brew of the early oceans provided a likely environment for the development of simple living cells. Thus Carson's first evocation of the "Mother Sea" effectively illustrates this conception of the ancient waters as a nutrient-rich environment affording protection, stability, and raw materials to burgeoning organisms.

In a similar vein, Carson stresses the close connection between the physiology of land organisms and the seawater from which they once emerged: "the animals that took up a land life carried with them a part of the sea in their bodies, a heritage which they passed on to their children and which even today links each land animal with its origin in the ancient sea. Fish, amphibian, and reptile, warm-blooded bird and mammal—each of us carries in our veins a salty stream in which the elements sodium, potassium, and calcium are combined in almost the same proportions as in sea water" (*Sea* 13–14). She extends this evolutionary insight by critiquing the fantasy of controlling nature, made absurd and impossible by the immensity and power of the sea. The ocean is a constant reminder to us that our "world is a water world, a planet dominated by its covering mantle of ocean, in which the continents are but transient intrusions of land above the surface of the all-encircling sea" (15). The scientific impulse to explore and understand the sea, in this view, is an unconscious effort to return to our beginnings, and any fantasy of control or manipulation is quite misguided. In short, the trope "Mother Sea" in *The Sea around Us* does not replay past representations of nature but rather reworks them to paint a compelling portrait of evolution and comment upon the relation between science and nature.

Like Carson, Eiseley displays traces of his era's gender conventions in his writing: he uses the universal "man" to signify humanity (as does Carson), and when his essays and anecdotes make reference to people (whether real or fictional, scientists or laypersons), they are men and not women.[9] On the surface, it would seem, Eiseley's textual world is a man's world, in much the same way that Antarctica in the early twentieth century was a place characterized by the presence of men and the absence of women. Nevertheless, Eiseley's representation of nature itself is not gendered, nor does he cast the relation between humanity and the environment in gendered terms. Like Carson, Eiseley portrays the physical world in ecological terms of complexity, interconnection, probability, and change, while simultaneously analyzing and rejecting mechanistic metaphors and models. Fundamentally shaping his view of nature, as with Carson, are the combined insights of ecological relationships and evolutionary biology.[10] While these ideas permeate Eiseley's many essays, one in particular from *The Immense Journey* illustrates the point quite well. In "How Flowers Changed the World," Eiseley reviews millions of years' worth of evolutionary history, underscores the myriad ways in which nature is shaped by change in the relations among organisms, and, as critic Mary Ellen Pitts argues, "undermines the deeply embedded notion of human dominance" of nature (151).

In this remarkable essay, Eiseley draws our attention to the angiosperms, the flowering members of the plant kingdom (typical examples include grasses or deciduous trees) that encase their seeds in nutritive coverings. He points out that while they "now seem part of man's normal environment . . . there is nothing very 'normal' about nature. Once upon a time there were no flowers at all" (63). The obvious meaning here is a typical theme of Eiseley's—nature did not evolve *purposefully* to the state we now recognize, with us at the summit of creation and complexity. Rather, what seems an eternal fact, a necessary outcome, is a product of natural selection and trial-and-error adaptation. A more subtle implication, though, is that nature as we see it is not stable or predictable—whatever metaphors we construct for nature, given this fact, are subject from the start to oversimplification and distortion. Eiseley here shows us how, if we become attuned to the "enormous interlinked complexity of life" (63), we can connect the development of flowering plants in the Cretaceous era to the subsequent evolution of humans. The subtle point he makes in the history lesson, though, is that this evolution, while it has definite causal structure, is not a teleological journey.

According to Eiseley's condensed evolutionary narrative, the emergence of flowering plants had a profound effect on the planet's web of life: flowers enabled plants to fertilize each other without the aid of an ever-present watery environment; the fertilized egg (the seed) itself soon becomes a tiny plant, one equipped with a substantial food supply to get it started in its growth; and this seed is enclosed in an amazing variety of dispersal systems (such as exploding seed pods or juicy fruits). In this way, the flowering plants were great and efficient reproducers and quickly became the dominant form of plant life over much of the earth's surface. But this development did not occur in isolation from the evolution of the animal kingdom. Eiseley stresses that the evolution of warm-blooded animals (which maintain a steady internal temperature by metabolic adjustments, as opposed to cold-blooded animals, which take their temperature from their surroundings) is linked closely to that of the flowering plants: the tremendous energy requirements of these animals found a welcome resource in the highly nutritious, concentrated food of the angiosperms' seeds, fruits, and nectar. The result was an explosion in the number and diversity of such animals, including birds and mammals. Conversely, the flowering plants, already assuming dominance through wind-based dispersal strategies, benefited from the feeding action of insects, birds, and mammals, who distributed seeds encased in fruits and transported pollen from one plant to another. These new flows of energy opened up even more possibilities for life to expand and diversify, as certain animals specialized as plant eaters, converted the angiosperms' tissues to flesh, and in turn passed on those energy reserves to carnivorous predators.

Thus was the stage set for "a strange, old-fashioned animal" accustomed to climbing trees and ill at ease on the ground (74). If the evolution of life is a grand historical drama, a story continually being written, then humans are mere bit players—neither stars nor the director. In Eiseley's essay, the evolution of humans from apes and the subsequent emergence of humans as the dominant mammal is not a miraculous transformation or a scripted victory of intelligence over ignorance—it is a gradual shift from a humble foraging strategy to a life of the hunt. Just as birds found ways to convert the stored energy of the angiosperms, so humans captured and consumed the large plant-eating animals, such as giant bison and woolly mammoths, which harbored tremendous energy reserves. Later, with available game depleted in the midst of the Ice Age, humans turned to agriculture to directly tap the stored energy of grasses. "How Flowers Changed the World" is thus a story of how ecological relationships shape evolution processes—and vice versa. The essay ends with a tribute to randomness worthy of contemporary chaos theory: "The weight of a petal has changed the face of the world and made it ours" (77). Despite the connotations of that last phrase, which obliquely refers to our contemporary efforts to control the earth by industrial agriculture and resource management, Eiseley deftly punctures any hint of a belief in human self-importance by making it clear that our existence is rooted in our most basic impulses: the need for energy and the consequent drive to eat. Rather than set humanity in opposition to nature by casting the environment in feminine garb and contrasting it with a detached, abstract portrait of human intelligence, Eiseley depicts the evolving *Homo sapiens* as much a part of nature and influenced by evolution as any other organism.

This ecological/evolutionary perspective on humanity within nature contrasts markedly with nineteenth-century portraits of a gendered or mechanistic nature, both of which tended to represent humanity and nature as two separate, distinct entities in an unequal relationship (with humanity and science exerting control over nature as woman or machine). While "How Flowers Changed the World" addresses this issue indirectly, in still another (and often-anthologized) essay from *The Immense Journey*, "The Bird and the Machine," Eiseley explicitly analyzes and rejects the mechanistic approach to the physical world.[11] "The engineers," he writes, setting the stage, "have its [the brain's] basic principles worked out; it's mechanical, you know; nothing to get superstitious about; and man can always improve on nature once he gets the idea" (180). Next comes a brief discussion of the history of the machine metaphor, which he roots not in theoretical physics but in applied engineering of the eighteenth century and cell biology of the nineteenth—both examples of how an increase in knowledge is tempered by the ghost of reductionism. As Eiseley notes ironically, "The wheels and the cogs are the secret and we can make them better in time—machines that will run faster and more accurately than real mice to real cheese" (182). Yes, he implies, the mechanistic vision of nature is a powerful tool, and its accompanying reductionistic perspective enables us potentially to extend our engineering powers to the workings of life itself—but to what end? Eiseley lacks faith in mechanism's ability to explain and accommodate change: "what man will do to himself he doesn't really know. A certain scale of time and a ghostly intangible thing called change are ticking in him" (182). The sly reader, of course, will catch Eiseley's final dig—his dismissal of the machine metaphor is completed by evoking the image of human as clock, with the latter serving as the ultimate eighteenth-century symbol of the mechanical worldview.

In the last section of "The Bird and the Machine," Eiseley recounts a personal experience, a compelling rejoinder to the dominant mechanistic view of nature, during a field expedition from his early days as a researcher. Instructed to capture some representative specimens of wildlife, Eiseley traps a male sparrow hawk within a deserted cabin (though not without some pain and loss of blood) while the hawk's mate escapes. Catching one is a good accomplishment, he thinks, though it would have been better to get both. However, the next day he brings the captured bird back to the cabin, which the female sparrow hawk had apparently abandoned—and, though it was an idea he "never let . . . come up into consciousness," he decides to free the bird, saddened by the realization that the female must be "in the next county by now" (190–91). However, soon after the male takes joyous flight up into the bright sky, the cry of his mate sounds, greeting his return. To the older Eiseley, the reuniting of the hawks signifies the presence of a consciousness we have yet to characterize adequately, for a "machine does not bleed, ache, hang for hours in the empty sky in a torment of hope to learn the fate of another machine, nor does it cry out with joy nor dance in the air with the fierce passion of a bird" (193).

In the year 2002, two generations removed from the publication of *The Immense Journey* and *Silent Spring*, we still struggle in technology-laden Western society with conflicting impulses about nature and science: some worship a deified Mother Earth as a source of power or a being in need of protection; others treat it like a machine to be controlled and, if necessary, modified to run more efficiently. We look to contemporary ecologists, the heirs of Carson and Eiseley, as the potential saviors of the environmental crisis, yet we bemoan the damage wrought to the earth by the tools of technoscience—interstate highways, hydroelectric dams, nuclear power plants, synthesized chemicals, fusion bombs. How can we move forward in solving pressing environmental problems and living more within our means while locked within these conflicting and limiting viewpoints? My argument thus far suggests that the work of Rachel Carson and Loren Eiseley provides one resolution to this dilemma. They free nature from the loaded nineteenth-century metaphors of gender and machinery, and in doing so they open up space for a different kind of relationship between science and nature.

Environmentalism and the Critique of Science

Much of the power and significance of Carson's and Eiseley's work resides in their vigorous environmental ethic and incisive critiques of science. Both stress how science is fundamentally a social process rather than an objective method floating free of outside influences, how the ways we characterize science matter greatly, and how the practice of science must be rooted both in a personal engagement with nature and an ethical attitude toward the environment. Good science, in the end, is both an imaginative endeavor and an act of stewardship—a characterization that constitutes an important alternative voice to the discourse and practices of "Big Science," which values innovation over contemplation, potential profits over ethics, environmental control over preservation and protection, corporate conformity over individual creativity. For Carson and Eiseley, the investigation of nature is not simply the means of acquiring knowledge, but a starting point for radically revising the relation between humanity and nature. Their ideas echo the spirit of Gilman's and Powell's reformist visions, even as they reject the doctrine of nature's control.

It is tempting to contrast the approach of Carson's sea books with that of *Silent Spring*, her most famous and influential creation: the trilogy is the work of a gifted and scientifically informed nature writer, while in her last book Carson emerges as powerful advocate and prototype of the soon-to-emerge 1960s eco-warrior. But though the texts are much different from a rhetorical standpoint, this contrast is overdrawn. True, Carson's views become much more politically charged and polemical in *Silent Spring*—for her goal is not just to inform, but to persuade and bring about profound change—but her fundamental attitudes about science and the relationship it can foster between humans and their environment remain consistent throughout her work. Carson maintains a healthy amount of skepticism about science, for she views it as an ongoing process, not a finished product; she recognizes the inherent limitations of science long before she becomes the outspoken critic of the chemical industry and, more broadly, the control of nature. Far from condemning or rejecting natural science, as sometimes was the case with subsequent "environmentalists" who viewed it as the avowed enemy of nature, Carson until her death remained dedicated to the belief that the empirical study of life and its environment can foster a vital, healthy interaction between humanity and the earth.

Throughout her career Carson remained a dedicated proponent of "good science": she never doubts the value of science done thoroughly, ethically, and without outside influence, and she retains faith in the solidity of fact, the accumulation of data, the imposition of order through theory and interpretation. *The Sea around Us* illustrates this point quite well: not only does the book impart varied information about the ocean—in terms of its biota, its physical characteristics, and its relationship to human economies—but it also discusses how data are gathered and scientific theories constructed. When, for instance, Carson describes the turbulent behavior of waves on the ocean's surface, she tempers this portrait of "seemingly hopeless confusion" with "the patient study of many men over many years [which] has brought a surprising amount of order. While there is still much to be learned about waves, and much to be done to apply what is known to man's advantage, there is a solid basis of fact on which to reconstruct the life history of a wave, predict its behavior under all the changing circumstances of its life, and foretell its effect on human affairs" (116). This passage neatly summarizes Carson's view of science in her sea trilogy: nature may seem chaotic and without purpose to us at first glance, but with disciplined observation and experimentation, science can reveal the inherent order in nature. She also stresses the ongoing nature of scientific inquiry: while we can get a "solid basis" of fact, we never gather all the facts or paint a complete, comprehensive picture of natural phenomena; nevertheless, this solid foundation and the predictive powers it gives us are impressive and valuable. *The Sea around Us* points out many examples of productive research techniques and projects aimed at increasing our understanding of the ocean as well as gaining information useful in harmonizing human communities with their immediate environment. For example, she notes how we are "turning to the waves of the sea for practical purposes," such as monitoring the physical characteristics of waves from a sensor in the open Atlantic waters in order to gather data relevant to reducing "the rate of erosion along the New Jersey Coast" (115).

Tempering her steadfast faith in the scientific process, though, is the recognition that science proceeds by the proposition, testing, and subsequent acceptance, rejection, or revision of theories. Such is both the strength and limitation of the scientific method, for while competition among theories promotes both openness and innovation, it also points out the inevitable lack of a final answer.[12] Consider Carson's discussion of "the origin of the drifting weeds of the Sargasso Sea": she notes that there are two major ideas proposed to explain this peculiar occurrence that has mystified sailors and naturalists for centuries, and that "there is truth in both ideas" (*Sea* 26). This technique of presenting several explanations or theories for a particular phenomenon and then discussing the available evidence in support of the respective theories not only deepens our understanding of oceanography but also models the ideal approach to scientific inquiry. Carson portrays science not as a fixed body of knowledge, a static edifice, but rather as a process, an ongoing conversation among authorities, a continual testing and reformulation of hypotheses. *The Sea around Us* thus paints a realistic picture not only of the ocean and its resident life, but also of the way science itself proceeds. The result is a spirited celebration of the openness of scientific discourse, a delight in the excitement that results from continual debate and inquiry. At the same time, Carson does not hesitate to point out the limits of oceanographic knowledge, whether it be the details concerning the origin of life in the oceans (7), the diving capabilities of whales (46), the length of time required for plants and animals to colonize a newly emerged island (89), or the effects of submarine waves upon creatures existing far below the ocean surface (133).

Carson's environmental values are shaped in particular by a crucial theme of the sea books: the endlessly flowing cycles and complex interdependencies of the ocean. As she states early on in *The Sea around Us*, "Nothing is wasted in the sea; every particle of material is used over and over again, first by one creature, then by another" (29). Elsewhere, she notes the commonality of all animals in their dependence, "directly or through complex food chains, on the plants for food and life" (8); the interdependence of plants and animals in the evolutionary transition from sea to land habitats (12); the connection between land-based and undersea rivers (61); and the ultimate unity of all ocean currents (150). Emerging from these commentaries is the notion of the sea as ecological utopia: a place where nothing is "garbage," where life's origins took place and evolution still occurs, where mineral and organic substances trade places freely, easily, and necessarily—and where the impact of human civilization, the ecological wildcard of the twentieth century, has been minimal.

Yet, of course, humans do enter this utopian realm. A brief look at how Carson characterizes individuals and human culture in general illuminates a key tension in the sea trilogy: on one hand, the sea is an inexhaustible resource that dwarfs human industry, making the potential threat of human abuse of the oceans almost inconceivable; on the other, Carson recognizes the damage that may be done to local marine ecosystems, such as small islands, an insight that prefigures her systemic critique in *Silent Spring*. In *Under the Sea-Wind*, among the few humans portrayed are fisherman, who capitalize upon the ocean's resources while staking their livelihood upon the health of the entire system, from the tiny floating phytoplankton near the water's surface to the large predator fish below. One such fisherman is relatively new to his profession, having spent only two years working the ocean—"not long enough to forget, if he ever would, the unslakable curiosity he had brought to his job" (200). Carson presents the young fisherman as one who cultivates a cross-species empathy for the mackerel, which dramatically escape the draw of his net. Such a view, cultivated throughout Carson's narrative, fosters one kind of environmental ethic—a respect for the pulse of life exhibited in other creatures, an unwillingness to divorce the "unslakable curiosity" about nature from the job of harvesting life from the sea.

Ultimately, Carson moves from this snapshot of one man's life to viewing human civilization itself in the grand context of geologic time, a perspective that is not only humbling but also indicative of the contrast between the vast power and immense age of the sea, on one hand, and the youth and possible impermanence of the human species, on the other. This point is underscored in the dramatic ending to *Under the Sea-Wind:* Carson suggests that the ebb and flow of a species' life cycle, such as that of the mysterious eel, enacts on a small scale the grand cycles of geologic time, in which the present "relation of sea and coast and mountain ranges was that of a moment. . . . For once more the mountains would be worn away by the endless erosion of water and carried in silt to the sea, and once more all the coast would be water again, and the places of its cities and towns would belong to the sea" (271).

In contrast to *Under the Sea-Wind* and *The Edge of the Sea*, which contain relatively few references to human cultural and technological practices, the last major section of *The Sea around Us* is entitled "Man and the Sea about Him" and thus serves as a useful barometer of how Carson in the early 1950s assessed the relation between humanity and the ecological utopia of the sea. Surprisingly, perhaps, to those more familiar with *Silent Spring*, the dominant theme of her analysis is the recognition that the impact we are capable of having upon the sea is negligible. In discussing a German chemist's scheme in the early twentieth century to filter and collect the precious metals known to be dissolved in the ocean, Carson notes that "in a cubic mile of sea water there is about $93,000,000 in gold and $8,500,000 in silver. But to treat this volume of water in a year would require the twice-daily filling and emptying of 200 tanks of water, each 500 feet square and 5 feet deep. Probably this is no greater feat, relatively, than is accomplished regularly by corals, sponges, and oysters, but by human standards it is not economically feasible" (192). Elsewhere Carson discusses how natural processes facilitate the "evaporation of salt on a scale far greater than human industry could accomplish" (194), how humanity "cannot control or change the ocean" as it has, unfortunately, "subdued and plundered the continents" (15). Such a view may seem surprising today, given the fact that urban and suburban development along coastlines, pollution from point sources (such as sewage discharge) and nonpoint sources (nutrient and sediment loading from river deltas), and widespread overfishing have seriously threatened the overall health of many marine ecosystems. Yet this situation has arisen, at least with respect to fisheries, after Carson published her last two sea books in the 1950s: whereas very few ocean species of fish were overfished in 1950, by the mid-1990s over a third of commercial species were overexploited; 25 percent more were in danger of becoming overfished (Worldwatch 79).[13] Had Carson lived to see the effects of cumulative overexploitation, she almost certainly would have revised her views on the seeming invulnerability of the oceans to human impact.

Likewise, an analysis of the uncritical stance on oil and mineral prospecting by Carson in *The Sea around Us* must take into account her belief in the immensity and vast power of the ocean ecosystem, a symbol of human impermanence and insignificance within the scope of geologic history. The place where everything returns to its origin, where nothing is wasted, the ocean is a seemingly inexhaustible source of minerals, precious metals, and other substances—everything from table salt to bromine to gold to petroleum—if only we can learn to re-trieve it economically and efficiently. On the potential pumping of oil from difficult-to-access undersea fields, Carson seems neutral: her multipage discussion evaluates the methods and challenges of extrac-tion but does not raise the specter of potential environmental damage—an omission curious to us in our age of heated debates over offshore drilling projects and ecologically disastrous oil spills from pipelines and tanker transports. Yet, as noted above with respect to fisheries, the eco-logical impact of such incidents, for example, increased dramatically in just the last two decades of the twentieth century: biologist Joanne Burger notes that of the seventeen worst oil accidents (by volume) in history, only one occurred as early as 1967, three years after Carson's death; the rest occurred from 1972 onward. Moreover, the typical oil tanker of 1977 had thirty times more capacity than its counterpart in 1945 (Burger 30–32). Thus, at the time of Carson's oceanographic re-search, oil spills probably were not perceived as a major ecological threat.

However, in "The Birth of an Island," one of the chapters in *The Sea around Us*, Carson recognizes and comes to terms with the profoundly damaging effects of some human activity. She assesses the impact of humans not upon the sea per se but on the small and ecologically sen-sitive land masses where many of the world's unique organisms have developed.

> But man, unhappily, has written one of the blackest records as a de-stroyer on the oceanic islands. He has seldom set foot on an island that he has not brought about disastrous changes. He has destroyed envi-ronments by cutting, clearing, and burning; he has brought with him as a chance associate the nefarious rat; and almost invariably he has turned loose upon the island a whole Noah's Ark of goats, hogs, cat-tle, dogs, cats, and other nonnative animals as well as plants. Upon species after species of island life, the black night of extinction has fallen. (93–94)

Carson's refrain in this chapter is that humans have interfered with or upset "nature's balance"—in contrast to the great imperturbability of the ocean, island ecosystems are vulnerable. Thus in "The Birth of an Island" and elsewhere in *The Sea around Us*, we detect a key tension in her characterization of the human-nature relation: on one hand, na-ture is a vast, limitless, all powerful entity, beside which human activity pales; on the other hand, nature is a balanced yet vulnerable system of checks and balances, which humans may disrupt even unintentionally with considerable consequences.

The full expression of this tension, as well as its resolution, would surface ten years later in *Silent Spring* (1962, originally titled "The Control of Nature"). In her landmark work, Carson shifts her focus from the ocean to the North American continent, educating her readers in basic ecological characteristics of soil, air, and freshwater; explaining the development and characteristics of various chemical pesticides; and evaluating the scientific evidence connecting their misuse with the harm or destruction of life. Carson writes not a celebration but a *defense* of nature—she argues that the Western impulse since World War II to control nature, to selectively destroy certain organisms (primarily insects) so that other "more desirable" organisms may flourish, is based upon profits and convenience rather than sound scientific knowledge. Even more importantly, such policies and attitudes evince a bankrupt environmental ethic. As she notes in the book's concluding paragraph, "The 'control of nature' is a phrase conceived in arrogance, born of the Neanderthal age of biology and philosophy, when it was supposed that nature exists for the convenience of man" (297).

Carson also bemoans the ties between, on one hand, science and technology and, on the other, politics and economics—such associations compromise the integrity of scientific research in both direct and subtle ways. Corporate-sponsored research proceeds with an implicit agenda, and all too often experimental results confirm the company line that chemical x is safe at level y of exposure. More indirectly, the pressures felt by scientists working for corporations or government agencies to avoid controversy and the lack of ready funding for independent research on the effects of various pesticides adversely affect the integrity of scientific investigations. Carson's critique of industry-sponsored science and technology, and the government's complicity in that sponsorship, suggests she was far from idealistic in her devotion to scientific progress. Instead, she thought it necessary to combine scientific inquiry with a broad-based understanding of ecological processes and an ethical commitment to preserving natural diversity. At the same time, she does not claim science is the main culprit in the tragedy of environmental degradation; in fact, Carson both relies upon the carefully documented research of many different scientists and places great faith in "new, imaginative, and creative approaches" to managing destructive organisms, such as the quickly developing field of biological pest control (*Silent* 296).

What Carson learned from the mid-1950s onward—from her reading of the scientific literature, from discussions with scientists in educational and governmental institutions, from garden clubs and letters from private citizens, and from her own explorations of natural areas—was that the indiscriminate use of chemical pesticides was damaging plant communities, destroying habitat, threatening wildlife, and engendering unhealthy living environments for people in their homes, workplaces, and public spaces. While Carson always had been mindful of conservation efforts and the need to protect nature from exploitation and abuse, even she was startled to learn of the extent to which pesticides were developed and marketed for use by individuals, businesses, and local governments, despite being largely untested. The result was a strong and systematic critique of "the chemical barrage . . . hurled against the fabric of life—a fabric on the one hand delicate and destructible, on the other miraculously tough and resilient, and capable of striking back in unexpected ways" (*Silent* 297).

This insight represents the culmination of Carson's study of nature and resolves the unspoken tensions present in her sea trilogy, not by choosing one interpretation over another but by embracing paradox. Just as light can be conceptualized and empirically demonstrated to be both a wave and a particle, so nature properly can be regarded as both strong and vulnerable, powerful yet fragile. Carson articulates both views in this discussion of nature's balance: "The balance of nature is not the same today as in Pleistocene times, but it is still there: a complex, precise, and highly integrated system of relationships between living things which cannot safely be ignored. . . . The balance of nature is not a *status quo*; it is fluid, ever shifting, in a constant state of adjustment. Man, too, is part of this balance; sometimes the balance is in his favor; sometimes—and all too often through his own activities—it is shifted to his disadvantage" (*Silent* 246). Two key ideas run through this concept of nature described in *Silent Spring:* first, nature is a system of checks and balances, of countervailing and interlocking forces, of complex webs—as such, it may absorb a certain amount of harmful impact before the balance is upset. Indeed, the idea of balance evoked here, in contrast to the typical view of an unchanging nature in steady state, highlights fluidity, flexibility, and adaptability.[14] Yet given enough pressure from, say, repeated pesticide applications to cornfields, nature can be thrown off kilter; excessive pesticides can destroy helpful populations of insects that would otherwise keep numbers of harmful bugs at a reasonable level. In this way is nature vulnerable. But at the same time, nature can retaliate with, as Carson puts is, "The Rumblings of an Avalanche" (262)—strains of harmful insects that demonstrate resistance to a given pesticide will grow abundantly in the absence of weaker strains already killed off. Natural selection occurs on a daily basis in farmers' fields, creating more and more resistant species of insects and other pests. In short, nature perturbed is powerful and resourceful—and it will evade our short-sighted plans of conquest, Carson assures us, if we do not work within the boundaries of natural fluctuations—the range of the acceptable balances.

Eiseley's environmental views began to emerge in the late 1950s with *The Immense Journey*, and these autobiographical musings represent the genesis of his later, more explicit discussions of ecological problems and their causes. Like Carson's viewpoint, Eiseley's perspective is rooted in a rejection of anthropocentrism and a vigorous critique of the supposed objectivity of science. However, whereas Carson concentrates on exposing the problematic linkages between science, government, and industry and suggesting new directions for ecological research and practice, Eiseley largely avoids discussions of policy and instead explores the connection between the practice of science and his own subjectivity. Carson never questions whether an objective scientific method exists; Eiseley does. The greatest power of Eiseley's work is his celebration of the imagination, the personal, the human touch in science as a necessary ingredient to foster humility toward nature, realism concerning our technological capabilities, and a responsible environmental ethic.[15]

For Eiseley, an evolutionary perspective and knowledge of the immense geologic sweeps of time in the earth's history provide the foundation for questioning our species' nearly unshakable belief in its inherent superiority, its manifest destiny to conquer and control all other forms of life, from bacteria to feed cattle to hardwood forests. He debunks the notion that humans are the crowning glory of evolution (*Immense* 57) and pointedly emphasizes that we, instead, are the chance products of natural selection (47, 122). The witty essay "Little Men and

Flying Saucers" examines the fallacy of a closely related and decidedly twentieth-century human tendency: to unconsciously assume that beings resembling ourselves populate the cosmos. Such expectations, rather than being realistic or scientifically credible, "equate neatly with our own projected dreams" (145).

A less silly but equally misguided version of anthropocentrism, according to Eiseley, exists in the view of nineteenth-century geologists and naturalists before Darwin, who were convinced that fossil evidence pointed to the eventual development of humanity. Even the views of proto-evolutionists, Eiseley suggests, were strongly anthropocentric; it remained for Darwin to see

> clearly that the succession of life on this planet was not a formal pattern imposed from without, or moving exclusively in one direction. Whatever else life might be, it was adjustable and not fixed. It worked its way through difficult environments. Every creature alive is the product of a unique history. . . . Life, even cellular life, may exist out yonder in the dark. But high or low in nature, it will not wear the shape of man. That shape is the evolutionary product of a strange, long wandering through the attics of the forest roof, and so great are the chances of failure, that nothing precisely and identically human is likely ever to come that way again. (*Immense* 160–61)

Eiseley indirectly comments on the anthropocentric perspective by exploring how the very concept of environment depends upon the position and viewpoint of the observer. In the essay "The Hidden Teacher," the narrator watches a female "orb spider" moving along her delicately spun web and benefits from "an unexpected lesson" (*Unexpected* 49). As is customary in Eiseley's essays, the insight connects a natural phenomenon with the scientist's imagination: "Spider was circumscribed by spider ideas; its universe was spider universe. All outside was irrational, extraneous, at best, raw material. . . . I realized that in the world of spider I did not exist" (50). This is not simply an experiment with perspective, an imaginative leap of seeing beyond the confines of human vision and experience; Eiseley realizes that he is part of the vast, outer, and largely unknown environment of the spider. His consciousness, his knowledge of human evolution and power in the world bear little upon the spider's existence. He is simply one additional potential sensory input for the arachnid attuned to vibrations of the web and what they might signify. Humbled by this insight, the narrator proceeds to look inward, to his very bloodstream. There he envisions the dynamic workings of his white blood cells to which he is merely "a kind of chemical web . . . , a natural environment seemingly immortal if they [the corpuscles] could have thought about it. . . . I began to see that among the many universes in which the world of living creatures existed, some were large, some were small, but that all . . . were in some way limited or finite. We were creatures of many different dimensions passing through each other's lives like ghosts through doors" (50–51). Cleverly, then, Eiseley uses this humble series of observations to deepen our notion of our place on earth, the profound interconnections among organisms, and the multiple, interlocking "environments" that exist side by side in nature. Eiseley's environmental ethic thus encompasses a healthy disrespect for anthropocentrism and an awareness of how creatures depend upon yet have limited knowledge of one another. He realizes that what we should recognize as the "environment" is far more complicated than simply the natural world outside our bodies, our homes, and our cities.

The Unexpected Universe and, particularly, *The Invisible Pyramid* go well beyond the lessons of spider and blood to assessing humankind's adverse affects upon the environment, from briefly bemoaning "the relentless advance of suburban housing" (*Unexpected* 196) to portraying humans as "planet changers" and "decimators" (99). With respect to the seemingly benevolent "green revolution" in agriculture, Eiseley suggests that the massive increase in farm production (due to mechanization, plant hybridization, and the use of pesticides) "would not long restore the balance between nature" and humanity (*Invisible* 106). Eiseley chafes at the reckless consumption of natural resources and the inherent wastefulness of that process as "over a billion pounds of trash are spewed over the landscape in a single year" (64). Such destruction spurs him to characterize *Homo sapiens* as a "planet virus"—our industrialized culture has become a "world eater," a metaphor that quickly becomes literal in Eiseley's critique (64).

Eiseley develops this bizarre yet apt analogy by describing, of all things, a slime mold:

> It came to me in the night, in the midst of a bad dream, that perhaps man, like the blight descending on a fruit, is by nature a parasite, a spore bearer, a world eater. The slime molds are the only creatures on the planet that share the ways of man from his individual pioneer phase

to his final immersion in great cities. Under the microscope one can see the mold amoebas streaming to their meeting places, and no one would call them human. Nevertheless, magnified many thousand times and observed from the air, their habits would appear close to our own. This is because, when their microscopic frontier is gone, as it quickly is, the single amoeboid frontiersmen swarm into concentrated aggregations. At the last they thrust up overtoppling spore palaces, like city skyscrapers. The rupture of these vesicles may disseminate the living spores as far away proportionately as man's journey to the moon. (*Invisible* 53)

Here Eiseley stretches the boundaries of metaphor, looking for a natural analog to the world-consuming tendencies of his favorite species, humans—though his careful qualifications indicate his reluctance to claim a perfect fit between us and them. I doubt Eiseley intends the comparison to be favorable to humanity, even though he does not seem anti-slime in the least. Slime molds rove about, take in nutrients, form "cities" by aggregation, and propagate themselves without motive; we, by contrast, must question our means of propagation, our relentless drive to consume natural resources. We simply cannot afford to be too much like slime molds, Eiseley implies, for it is then we truly become world eaters.

In an uncustomary bit of political commentary, he seriously questions our drive to reach out to the moon—a technological undertaking that was the logical consequence of the Cold War–driven space race of the 1960s and that galvanized the nation in a heady burst of patriotism even as the Vietnam War raged amidst spirited domestic protests. On one hand, Eiseley the anthropologist, in the essay "The Spore Bearers," views the race to conquer space as an extension of humans' consumptive nature: when resources run out, the species must move on to new territory and populate new worlds, and in this respect, humans are merely duplicating the workings of nature. Consider the fungus *Pilobolus*, whose ability to fire "its spore capsule, constitutes a curious anticipation of human rocketry" (*Invisible* 75). Indeed, he admits that "[t]here is a certain grandeur . . . in the thought of . . . battling against oblivion by launching a final spore flight . . . through the galaxy—a haven-seeking flight projected by those doomed never to know its success or failure" (81).

Eiseley the writer-philosopher, however, has great reservations about the space program and how it reflects both our misplaced scientific priorities and our lack of ecological responsibility. Space exploration, while romantic and exciting in its dependence upon astounding technological innovations, "constitutes a public sacrifice equivalent in terms of relative wealth to the building of the Great Pyramid at Giza almost five thousand years ago. Indeed, there is a sense in which modern science is involved in the construction of just such a pyramid, though an invisible one" (*Invisible* 87). Eiseley not only recognizes that the incredible cost of the space program indicates our lack of reasonable attention to vital ecological matters, as "elected officials frequently boggle over the trifling sums necessary to save a redwood forest or to clear a river of pollution" (90); he also claims that we have not examined adequately our motivations and objectives for such massive endeavors. The moon landings represent an uncritical, underdeveloped view of science: while the space missions dramatize science's impressive rise in prestige and political power, they also demonstrate our untempered faith in science "as the solution for all human problems" (90).

Such a view is both limiting and destructive. Eiseley's own complex attitude toward science, developed over many years as a researcher, historian, and creative writer, rests on the recognition that "Science, in spite of its awe-inspiring magnitude, contains one flaw. . . . It can solve problems, but it also creates them in a genuinely confusing ratio" (*Invisible* 92). Such a statement had been made a few years before by Rachel Carson, of course, and most scientists admit that scientific research frequently produces unanticipated difficulties and challenges. Eiseley's contribution to this conversation, though, is special in his insistence on questioning not just the results of scientific investigation but the very way in which science is *practiced*, both in general and on the individual level. I have already discussed how Eiseley's view of nature is at odds with the mechanistic paradigm prevalent in eighteenth-century physics and twentieth-century biology. He recognizes, too, that the vaunted objectivity of the scientific method—so dramatically depicted in Frémont's explorer-hero's attitude toward nature, formalized in Powell's dispassionate assessment of the West's natural resources, and clung to by Byrd in his moments of despair in the Antarctic winter—is a myth.

This insight in no way diminishes Eiseley's respect for (and, in some cases, fear of) science's technological achievements, its capacity to control and modify nature—but it leads him to the observation that science is much more than a prescriptive method available to all; it is an intensely personal endeavor, rooted in the (fallible) human senses and, even more importantly, in the imagination. Just as we cannot separate observation from interpretation, as our senses must interpret the empirical data derived from microscope or telescope, we also cannot separate scientific investigation from the exercise of our imaginative engagement with the natural world. Seen in this light, Eiseley's unusual and provocative essays do not represent the musings of an eccentric thinker, an exception to the rule; rather, they dramatize in great detail the flash of insight, the moments of doubt, the leaps from theory to data and back to theory that take place in the course of the scientific approach to studying nature. Eiseley is one who has "pressed his hands against the confining walls of scientific method" (*Invisible* 13) and found it lacking complete answers.

Though the link between science and the imagination, between empirical observation and personal engagement, is a theme that runs throughout Eiseley's work, he expresses it perhaps most eloquently in *The Immense Journey*. On one level, Eiseley claims that the theoretical work of science, however well informed by factual evidence, involves a great measure of creative speculation: he cites the abyss of the ocean, "the sole world on the planet which we can enter only by a great act of the imagination" (34). He tells the story of how several eminent nineteenth-century biologists, including Ernst Haeckel, Thomas Huxley, and Charles Thomson, were convinced they had isolated a primitive life form, a gelatinous ooze native to the ocean floor that represented a transition form between living and nonliving matter. Such a conclusion, however, proved to be merely imaginative in the pejorative sense, as another biologist demonstrated that the apparently mobile and food-ingesting slime was nothing but an artifact of adding alcohol to ordinary seawater (35–36). Eiseley's point here is not to ridicule the misguided theorizing of past scientists, for the history of science is full of similar turns of events, but to emphasize the profound connection between observation and imagination—to stress that one cannot proceed without the other.

By effectively fusing artistic perception, scientific knowledge, and a passion for the study of nature, the writings of Rachel Carson and

Loren Eiseley resonated with great force within American culture. At a time when the practice and language of science had become more specialized and thus less accessible to the public, Carson and Eiseley eloquently explored the insights of ecology and evolution and set standards against which today's popular scientific and environmental writings are measured. More importantly, their passionate and imaginative engagement with the natural world and their critiques of scientific progress greatly influenced the nascent environmental movement of the 1960s. Yet, unlike those who blamed Science (with a capital *S*) for all of society's ills and advocated returning to a pre-technological state, Carson and Eiseley saw great value in the scientific investigation of nature, provided it was combined with a responsible environmental ethic and the realization that the technological domination of nature was both misguided and dangerous. The fact that their views went against the grain of the scientific establishment and the culture at large made their voices all the more important.

Afterword

From the vantage point of 2001, as I sit writing at my desk at home in Chicago, nature seems to be more than ever a place of contested agendas and representations—at times a site of renewal and at others a place of continued exploitation. On one hand, within this sprawling, heavily industrialized urban region, nature is undergoing a revival. Local leadership, proud of Chicago's historic vision of itself as a "city in a garden," funnels impressive sums into landscape beautification with trees and flowers, and the City with Big Shoulders hasn't looked so green in thirty years or more. Environmental education programs have taken root and flourished in local school systems and park districts; canoes ply the water of rivers that have partially rebounded from a legacy of pollution. And at the fringes of the southwestern suburban region, near my hometown of Joliet, Illinois, a dramatic long-term prairie restoration project is underway at Midewin National Tallgrass Prairie—an effort that is transforming over nineteen thousand acres of former farmland and munitions factory into a living example of the state's ecological heritage.

Such developments signal the growing awareness of nature as something to be valued, conserved, and even restored; but counterbalancing them is the persistent consideration of the environment as a resource to be exploited, an impulse evident not only within my home community but on national and global levels. In Chicago and other metropolitan areas, urban sprawl continues to chew up farmland, wet-lands, and other open spaces while discharged waste from industrial and residential sources degrades air and water quality. Our nation's consumption of fossil fuels continues to increase, despite soaring gas prices and dependence upon foreign imports of oil; chemically inten-sive, industrialized agriculture remains the dominant mode of food production; national forests are managed as much for lumber produc-tion as for recreation and wildlife habitat; wildlife refuges and wilder-ness areas are repeatedly eyed as sources for ore, wood, or oil, despite significant public support for the preservation of such lands. On a global scale, average temperatures and greenhouse gas levels rise in re-sponse to ever-increasing factory and auto emissions, even as scientists and politicians confer at multinational conferences and wrangle over environmental protocols. Meanwhile, deforestation, habitat destruc-tion, and pollution continue at ever-accelerating rates. That such trends exist despite thirty-plus years of environmental reform, educa-tion, and activism is a humbling reminder of how far we have to go to-ward effective environmental stewardship.

Closely linked to our conflicted ideas about nature are tacit contra-dictions within our attitudes about the possibilities and power of sci-ence. This centuries-old tension between benefiting from the tangible fruits of scientific research and fearing its unintended consequences shapes our attitudes about science's influence upon our relationship with nature. Natural history, biology, paleontology, and ecology have given us a profound appreciation for the beauty, complexity, and di-versity of organisms and ecosystems as well as teaching us we are part of, not separate from, the web of life. Embracing science as an instru-ment of knowledge, progress, and hope, we turn to environmental sci-entists—ecologists, wildlife biologists, climatologists, oceanographers, and others—as potential saviors who can craft practical solutions to en-vironmental problems. At the same time, we recognize the limitations of scientific inquiry in the face of economic barriers, political pressures, and nature's inherent complexity, and we rue the environmental dam-age wrought by technology-based societies. Our faith in science is tem-pered by the realization that it has given us the tools to modify or de-stroy organisms, habitats, ecosystems—even the biosphere itself. Even when used for beneficial ends, such tools exact a substantial price we are only now beginning to comprehend. Vast irrigation projects control flooding, provide electricity, and supply water for farms and communities but also alter the biology and aesthetics of rivers; chemically intensive agriculture increases crop yields even as it impoverishes soils and pollutes surface waters with pesticides and excess fertilizers; atomic power plants provide cheap electricity to millions, but scientists and governments have failed to devise safe and effective long-term storage of nuclear waste.

The diverse group of scientist-writers examined here, from Frémont and Cooper in the mid-nineteenth century to Carson and Eiseley at the dawn of the modern environmental movement, provide a useful vehicle for analyzing our shifting and sometimes conflicting views about science and nature. These tensions are rooted in the rhetoric of heroic exploration narratives and its feminist critique, the scientific management of nature and its concomitant faith in progress, and the holistic discourses of nineteenth-century natural history and twentieth-century ecology. Each case study in the preceding chapters illustrates both the possibilities and limitations of various scientific perspectives on the natural world. Such an analysis is partial rather than exhaustive, suggestive rather than historically definitive—nevertheless, these writings provoke a critical examination of our views of nature, our ideas about the proper human relationship with the environment, and our practice of science in service of these ideas.

John Charles Frémont and Richard Byrd construct a romance of the scientist-hero exploring and conquering the wilderness—mapping its contours and limits, defining it in empirical and cartographic terms, making nature a known quantity in the eyes of science. Within their exploration narratives, the notion that the seemingly limitless open spaces of the North American Plains or the forbidding Antarctic ice fields would require conservation or protection never surfaces. Such a concept is incompatible with the quest of the rugged male explorer who challenges the strength and limits of a feminized nature and withstands harsh conditions in order to gather valuable data. Consequently, nature becomes a passive object of scientific analysis, which in turn creates a conceptual separation between humans and their environment. Yet even within this drama of science conquering the wilderness, brief glimpses of a potentially more equitable relationship between science and nature emerge. Byrd's experiment in solitude, for example, is not just a meteorological mission, but also a Thoreau-like effort at self-examination and an attempt to achieve a state of harmony with the polar environment. Likewise Frémont, vanguard of frontier military power, western settlement, and political expansion, nevertheless displays an abiding respect for the power and inherent beauty in nature.

Charlotte Perkins Gilman's fictional all-female society and John Wesley Powell's reformist vision of the American West illustrate the progressive possibilities of a community committed to living wisely within the landscape. Each constructs an ecological utopia in which humans adapt to the particular limits of their environment; within such frameworks, nature nearly achieves agency, an independence outside the realm of human use or interest. Gilman explicitly critiques the values underlying Euro-American exploration science by spoofing the figure of the explorer-hero and questioning the conventional association of women with nature; Powell's technocratic perspective renders the hero obsolete by replacing him with the government-sponsored institution of science in the settlement of the West's arid regions. However, the primary legacy of Gilman's and Powell's progressive visions is the idea that nature requires scientific control and technological manipulation in order to function most efficiently and for maximum benefit to its inhabitants. Science directs the cultivation of crops, the pattern of land distribution, the use of resources such as soil, timber, water, and minerals, even the political fabric of communities. Buttressing this optimistic view of the human-nature relation is, particularly in Powell's case, the representation of nature as a machine that can be tinkered with and improved, and the belief in science as the ultimate problem solver. Though they shift the focus from the scientist-hero's romantic engagement with nature to the process of scientific management, their emphasis upon controlling the environment as resource is a logical extension of the explorer's impulse to conquer nature. Consequently, while Gilman and Powell offer positive examples of how we may radically reimagine the structure and functioning of human communities within an environmental context, their views of nature and faith in science preclude them from considering the possible drawbacks of intensive scientific management.

The discourses of natural history and, later, ecology—as exemplified in the writings of Susan Cooper, Rachel Carson, and Loren Eiseley—reject both the heroic persona of the Frémontian explorer and the scientific manager of Progressive-era utopias in favor of the empathetic naturalist who seeks both scientific knowledge of and a more spiritual connection to the natural world. Cooper's mid-nineteenth-century seasonal journal is an important part of the natural history tradition that places value on nature experiences, fosters early concern for wildlife and habitat conservation, uncovers the interconnections between organisms and the physical environment, discovers moral lessons in the design and operations of nature, and lays the groundwork for ecology's development as an influential science in the twentieth century. Within this benign vision of rural America living peacefully within nature, however, resides a tension between the desire to preserve certain aspects of wilderness and the tendency to idealize a pastoral version of the landscape. In the mid-twentieth century, Carson and Eiseley's popular writings revitalize the naturalist persona in an age of scientific specialization; reject gendered and mechanistic metaphors for nature in favor of a representation based on integration, interconnection, complexity, and change; and explicitly critique the hubris of science and the dream of infinite progress. At the same time, they affirm an ethical approach to scientific inquiry, one that values the power of empirical methods even as it rejects the vision of a purely objective, innocent science. Carson and Eiseley thus foster an ecocentric view in which science—practiced with imagination and a necessary realization of its limits—can craft a productive and more equitable relation between humanity and nature.

Carson's and Eiseley's ethical engagement with the values and methods of science mirrors a fundamental concern of ecocriticism and the overarching purpose of this study: to examine the relation of literature and science to the physical world we inhabit, with the conviction that such work can reveal the texture and patterns of our beliefs about nature. Neither these critical readings nor the ongoing project of ecocriticism constitutes a blueprint for reforming science and restoring the environment—such concrete plans can emerge only from the combined work and knowledge of environmental advocates, historians, politicians, scientists, literary critics, engineers, economists, business leaders, and others. However, such efforts cannot take place within a historical and intellectual vacuum: they require analyzing how past ideas, stories, and assumptions about the power of science and the character of nature have shaped our present views. By critically evaluating the many ways nature has been seen through the eyes of science, we can move beyond limiting models of nature, whether gendered or mechanistic, which define the environment as mere resource; temper the scientific hubris exemplified by the explorer-hero and countered by the empathetic naturalist; and imagine an environmentally engaged scientific outlook based not upon the desire to control and reshape the earth but upon the goal of restoring health and equity to our relationship with nature.

Notes

Introduction

1. Among works of environmental studies I have found particularly valuable are Carolyn Merchant's *Ecological Revolutions* (1989) and *The Death of Nature* (1980), Patricia Nelson Limerick's *The Legacy of Conquest* (1987) and *Desert Passages* (1989), Donald Worster's *Under Western Skies* (1992) and *Nature's Economy* (1994), William Cronon's *Changes in the Land* (1983), Roderick Nash's *Wilderness and the American Mind* (1967), Paul Brooks's *Speaking for Nature* (1980), and Daniel Botkin's *Discordant Harmonies* (1990).

2. The Association for the Study of Literature and Environment (ASLE) fosters ecocriticism, maintains a comprehensive Web site, publishes an excellent journal, *ISLE* (*Interdisciplinary Studies in Literature and Environment*), and sponsors a biannual conference for scholars, writers, scientists, activists, and others. Representative works of scholarship include Ian Marshall's *Story Line* (1998), Patrick Murphy's *Farther Afield in the Study of Nature-Oriented Literature* (2000), Scott Slovic's *Seeking Awareness in American Nature Writing* (1992), Robert McGregor's *A Wider View of the Universe* (1997), James McClintock's *Nature's Kindred Spirits* (1994), and Frank Stewart's *A Natural History of Nature Writing* (1995). Key critical anthologies include *The Ecocriticism Reader* (edited by Cheryll Glotfelty and Harold Fromm, 1996), *Reading under the Sign of Nature* (edited by John Tallmadge and Henry Harrington, 2000), *Writing the Environment* (edited by Richard Kerridge and Neil Sammells, 1998), *Ecofeminist Literary Criticism* (edited by Greta Gaard and Patrick Murphy, 1998), and *Reading*

the Earth (edited by Michael Branch, Rochelle Johnson, Daniel Patterson, and Scott Slovic, 1998).

3. In his 1978 review essay "Literature and Science," G. S. Rousseau claims that the field has a long historical tradition dating back at least to Matthew Arnold's 1882 essay "Science and Literature." By 1978, science and literature studies were grappling with a question of influence. Although the traditional direction of influence went from science theories to literary works, Rousseau saw a need for an investigation in the opposite direction, from literary studies to scientific practice and texts. A sizeable body of critical studies in the 1980s and 1990s—in fields as diverse as literary theory and criticism, sociology, anthropology, history, and philosophy—have begun investigating these other "directions." Key works include Gillian Beer's *Darwin's Plots* (1983), Donna Haraway's *Primate Visions* (1989), *One Culture* (edited by George Levine, 1987), N. Katherine Hayles's *The Cosmic Web* (1984) and her edited collection *Chaos and Order* (1991), Alan Gross's *The Rhetoric of Science* (1990), and John Limon's *The Place of Fiction in the Time of Science* (1990). For an exhaustively researched bibliography of science and literature scholarship, see *The Relations of Literature and Science* (edited by Walter Schatzburg, Ronald Waite, and Jonathan Johnson, 1987). A forum for scholars is the journal of the Society of Literature and Science, *Configurations: A Journal of Literature, Science, and Technology*, published by Johns Hopkins University Press. *Configurations* also publishes an annual comprehensive bibliography of Sci-Lit scholarship.

4. Joseph Rouse's essay "What Are Cultural Studies of Scientific Knowledge?" suggests that "significant common themes" link this diverse body of scholarship: "antiessentialism about science; a nonexplanatory engagement with scientific practices; an emphasis upon the materiality of scientific knowledge; an even greater emphasis upon the cultural openness of scientific practice; subversion of, rather than opposition to, scientific realism or conceptions of science as 'value-neutral'; and a commitment to epistemic and political criticism from within the culture of science" (7). A more recent anthology, *The Science Studies Reader* (edited by Mario Biagioli, 1999), presents the thinking of some of the field's most noted scholars.

5. Key works include Evelyn Fox Keller's *A Feeling for the Organism* (1983) and *Secrets of Life, Secrets of Death* (1992), Susan Squier's *Babies in Bottles* (1994), Sandra Harding's *Whose Science? Whose Knowledge?* (1991) and *The Science Question in Feminism* (1986), Helen Longino's *Science as Social Knowledge* (1990), and Londa Schiebinger's *The Mind Has No Sex?* (1989) and *Nature's Body* (1993).

6. Two excellent studies in this vein are Vera Norwood's *Made from This Earth* (1993) and *Natural Eloquence* (edited by Barbara Gates and Ann Shteir, 1997).

7. See Evelyn Fox Keller's *Secrets of Life, Secrets of Death* (1992) and Donna Haraway's *Simians, Cyborgs, and Women* (1991).

Chapter One

1. Edited versions of these narratives as well as other writings of Frémont are collected by Allan Nevins in *Narratives of Exploration and Adventure* (1956). Throughout this chapter, internal citations of Frémont will be from the Nevins edition.

2. For a useful introduction to and informative analysis of the language of seventeenth-century English narratives of discovery and exploration, see Wayne Franklin's *Discoverers, Explorers, Settlers* (1979). Tzvetan Todorov examines Spanish exploration discourse and, in particular, the writings of Christopher Columbus in his postcolonial cultural study *The Conquest of America* (1984).

3. According to historian George Daniels, the mid-nineteenth century was the "Reign of Bacon" (63). The transformation of physical objects and natural processes into quantitative data as well as strict adherence to the scientific method ostensibly results in the exclusion of messy individual subjectivity. For Bacon, method, not the scientist, is primary; good science means trusting in and listening to experimental data, performing multiple trials, reducing systems to their smallest components, and, finally, distrusting the vagaries, inconsistencies, and imprecision of words. In his *Novum Organum* (1620), Bacon insists that language is the weak link of the scientific process: "when a more acute understanding, or more diligent observation is anxious to vary these lines, and to adapt them more accurately to nature, words oppose it" (27). This is because, for Bacon, "[t]here are . . . different degrees of distortion and mistake in words" (29). The resulting benefits from such a scientific philosophy include increased precision (via the standardization of method), knowledge about universal processes (via the measurement of "real" objects and natural phenomena), and the universality of the scientific process (anyone, properly trained, supposedly can utilize the experimental method and get results). In Bacon's words: "Our method of discovering the sciences is such as to have little to the acuteness and strength of wit, and indeed rather to level wit and intellect" (30).

4. A key figure who helped instigate the historical shifts I outline here is Thomas Jefferson, who was a motive force behind the push toward scientific empiricism and the professionalization of the scientist. Parts of his *Notes on the State of Virginia* (1787) anticipate the scientific rhetoric of the nineteenth century. In broad, political terms, Jefferson's impact was profound in constructing an explicit national agenda for science. Science historian John Greene credits Jefferson with dramatically transforming the scene of American science by acting as both "spokesman and symbol" (4). Jefferson served, for example, as president of the prototype American scientific group, the American Philosophical Society in Philadelphia, from 1797 to 1815. The most tangible example of Jefferson's vision and influence is, of course, the Lewis and Clark expedition of

1803–6, the event that another historian calls Jefferson's "dream brought to fruition" (Benson 71).

5. See also John D. Unruh Jr.'s *The Plains Across* (187–88). In a letter to Frémont sent just before his first expedition (to the Rockies in 1843), Thomas Hart Benton writes: "In the very important expedition which you are fitting out to the region beyond the *Rocky Mountains,* and to complete the gap in the Surveys between the South Pass and the head of tidewater in the Columbia, the officer in command has to appear to the Indians as the *representative of the government,* and not as the officer of a bureau. To them he represents the government, and as such he must make presents, or bring both himself and his government into contempt" (Benton, qtd. in Jackson and Spence, 1:164). The emphases are Benton's.

6. These reports were combined and reprinted by Congress in 1845 under the title of *Report of the Exploring Expeditions to the Rocky Mountains in the Year 1842, and to Oregon and California in the Years 1843–44. By Brever Capt. J. C. Frémont.* Many unofficial abridged versions subsequently appeared.

7. Unruh is even more specific in his appraisal of Frémont's work: "His real impact came not in the discovery of new and better trails. . . . Rather, Frémont's importance came through publicity. . . . Frémont always sought, in concert with his expansionist father-in-law . . . to go beyond simple surveys or explorations. His expeditions invariably were aimed at the furtherance of broader national goals" (187).

8. Speaking of Frémont's first report (published in 1843), Jessie Benton Frémont's biographer, Pamela Herr, notes that the "report was a unique document. Previous accounts of the West had been either dryly scientific or exciting but factually unreliable. In contrast, Frémont's report combined accuracy with narrative power. It was both a keenly observed description of a western journey by a trained scientist and a dramatic adventure story buffed to a high literary polish. . . . The report was an immediate success. Newspapers throughout the country were soon printing excerpts. . . . [I]t touched the restless heart of America" (82).

9. This map is reprinted as map 4 (in seven sections) in the *Map Portfolio* volume of Donald Jackson and Mary Lee Spence's *The Expeditions of John Charles Frémont* (1970).

10. As Thomas Jefferson had demonstrated in the late eighteenth century, a graph or table speaks volumes, in terms of persuading an audience that a particular interpretation is true, and that its truth is based on empirical observations. In *Notes on the State of Virginia,* Jefferson uses tabular information brilliantly in his refutation of the French naturalist Buffon's claim that New World animal species are small and even degenerate in comparison to Old World varieties due to the fact that America's climate is cold and damp (47). Offended by such assertions, Jefferson states that "our only appeal on such questions is to ex-

perience; and I think that experience is against . . . [Buffon's] supposition" (48). Jefferson then directs the reader to his amassed data, "a comparative view of the Quadrupeds of Europe and America, presenting them to the eye in three different tables" (49). Table 2 ("Aboriginals of one only," 50–52) is particularly impressive, for it lists 18 European species alongside 84 American species and arranges the columns in descending order of body weight, so that the European wild sheep (56 pounds) is juxtaposed, in the table, with the American Elk (450 pounds)! The effect is that the table visually (and somewhat deceptively) suggests that America produces a far greater number of and far more massive species than does Europe.

11. Near the beginning of the report of his second expedition (1843–44), Frémont reprints the comments of a Senator Linn, who calls for a reprinting of Frémont's first expedition report. The document, according to Linn, "proves conclusively that the country for several hundred miles from the frontier of Missouri is exceedingly beautiful and fertile; alternate woodland and prairie, and certain portions well supplied with water. It also proves that the valley of the River Platte has a very rich soil, affording great facilities for emigrants to the west of the Rocky Mountains" (*Narratives* 184).

12. As Pamela Regis points out, the practice of natural history "employed two basic procedures: collecting and observing" (6). In the Linnaean method, a "name is assigned that applies to a member of that species and to none other. The thing referred to, as well as the kind of thing referred to, is fixed for all time" (19). Regis's summary is an echo of earlier ideas by philosopher Michel Foucault, who observes that "the locus of this [natural] history is a non-temporal rectangle in which, stripped of all commentary, of all enveloping language, creatures present themselves one beside another, their surfaces visible, grouped according to their common features, and thus already virtually analysed, and bearers of nothing but their own individual names" (*Order* 131).

13. Both Frémont and Jefferson see in nature the characteristics of what Edmund Burke called the "Sublime" in his *Philosophical Enquiry into the Origin of our Ideas of the Sublime and the Beautiful* (1757). These characteristics include power, vastness, and magnificence, and they produce two levels of effects in the human observer. The primary effects are those of astonishment and "delightful horror" (Burke 73); the secondary effects are admiration, reverence, and respect (57).

14. See Mark Warhus's 1993 article "Cartographic Encounters." This exhibition was displayed in 1992 by the Herman Dunlap Smith Center for the History of Cartography at the Newberry Library in Chicago.

15. See chapter 1 ("Adventure, Manliness, Nationalism") from Martin Green's *The Great American Adventure* (1984, esp. 2). Green argues that the adventure story—as created by male writers such as Cooper, Irving, Bird, Dana,

Melville, Parkman, Carson, and Twain (among others)—"constitutes the central achievement of American letters" (19). While I disagree with Green's hierarchy of importance in American literary forms, his observations about how the notion of "manliness" is variously developed by these authors is informative.

16. Historian Richard Slotkin has traced the influence of the Bumppo persona in our cultural myths and narratives in his important 1973 study *Regeneration through Violence* (see, in particular, chapter 13).

17. Along these lines, Lisa Bloom has this to say about British explorer Robert F. Scott (who died on the return trip from his 1911 trek to the South Pole) in her 1993 study *Gender on Ice:* "Scott is concerned above all with constructing an image of noble struggle. . . . He is someone who prefers adventure to anything else. Adversity and setback almost become morally desirable. He shuns the use of dogs because they would make the obstacle seem less formidable. Why? For Scott the basis for all this is the Englishman's ever-present willingness to prove his superiority. . . . Dogs would compromise this heroic image" (122).

18. As recent biographical work has suggested, Frémont was far from innocent in the violent aspects of his expeditions, and thus the rigid contrast drawn between himself and Carson in the narratives is somewhat disingenuous. Frémont had knowledge of and sanctioned much of the "retribution" carried out by Carson and others. Certainly, if he did not order it, he often condoned it by his silence. The atrocities committed by Carson and others have been well documented. See Rolle (70–75).

19. In *The Lay of the Land* (1975), Annette Kolodny argues that from the colonial times onward, American writers of various literary forms have coded the land "female." Kolodny contends that the literature of European exploration and colonization of North America from 1500 to 1740 draws heavily on gendered metaphors in descriptions of the land (chapter 2). Utilizing a psychoanalytic approach, she also investigates writers in the nineteenth century, including John James Audubon, James Fenimore Cooper, and Washington Irving. Kolodny points out that this gendering of the landscape is a complex process: the land may be personified maternally (as a source of abundance and sustenance) or erotically (as a virginal object of domination and exploitation) (5). In her words: "Implicit in the metaphor of the land-as-woman was both the regressive pull of maternal containment *and* the seductive invitation to sexual assertion: if the Mother demands passivity, and threatens regression, the virgin apparently invites sexual assertion and awaits impregnation" (67).

20. For an excellent historical analysis of how Western science has defined nature as both a woman and passive object, see Carolyn Merchant's *The Death of Nature* (1980).

21. Some of Jessie Benton Frémont's book-length publications include *The Story of the Guard* (1863), *A Year of American Travel* (1878), *Souvenirs of My Time*

(1887), *Far West Sketches* (1890), and *The Will and the Way Stories* (1891). She also published numerous shorter articles for publications such as the *Historical Society of Southern California Quarterly* and the *New York Ledger*. In the 1870s, when the Frémonts fell upon hard financial times, the family lived on the proceeds from Jessie's literary efforts.

22. See, for example, Henry Nash Smith's *Virgin Land* (27).

23. Men, so this outdated version of American literary history goes, wrote tales of action and adventure (James Fenimore Cooper's Leatherstocking Tales, Herman Melville's *Moby-Dick*) or "serious" literary or philosophical works (Ralph Waldo Emerson's essays, Nathaniel Hawthorne's *The Scarlet Letter*, Walt Whitman's *Leaves of Grass*). Women, by contrast, wrote "trivial" (and tremendously popular, to Hawthorne's great dismay) domestic, sentimental fiction (Susan Warner's *The Wide, Wide World*) that often performed powerful political work (Harriet Beecher's Stowe's *Uncle Tom's Cabin*, a novel that was long dismissed on account of being domestic and political). These distinctions say far more about the political values of writers of American literary history in the twentieth century (and what they consider "serious," "trivial," and so forth) than about nineteenth-century literary artists themselves.

24. This peculiar anxiety of King's is a tension that has caught the eye of other readers; see literary critic John P. O'Grady's book *Pilgrims to the Wild* and the chapter entitled "The Subterranean Clarence King" (esp. 100–103).

25. In his landmark 1964 study *The Machine in the Garden*, Leo Marx articulates a defining tension in American culture, namely between an ever-growing technological base of society and a traditional pastoral vision of the American land. Marx deals with the complex dichotomy of nature and culture, where the "machine," i.e., technology, is alternately seen as effectively taming or aggressively threatening a pristine wilderness, i.e., the pastoral ideal (7–16).

26. In Ihde's terminology, the "human-instrument" complex perceives—indeed, constructs—the "lifeworld." Such a lifeworld could not exist as particular data points, maps, etc., without that specific human-instrument relation. Ihde describes this type of relationship between human and instrument as an "*embodiment relation* [emphasis mine], because in this use context I take the technologies *into* my experiencing in a particular way by way of perceiving *through* [emphases his] such technologies and through the reflexive transformation of my perceptual and body sense" (72).

Chapter Two

1. Lisa Bloom makes a similar point about the northern polar regions in her recent study *Gender on Ice:* "[A]s pointless as a trek across a barren wasteland may have seemed to those concerned with financial gain, such an exploit had a

pervasive scientific appeal. It literalized the colonial fantasy of a tabula rasa where people, history and culture vanish. The absence of land, peoples, or wildlife to conquer gave polar exploration an aesthetic dimension that allowed the discovery of the North Pole to appear above political and commercial concerns" (2–3).

2. For an informative overview of early-twentieth-century geopolitical conflicts and issues, see Pyne's chapter "Geopolitics" (esp. 330–41). I also recommend Fogg's discussion of nationalistic and imperialistic influences upon Antarctic science (155–61).

3. Byrd procured funding for both the Discovery and Little America expeditions through private sources, both corporations and individuals. His total capital resources for Discovery were $150,000; contributors included Edsel Ford and the National Geographic Society. Active government involvement in providing funds and support for Antarctic exploration did not commence until 1939, with the formation of the United States Antarctic Service.

4. The 1928–30 and 1933–35 expeditions are thoroughly documented by Byrd in *Little America* (1930) and *Discovery* (1935), respectively.

5. For an illustration of the extent of media coverage enjoyed by Byrd in the late 1920s, consult Joerg's *The Work of the Byrd Antarctic Expedition, 1928–1930* (a collection of *New York Times* articles from 1928 to 1930 that forms a running account of the first expedition).

6. Though his claims are symbolic (i.e., not officially sanctioned by the U.S. government), Byrd is an integral part of what Bloom describes as U.S. "empire building activities" in the early twentieth century (4). The subsequent geopolitical history leading up to the International Geophysical Year of 1957–58, the activation of the Antarctic Treaty in 1961, and the current regulation of Antarctic activities by the multinational (and constantly evolving) Antarctic Treaty Organization is complex and thus difficult to summarize. In very general terms, the Antarctic Treaty signals both an active spirit of international scientific collaboration and cooperation as well as a "putting on ice" (but not formal annulment) of individual nationalist claims upon territory. See Pyne, chapter 8, for a detailed treatment of this subject. Siple's *90° South* provides a revealing, decidedly American (and relentlessly pro-Byrd) perspective on Antarctic science and exploration leading up to and including the work of the 1957–58 IGY. For a historical overview of the Antarctic Treaty System, see Kimball's "The Antarctic Treaty System."

7. Though Shackleton equipped his 1921–22 expedition with radio, Byrd was the first to effectively implement radio communication between his main base and various field and air parties (Fogg 135).

8. An example of such an approach is the project description of a joint ecological research team from Woods Hole Oceanographic Institute and the U.S.

Geological Survey. (I was part of this team on an expedition to Antarctica in October–December of 1991.) Entitled "Biogeochemistry of Antarctic Dry Valley Lakes: Seasonal and Feed-back Processes in Amictic Lakes Dominated by Internal Cycling," the summary states: "In temperate regions, . . . [t]he mixing and diluting of lake water . . . can obscure the importance of some biogeochemical processes. The lakes of the McMurdo Dry Valleys sharply contrast with temperate-zone lakes but are uniquely suited for studying internal production and degradation of organic material. . . . Data from this project will help us to understand internal biogeochemical cycling in non-Antarctic lakes" (Howes, McKnight, and Smith 3–4).

9. In chapter 9 of *Discovery*, Byrd introduces the purpose and strategy of the Advance Base project (162–65). The next three chapters are written by C. J. V. Murphy and narrate the events at Advance Base from Little America's perspective. Resuming the role of narrator in chapter 13, Byrd summarizes his experience as follows: "From June on, till the tractor arrived in August, it was very tough sledding. The chances of my survival seemed very slim. But March, April, and May were more than all right. I had a great time. The trying months that followed have never succeeded in taking away the joyful memory of the earlier period. . . . The meteorological records are now in the possession of government meteorologists" (248). The passage is just as notable for what Byrd *doesn't* tell us as for what he does.

10. All this, of course, necessitates our taking Byrd at face value, for the question of textual authority, reliability, objectivity (take your pick) is always a complex matter when considering autobiographical texts. Which life story is more authoritative—the subject's own version, told through his or her highly personal filter, or a biographer's version, "objectively" told with the aid of interviews, letters, documents, etc.?

11. Thoreau's solitude is more symbolic than actual. His house is a short walk from the village center of Concord, and he strolls into town frequently. He also meets with visitors now and then at his pond-side residence.

12. In her analysis of the texts of mid-nineteenth-century British explorers searching for the source of the Nile in central Africa (chapter 9 of *Imperial Eyes*), Mary Louise Pratt notes a similar phenomenon, in which the act of discovery is bound up with a particular way of visualizing nature. Three salient features characterize what she calls a "rhetoric of presence" within Victorian discovery narratives: "the landscape is *estheticized*"; "*density of meaning* in the passage is sought"; and "the relation of *mastery*" is "predicated between the seer and the seen" (Pratt 204–5). All three of these features characterize the quote from Byrd as well.

13. For an illuminating discussion of masculinity and polar exploration, see Lisa Bloom's *Gender on Ice* (1993).

14. Paley proposed his "watchmaker" thesis in his 1802 treatise *Natural Theology—or Evidences of the Existence and Attributes of the Deity Collected from the Appearances of Nature*. An excellent critique of Paley's position is provided in Richard Dawkins's *The Blind Watchmaker*.

15. In the Anglo-American tradition of polar exploration narratives, to be "defeated" by the harsh environment does not necessarily negate one's status as a hero. Indeed, the tragic failure of Robert F. Scott's party to return safely from the South Pole in 1912 is perhaps the most mythologized and enduring chapter of this history. The popular story, based on the contents of Scott's diary, suggests that character and personal honor are the ultimate hallmarks of heroism. As Lisa Bloom notes, "Scott's masculine performance depended simply upon the integrity and honor of being a British gentleman. In Scott's view, British minds and bodies alone were enough to display the superior capabilities of the male hero" (112). Bloom goes on to contrast the British heroic myth with an American narrative "that is part of a scientific tradition. There is a larger emphasis on exteriority. Performance and achievement matter most. The scientific ideal calls for professional detachment and scientific proofs. The rhetoric of science does not allow for subjectivity except in the form of 'genius,' or for a sacrifice for a collective identity" (128). In this interpretative framework, *Alone* is somewhat of an aberration, for the issue of subjectivity is highly foregrounded in the narrative. Yet, it is precisely Byrd's lack of detachment, his inability to achieve the position of authority relative to the instrumentation he utilizes, that ultimately prevents him from fully achieving the status of "hero" in the Frémontian sense. This point verifies Bloom's claim that in American polar discourse, the heroic is linked closely with the operations of science (116–28).

Chapter Three

1. *Herland* did not reach a wide audience until its republication in book form by Pantheon in 1979. Brief but informative discussions of Gilman's life and career can be found in Ann L. Jane's introduction to the 1979 edition of *Herland* and in a recent anthology of Gilman's work, *Charlotte Perkins Gilman* (edited by Larry Ceplair, 1991).

2. The feminist movement in the 1960s spurred a renewed interest in Gilman's work. Since then, Gilman has been widely regarded as a key figure in American literary and social history. George Cotkin, for example, in his 1992 study *Reluctant Modernism*, cites Gilman as a key figure in the transition from Victorian to modernist culture in fin-de-siècle America. Cotkin maintains that Gilman, along with William James, John Dewey, Franz Boas, and Neyman Smyth, were among "the most challenging and original thinkers of the age" (xii).

3. In her 1989 essay "The Disoriented Male Narrator and Societal Conversion," Marsha A. Smith discusses the function of the male narrators in *Herland* but does not examine the scientific-exploration frame of the novel.

4. Cinnabar is mercuric sulfide, a primary natural source of mercury present as a reddish coloring in water.

5. Peyser is one of the few critics to highlight how *Herland* reproduces the dominant ideologies it ostensibly critiques. Other commentators on Gilman, however, have brought attention to the often not so subtle racism present in her other writings: see, for example, Polly Wynn Allen, *Building Domestic Liberty* (1988, 173), and Ann Jane's introduction to *Herland* (xvii–xviii). See also Gilman's short essay "A Suggestion on the Negro Problem" (1908), reprinted in Ceplair's *Charlotte Perkins Gilman* (176–82).

6. For a more detailed discussion of these issues, see chapter 4, "A Manly Profession," in Rossiter's *Women Scientists in America*.

7. "Hard" and "soft" designations have certain denotations in popular scientific discourse. Hard sciences are those historically associated most strongly with men—they also enjoy the greatest scientific legitimacy. Soft sciences, besides linking a certain discipline to women and supposed feminine "weakness," have often been so named as a way of highlighting their lack of rigor, empiricism, and ability to make quantitative predictions. In fact, such labels have functioned historically to marginalize certain ways of producing knowledge in preference to other, more established, ways.

8. For a historical analysis of European women's participation in botany and medicine and how those disciplines were co-opted by men, see Londa Schiebinger's *The Mind Has No Sex?* (1989, esp. 104–12, 241–43).

9. For other documents and essays on the application of Darwinism to social thought, see part 5, "Darwin and Society," in *Darwin* (edited by Philip Appleman, 1979).

10. Several scholars have discussed Gilman's views on social Darwinism. Larry Ceplair points out that Gilman was highly influenced by Lester Ward (1841–1913), who not only helped establish sociology as a discipline but also led the American countermovement to social Darwinist thought (the latter was championed by the conservative social theorist William Sumner, 1840–1910). Ward distinguished natural evolution ("genesis") from social evolution ("telesis") and was committed to "the conscious alteration of the environment through the operation of human intellect" (Ceplair 26). Gilman and other women "independently assessed the value for the feminist cause of Darwin, evolutionary theory, and the scientific method" (28). Also see Lois Magner's essay "Women and the Scientific Idiom" (1978, 68–77) and Ann Jane's introduction to *Herland* (ix–xi).

The literature on social Darwinism in America—as well as the wider influence of Darwin in general—is voluminous. Good reference points include George Cotkin's *Reluctant Modernism* (1992), an intellectual-cultural history of America from 1880 to 1900 that defines modernism chiefly in terms of the Darwinian revolution. Chapter 4, "Woman as Intellectual and Artist," contains an informative discussion of Gilman. *Darwinism Comes to America* (edited by George Daniels, 1968) is a useful documentary history on the general impact of Darwin on American culture.

11. Gilman, of course, is going out of her way to dispel so-called natural characteristics of women, but the point I want to stress is the continual references to behaviors and attitudes that could be roughly called "objective."

12. Gilman elsewhere discusses the "scientific mind," which sheds light upon what she considers to be effectively objective inquiry. She states that the "scientific mind has developed a new attitude—that of hypothesis. It assumes certain things to be true and tests them, quite willing to relinquish and to change that assumption if proven false. But of believing, in the cast-iron way that a religion must be believed, the truly scientific mind is incapable. . . . For health and vigor, for growth and progress, the mind must keep a steady watch on its beliefs, continually discarding errors freely, accepting new truths, always ready to change" ("Our Brains and What Ails Them" [1912], reprinted in Ceplair).

13. As it turns out, it is important that Gilman questions this specific view about inherited traits, since Weismann's theory conflicts with her fundamental belief in the capability of the human race to progress. Thus, like Lester Ward and as a committed social progressive, she distinguishes between acquired and transmissible traits in humans and the biological evolution driven by natural selection.

14. Gilman is grappling with questions of great import in current feminist discourse on the problems and potentials of doing science: Is there an alternative, distinctly female, way of doing science? If so, what would such a scientific practice look like? In her 1986 book *The Science Question in Feminism*, Sandra Harding discusses several types of feminist responses to issues of social change and the effort to increase science's objectivity. *Feminist empiricism* is a view that considers that "sexism and androcentrism are correctable" within standard science norms (24). The *feminist standpoint* position considers the male dominant position as producing false and distorted data. Standpoint theorists feel that an anti-empiricist perspective can offer an alternative solution to the limitations of normal (i.e., male) scientific practices. This dichotomy in feminist theorizing can be summarized as such: in the first view, the scientists (their beliefs and biases) themselves pose the problem to be corrected; in the second, it is science itself that is flawed. Harding considers both of these views to be limiting and instead looks toward *feminist postmodernist* critiques of science—which share a distrust of essential or universal claims to truth and knowledge—to have a greater

potential of producing viable alternatives to current scientific practices. Donna Haraway's *Primate Visions* (1989) is a notable example of this last approach.

15. In her desire to scientifically manage domestic duties, Gilman is revising the program of domestic science articulated in the mid-nineteenth century by Catherine Beecher. Though Gilman and Beecher share a vision of a household under scientific control, Gilman contests Beecher's view that women are properly confined to the "domestic sphere." Indeed, in Herland society, there is no differentiation between "home" and "society"—as Celis explains to the men, "Our work takes us all around the country. . . . We cannot live in one place all the time" (96).

16. Other commentators have noted Gilman's rather extreme views in this regard. See, for example, Polly Wynn Allen, *Building Domestic Liberty* (101–2).

17. Probably the most important signpost on the road to late-twentieth-century environmental awareness is Rachel Carson's *Silent Spring* (1962). Carson's widely read text was an eloquent exposure of the hazards of insecticide use in the United States and served as a springboard for other investigations into the environmental effects of industrial waste and chemical fertilization of farmland (see chapter 6). Another landmark work is Barry Commoner's *The Closing Circle* (1971).

18. This equilibrium is detected by the three men in their initial forays into Herland territory, as they admire the skilled architecture of the country. They are struck by the harmonious fit between the architecture and the surrounding environs, as opposed to "the offensive mess man made in the face of nature" (18). Such an aesthetically pleasing arrangement is indicative of Gilman's fascination with what Polly Wynn Allen calls "an environment in which nature and culture coexist . . . in beautiful harmony" (86).

Chapter Four

1. In 1978, seventeen western states contained over 43 million irrigated acres, or one-tenth of the world's total acreage under irrigation. Moreover, nine of the top ten agricultural counties in the United States were in the western states (Worster, *Under* 28–29).

2. See William Smythe's *The Conquest of Arid America* (1905).

3. A bit of context: historian John D. Unruh Jr. notes that 18,847 people emigrated overland to Oregon, California, and Utah in the period 1840–48. From 1849 to 1860, the number of emigrants increased to 296,259 (84–85).

4. See, for example, Worster's *An Unsettled Country* (17).

5. Two excellent sources on Powell's life and work as well as western exploration after 1860 are Wallace Stegner's *Beyond the Hundredth Meridian* (1954) and William Goetzmann's *Exploration and Empire* (1966). Hayden led expeditions

to Yellowstone beginning in 1871, and his reports were instrumental in the subsequent designation of the area as America's first national park; King (discussed in chapter 1) conducted a monumental survey in 1867 of a hundred-mile swath of territory along the transcontinental railroad route, as well as other explorations of the Sierra Nevada; and Wheeler headed the "U.S. Geological Surveys beyond the Hundredth Meridian" beginning in 1871, which divided the West into 94 quadrants for definitive, systematic mapping (Goetzmann 392). Josiah Whitney also bears mention as a predecessor to these projects, as his California Survey in the mid-1850s perfected instrumental surveying techniques and explored the Yosemite Valley (later designated a park in 1864).

6. *The Explorations of the Colorado River and Its Canyons* was revised in 1895 and combined essays on geology, geography, and ethnology with the original exploration narratives. George Crossette has assembled an invaluable volume of Powell's shorter writings in an anthology entitled *Selected Prose of John Wesley Powell* (1970).

7. All subsequent references are to the 1983 edition of Powell's *Report*, edited by T. H. Watkins; this edition is a facsimile of the 1879 printing.

8. Several commentators have discussed Powell's battles with a recalcitrant Congress; see Watkins (xvi-xx); Worster, *An Unsettled Country* (13); and H. N. Smith (199).

9. For in-depth analyses of Powell's influence and political legacy, see Wallace Stegner's *Beyond the Hundredth Meridian* (351–67), and Donald Worster's essay "The Legacy of John Wesley Powell" (in Worster's *An Unsettled Country*, 1–30).

10. Interestingly, the "literature" cited by Powell is George P. Marsh's *Man and Nature* (1864). Marsh examined irrigation and agricultural practices in Europe and elsewhere, and his work is widely recognized as one of the first detailed analyses of the impact, both historical and potential, of human activity on natural systems.

11. Sociologist of science Bruno Latour analyzes the shifting balance of objectivity and subjectivity within scientific discourse in seeking to understand how "facts" are constructed. In Latour's view, a spokesperson of science is, to varying degrees, objective or subjective depending on the "trials of strength" that she or he is able to assemble. "Being objective means that no matter how great the efforts of the disbelievers to sever the links between you and what you speak for, the links resist. Being subjective means that when you talk *in the name* of people or things, the listeners understand that you represent only yourself" (78). In other words, the authority of one's rhetoric hinges upon the degree to which a scientist can render himself or herself "invisible" and thus speak directly for the facts.

12. Pinchot articulated American policies of nature conservation during the early-twentieth-century Progressive movement. His philosophy of land use and

development was rejected as anthropocentric by more radical thinkers like John Muir, who advocated a no-holds-barred program of wilderness preservation (Opie 32, 40). Nevertheless, Pinchot's ideas became dominant because of his powerful government position (he became head of the Department of Forestry in 1898), his close association with Theodore Roosevelt (Limerick, *Legacy* 296–98), and the fact that his views rested comfortably within market capitalism's view of nature as first and foremost an economic resource. Conservation for Pinchot thus meant the development of resources, with a view to present as well as future use; the prevention of waste (i.e., from forest fires); and the consideration of the needs of the many rather than the few (42–46).

13. Although the phrase "quasi-ecocentric" sounds odd, I think it is appropriate, for Powell's discussions of the environment were almost always linked to speculation on how such lands could be used and what economic resources (timber, minerals, water) they could provide. Additionally, Powell did not advocate the setting aside of wilderness areas for preservation, a key tenet of John Muir's radical preservationism. Nevertheless, Powell's characterization of nature as a self-regulating, independent system is a significant step in the direction of an ecocentric viewpoint.

14. Insightful analyses of the mechanistic model of nature are provided in Daniel Botkin's *Discordant Harmonies* (1990) and Rupert Sheldrake's *A New Science of Life* (1981).

15. See, for example, Powell's essay "From Barbarism to Civilization" (in his *Selected Prose*).

Chapter Five

1. Vera Norwood's analysis (see *Made from This Earth* 25–53) was one of the first to seriously examine Susan Cooper as a scientist. Also see Michele Aldrich's essay "Women in Geology," in *Women of Science* (edited by G. Kass-Simon and Patricia Farnes, 1990, 50).

2. See Levin's "Romantic Prose" (183–84), Lucy Maddox's essay "Susan Fenimore Cooper and the Plain Daughters of America" (141), and Norwood's *Made from This Earth* (26).

3. For a wide-ranging and thorough discussion of women's contributions to natural history and popular science writing, see *Natural Eloquence* (edited by Barbara Gates and Ann Shteir, 1997).

4. The full title of the book is rather impressive and conveys the scope and depth of Phelps's knowledge: *Familiar Lectures on Botany, Explaining the Structure, Classification, and Uses of Plants, Illustrated upon the Linnaean and Natural Methods, with a Flora for Practical Botanists. For the Use of Colleges, Schools, and Private Students.* For sales figures, see Norwood's *Made from This Earth* (19).

5. Norwood also reads *Rural Hours* in the context of nineteenth-century separate sphere ideology, suggesting that Cooper fashioned a proto-ecological vision of the earth as "home" and thus appropriated dominant cultural metaphors into her analysis of nature.

6. See Marcia Myers Bonta's *American Women Afield* (1995, 9–12, 17–20, 95–98) and Paul Brooks's *Speaking for Nature* (1980, 166–68, 171–75). Both texts are excellent introductions to the work of nineteenth-century women naturalists; Bonta's anthology includes samples from the writings of each naturalist. Additional biographical and historical information can be gleaned from Bonta's *Women in the Field* (1991), a companion volume to the above-cited work.

7. While nature writing, in the broadest sense, has been popular in America for over two centuries, this diverse literature was for many decades relegated to the margins of the American literary tradition, despite the appearance of nature writing anthologies in the mid-twentieth century—William Beebe's *The Book of Naturalists* (1944), Joseph Wood Krutch's *Great American Nature Writing* (1950), and John Kiernan's *Treasury of Great Nature Writing* (1957). The rise of the contemporary environmental movement in the 1960s and 1970s, and the subsequent development of ecocriticism in the 1990s, produced not only a resurgence of interest in past nature writers but also an explosion of critical activity on environmental themes in all literary genres as well as nature writing in particular. Early anthologies of nature writing emphasized male writers of nonfiction over women writers and other genres, creating a sort of malleable "canon"; subsequent anthologies, encyclopedias, and critical studies have opened up the category and explored the work of marginalized authors. A good starting point for exploring ecocriticism is *The Ecocriticism Reader* (edited by Cheryll Glotfelty and Harold Fromm, 1996). Thomas J. Lyon's essay from this volume, "A Taxonomy of Nature Writing," sketches a classification scheme for the many variants of the genre; Patrick Murphy provides a more detailed taxonomy in his important critical study *Farther Afield in the Study of Nature-Oriented Literature* (2000). More recent anthologies of nature writing include Robert Finch and John Elder's *The Norton Book of Nature Writing* (1990), Lorraine Anderson's *Sisters of the Earth* (1991), and Daniel Halpern and Dan Frank's *The Nature Reader* (1996). A superb resource for students, scholars, and general readers is the two-volume encyclopedia *American Nature Writers* (edited by John Elder, 1996).

8. For a study of how eighteenth- and nineteenth-century natural history helped shape modern ecology, see Donald Worster's *Nature's Economy* (1994). Also consult Michael Branch's essay "Early American Natural History Literature" in Elder's *American Nature Writing* (1059–77).

9. Surprisingly, Cooper does not mention Jane Colden, a botanist who lived

and worked in New York's Hudson River valley in the 1750s and who has been called America's pioneer woman scientist (Rossiter 2).

10. Rochelle Johnson makes a related point in arguing that reading *Rural Hours* primarily in terms of domestic ideology can obscure "consideration of the ways in which nineteenth-century American women maneuvered their ways through dominant discourses in order to assert their criticisms of their culture" ("Placing" 80).

11. Cooper's literary output was, nevertheless, fairly substantial. After the original publication of *Rural Hours* in 1850, Cooper revised and reissued the book in 1868 and 1887. In addition, she published and edited a variety of works, including a novel entitled *Elinor Wyllys; or, The Young Folk of Longbridge*, published under the pseudonym "Amabel Penfeather" in 1845, and *Pages and Pictures from the Writings of James Fenimore Cooper* in 1861. She also edited a work by the English naturalist John Leonard Knapp, entitled *Country Rambles in England; or, The Journal of a Naturalist* (1853), as well as an anthology of poetry, *The Rhyme and Reason of Country Life; or, Selections from Fields Old and New* (1854). Finally, she composed a number of introductions to later editions of her father's novels, as well as a wide variety of biographical sketches and articles.

12. Two related parts of conventional attitudes concerning the roles of men and women in American society were the science of home economics and the notion that men and women should most properly inhabit separate spheres of life—i.e., the home and the world at large. The scientific management of the household had its early expression in the work of Catherine Beecher, who published her classic work of "advice literature" in 1841, *A Treatise on Domestic Economy*. Beecher's fundamental message was that women need to establish systematic and orderly habits in their management of the domestic space, but she did not connect her emphasis on scientific management of the household to women's liberation. Beecher instead advocated that women's proper sphere was the home (and proper object of influence, the family), and advised that women should remain subordinate to men in the affairs of business, politics, etc. (For a discussion of Beecher's views, see Gillian Brown, *Domestic Individualism*, 18.) Home economics eventually became an academic department in many American colleges in the late nineteenth century thanks to Ellen Swallow Richards, who, according to historian Margaret Rossiter, "between 1880 and 1910 . . . almost singlehandedly created the field" (68). Richards, a chemist, incorporated basic chemistry, nutrition, and scientific management techniques into her curricula in order to train women to make housework more efficient and productive.

13. These gendered characterizations of nature are analyzed in depth in Annette Kolodny's *The Lay of the Land* (1975) and Carolyn Merchant's *The Death of Nature* (1980).

14. Ralph Lutts analyzes this controversy in *The Nature Fakers* (1970).

15. See Lynn White Jr.'s 1967 essay "The Historical Roots of Our Ecologic Crisis" (reprinted in Glotfelty and Fromm, 3–14).

16. Also see Buell (189–200), who insightfully compares Burroughs the critic with Muir the practitioner of pathetic fallacy.

17. For a brief but perceptive overview of Cooper's approach to nature and her views on conservation, see Rochelle Johnson and Daniel Patterson's introduction to their 1998 edition of *Rural Hours* (xviii–xxi).

18. The term *ecology* was coined in 1873 by German biologist Ernst Haeckel.

19. For an insightful discussion of pastoralism in nineteenth-century America (and the tension between nature and culture in pastoral ideology), see Leo Marx's *The Machine in the Garden* (1964) as well as chapter 1 of Buell's *The Environmental Imagination*.

20. A classic example in early American literature of the identification of Native Americans as the human embodiment of nature as wilderness is Mary Rowlandson's *The Sovereignty and Goodness of God, Together with the Faithfulness of His Promises Displayed, Being a Narrative of the Captivity and Restoration of Mrs. Mary Rowlandson* (1682). Indeed, Rowlandson literalizes the association at times: "The Indians were as thick as trees—it seemed as if there had been a thousand hatchets going at once—if one looked before one there was nothing but Indians, and behind one, nothing but Indians, and so on either hand" (23).

Chapter Six

1. See *The Literature of Science* (edited by Murdo William McRae, 1993), a collection of critical essays on popular scientific writing.

2. For an excellent and comprehensive overview of environmental trends in the twentieth century, see the Worldwatch Institute's *The State of the World* (1999).

3. Of the several biographies of Carson, two that I found most valuable are Paul Brooks's *The House of Life* (1972), for many years the definitive study of Carson's life as a writer and scientist, and more recently, Linda Lear's *Rachel Carson* (1997). Brooks also has written an excellent, wide-ranging study of nature writing entitled *Speaking for Nature* (1980).

4. The term "concealed essay" is from Andrew Angyal's critical study of Eiseley's work, *Loren Eiseley* (1983). A watershed year in Eiseley studies, 1983 also saw the publication of E. Fred Carlisle's *Loren Eiseley* and Leslie Gerber and Margaret McFadden's *Loren Eiseley*, both literary-critical studies. A solid biographical treatment is *Fox at the Wood's Edge* by Gale Christianson (1991).

5. In his essay "Marginality, Midnight Optimism, and the Natural Cipher" (1992), Scott Slovic argues that the "concept of marginality . . . pervades nearly

everything he ever wrote. . . . The lonely wanderer is a common Eiseleyan image of marginality" (35).

6. See, for example, Roger Jones's intriguing study *Physics as Metaphor* (1982), as well as Alan Gross's *The Rhetoric of Science* (1990).

7. For a definitive history of mechanism's rise to scientific dominance, see Carolyn Merchant's *The Death of Nature* (1980). The mechanistic and organic worldviews are ably discussed and contrasted by ecologist Daniel Botkin in his book *Discordant Harmonies* (1990).

8. Vera Norwood's 1984 essay "Heroines of Nature" makes this point quite ably, when she discusses the diversity of views expressed by nineteenth- and twentieth-century women (including Carson) who wrote about the natural environment. Their views, Norwood argues, "complicat[e] the models that assume either a total acceptance or total rejection by women of the undeveloped natural environment" (326). The upshot is that although Norwood detects "differences between masculine and feminine environmental ethics," these viewpoints are not monolithic categories.

9. Lawrence Buell gives this interesting take on Carson's language: "A subtle but firm critique of homocentrism, more particularly a critique of 'man,' runs throughout all her work. Woman is rarely, if ever, nature's adversary in Carson's work, but 'man' often is. Carson adeptly exploits the protective coloring of the generic pronoun—a satirical obliquity no longer open to enlightened discourse" (292). I suspect Buell is giving Carson too much credit here, though his point about the nonadversarial relation between women and nature is perceptive.

10. As Leslie Gerber and Margaret McFadden note in their 1983 book *Loren Eiseley*, "evolution is the central unifying idea" of Eiseley's anthropological approach (35). I do not mean to suggest, however, that the theory and practice of evolutionary biology and anthropology are somehow free from gender biases, whether explicit or unconscious. In fact, historians of science have argued persuasively that studies of primate and human evolution, for example, have been shaped by both personal and cultural attitudes about gender. See Donna Haraway's excellent 1989 study of twentieth-century primatology, *Primate Visions*.

11. Mary Ellen Pitts's book *Toward a Dialogue of Understandings* contains an insightful and thorough discussion of Eiseley's critique of the mechanistic worldview.

12. See chapter 4 for a similar point about Powell.

13. Worldwatch also reports that "more than half of the world's coastlines and 60 percent of the coral reefs are threatened by human activities, including intensive coastal development, pollution, and overfishing" (79).

14. See Botkin's *Discordant Harmonies* (1990) and *Our Natural History* (1995) for his critique of the idea that nature exhibits balance as a fundamental characteristic.

15. In his 1999 essay "Coasts Demanding Shipwreck," critic Anthony Lioi provides an insightful analysis of Eiseley's work in relation to Plato, Descartes, and Darwin and suggests that Eiseley reacts against the dualism of Descartes and the Darwinian vision of nature as competition (52–53). More specifically, Eiseley's "rethinking proceeded not by rejecting rationality and the scientific method, but by interrogating them in light of the narrator's demand for loving engagement with the world" (56).

Bibliography

Primary Works

Anderson, Lorraine, ed. *Sisters of the Earth: Women's Prose and Poetry about Nature*. New York: Vintage, 1991.

Appleman, Philip, ed. *Darwin: A Norton Critical Edition*. 2nd ed. New York: Norton, 1979.

Audubon, John James. *Ornithological Biography*. 5 vols. Edinburgh: 1831–39. Selections rpt. in Sanders, *Audubon Reader*. 89–191.

Austin, Mary. *The Land of Little Rain*. 1903. Garden City, N.Y.: Doubleday, 1962.

Bacon, Francis. *Novum Organum; or, True Suggestions for the Interpretation of Nature*. 1620. London: William Pickering, 1850.

Bailey, Florence Merriam. *Among the Birds in the Grand Canyon Country*. Washington, D.C.: U.S. Government Printing Office, 1939.

Bartram, William. *Travels*. 1791. Ed. Mark Van Doren. New York: Dover, 1928.

Beebe, William, ed. *The Book of Naturalists: An Anthology of the Best Natural History*. New York: Knopf, 1944.

Beecher, Catharine. *A Treatise on Domestic Economy*. 1841. New York: Schocken, 1977.

Bellamy, Edward. *Looking Backward*. 1888. New York: New American Library, 1960.

Bergon, Frank, ed. *The Journals of Lewis and Clark*. New York: Penguin, 1989.

Bonta, Marcia Myers, ed. *American Women Afield: Writings by Pioneering Women Naturalists*. College Station: Texas A&M UP, 1995.

Buffon, Georges-Louis Leclerc. *Histoire naturelle, générale et particulière*. 44 vols. Paris, 1749–1804.

Burroughs, John. *Wake-Robin*. 1871. Boston: Houghton Mifflin, 1892.

———. *Ways of Nature*. Boston: Houghton Mifflin, 1905.

Byrd, Richard. *Alone*. 1938. Covelo, Calif.: Island P, 1984.

———. "Alone" (abridged). *Reader's Digest* 34 (Feb. 1939): 111–27.

———. *Discovery*. New York: Putnam's, 1935.

———. *Little America*. New York: Putnam's, 1930.

Byrd, William. *Histories of the Dividing Line betwixt Virginia and North Carolina*. 1728. New York: Dover, 1967.

Cabeza de Vaca, Alvar Nuñez. *Relation of Alvar Nuñez Cabeza de Vaca*. Seville, 1542. Trans. Buckingham-Smith. 1871. Ann Arbor, Mich.: University Microfilms, 1966.

Carson, Rachel. *The Edge of the Sea*. Boston: Houghton Mifflin, 1955.

———. *Lost Woods: The Discovered Writings of Rachel Carson*. Ed. Linda Lear. Boston: Beacon P, 1998.

———. *The Sea around Us*. New York: Oxford UP, 1951.

———. *Silent Spring*. Boston: Houghton Mifflin, 1962.

———. *Under the Sea-Wind: A Naturalist's Picture of Ocean Life*. 1941. New York: Oxford UP, 1952.

Ceplair, Larry, ed. *Charlotte Perkins Gilman: A Nonfiction Reader*. New York: Columbia UP, 1991.

Champlain, Samuel de. *The Voyages of Samuel de Champlain, 1604–18*. Ed. W. L. Grant. New York: Scribner's, 1907.

Columbus, Christopher. *Four Voyages to the New World: Letters and Selected Documents*. Ed. and trans. R. H. Major. New York: Corinth Books, 1961.

Cooper, James Fenimore. *The Pioneers*. 1823. New York: New American Library, 1964.

———. *The Prairie*. 1827. New York: New American Library, 1964.

Cooper, Susan Fenimore [Amabel Penfeather]. *Elinor Wyllys; or, The Young Folk of Longbridge*. Philadelphia, 1846.

Cooper, Susan Fenimore. *Pages and Pictures from the Writings of James Fenimore Cooper*. New York, 1861.

———. *The Rhyme and Reason of Country Life; or, Selections from Fields Old and New*. New York, 1854.

———. *Rural Hours*. 1850. Intro. Rochelle Johnson and Daniel Patterson, eds. Athens, Ga.: U of Georgia P, 1998.

Cooper, William. *A Guide to the Wilderness; or, The History of the First Settlements in the Western Counties of New York with Useful Instructions to Future Settlers*. New York: Gilbert and Hodges, 1810.

Crèvecoeur, J. Hector St. John de. *Letters from an American Farmer and Sketches of Eighteenth-Century America*. 1782. New York: New American Library, 1963.

Daniels, George, ed. *Darwinism Comes to America*. Waltham, Mass.: Blaisdell, 1968.

Darwin, Charles. *On the Origin of Species by Means of Natural Selection*. London, 1859.

Eiseley, Loren. *Darwin's Century*. Garden City, N.Y.: Doubleday, 1958.

———. *The Immense Journey*. New York: Random House, 1957.

———. *The Invisible Pyramid*. New York: Scribner's, 1970.

———. *The Unexpected Universe*. New York: Harcourt, Brace and World, 1969.

Filson, John. *The Discovery, Settlement, and Present State of Kentucke*. Wilmington: James Adams, 1784.

Finch, Robert, and John Elder, eds. *The Norton Book of Nature Writing*. New York: Norton, 1990.

Frémont, Jessie Benton. *Far West Sketches*. Boston: D. Lothrop, 1890.

———. *Souvenirs of My Time*. Boston: D. Lothrop, 1887.

———. *The Story of the Guard: A Chronicle of the War*. Boston: Ticknor and Fields, 1863.

———. *The Will and the Way Stories*. Boston: D. Lothrop, 1891.

———. *A Year of American Travel*. 1878. Intro. Patrice Manahan. San Francisco: Book Club of California, 1960.

Frémont, John Charles. *Memoirs of My Life*. Chicago: Belford and Clark, 1887.

———. *Narratives of Exploration and Adventure*. Ed. Allan Nevins. New York: Longmans, Green, 1956.

———. *Report of the Exploring Expeditions to the Rocky Mountains in the Year 1842, and to Oregon and California in the Years 1843–44. By Brever Capt. J. C. Frémont*. Washington, D.C., 1845.

Fuller, Margaret. *Summer on the Lakes*. 1844. New York: Haskell House, 1970.

Gilman, Charlotte Perkins. *Herland*. 1915. Intro. Ann L. Jane. New York: Pantheon Books, 1979.

———. *Herland and Selected Stories by Charlotte Perkins Gilman*. Ed. Barbara H. Solomon. New York: Penguin, 1992.

———. *The Living of Charlotte Perkins Gilman: An Autobiography*. New York: D. Appleton-Century, 1935.

———. *The Man-Made World; or, Our Androcentric Culture*. London: T. Fisher Unwin, 1911.

———. *Moving the Mountain*. Serialized novel. *The Forerunner* 2, 1–12, 1911.

———. *With Her in Ourland*. Serialized novel. *The Forerunner*, 7, 1–12, 1916.

———. *Women and Economics: A Study of the Economic Relation between Men and Women as a Factor in Social Evolution*. 1898. New York: Harper and Row, 1966.

———. "The Yellow Wallpaper." 1892. *Herland and Selected Stories*. 165–80.

Hale, Sarah Josepha. *Flora's Interpreter; or, The American Book of Flowers and Sentiments.* Boston: Marsh, Capen, and Lyon, 1832.

Halpern, Daniel, and Dan Frank, eds. *The Nature Reader.* Hopewell, N.J.: Ecco P, 1996.

Hawthorne, Nathaniel. "Rappaccini's Daughter." 1844. *Hawthorne: Selected Tales and Sketches.* Intro. Hyatt H. Waggoner. New York: Holt, Reinhart, and Winston, 1965.

———. *The Scarlet Letter.* Boston: J. T. Fields, 1850.

Hayden, Ferdinand V. *Preliminary Report of the Commissioner of the General Land Office for the Year 1867.* Washington, D.C.: 1867.

Holley, Mary. *Texas. Observations, Historical, Geographical and Descriptive, in a Series of Letters, Written during a Visit to Austin's Colony, with a View to a Permanent Settlement in that Country, in the Autumn of 1831.* Baltimore: Armstrong and Plaskitt, 1833.

Hooper, Lucy, ed. *The Lady's Book of Flowers and Poetry, to Which Are Added a Botanical Introduction, a Complete Floral Dictionary, and a Chapter on Plants in Rooms.* New York: J. C. Riker, 1848.

Howes, Brian, Diane McKnight, and Richard Smith. "Biogeochemistry of Antarctic Dry Valley Lakes: Seasonal and Feed-back Processes in Amictic Lakes Dominated by Internal Cycling." *United States Antarctic Program 1991–1992 Research Projects,* pp. 3–4. Xeroxed handout provided at the United States Antarctic Program's Orientation Conference, 9–12 Sept. 1991, Washington, D.C.

Jackson, Donald. "Maps of the John Charles Frémont Expeditions." Jackson and Spence.

Jackson, Donald, and Mary Lee Spence, eds. *The Expeditions of John Charles Frémont.* Vol. 1. *Travels from 1838 to 1884.* Vol. 3. *Map Portfolio.* Commentary by Donald Jackson. Champaign: U of Illinois P, 1970.

Jefferson, Thomas. *Notes on the State of Virginia.* 1787. Ed. William Peden. New York: Norton, 1954.

Joerg, W. L. G. *The Work of the Byrd Antarctic Expedition, 1928–1930.* New York: American Geographical Society, 1930.

Kiernan, John, ed. *Treasury of Great Nature Writing.* Garden City, N.Y.: Hanover House, 1957.

King, Clarence. "The Age of the Earth." *American Journal of Science* 45 (Jan. 1893): 1–20.

———. *Mountaineering in the Sierra Nevada.* 1872. Philadelphia: J. B. Lippincott, 1963.

———. *Systematic Geology.* Professional Papers of the Engineering Department, U.S. Army, #18. 1878.

Knapp, John Leonard. *Country Rambles in England; or, The Journal of a Naturalist.* Ed. Susan Fenimore Cooper. Buffalo, 1853.

Krutch, Joseph Wood, ed. *Great American Nature Writing.* New York: Sloane, 1950.

Leopold, Aldo. *A Sand County Almanac, and Sketches Here and There.* New York: Oxford UP, 1949.

Lewis, Graceanna. "Truth and the Teachers of Truth." *Friends' Intelligencer and Journal* (1896).

Marsh, George Perkins. *The Earth as Modified by Human Action.* 1874. New York: Arno P, 1970.

———. *Man and Nature; Or, Physical Geography as Modified by Human Action.* 1864. Boston: Harvard UP, 1965.

Maury, Matthew Fontaine. *The Physical Geography of the Sea.* New York: Harper, 1855.

Melville, Herman. *Moby-Dick.* 1851. New York: Bantam, 1967.

Merriam, Florence. *A-Birding on a Bronco.* Boston: Houghton Mifflin, 1896.

———. *Birds of Village and Field.* Boston: Houghton Mifflin, 1898.

Miller, Olive Thorne. *A Bird Lover in the West.* Boston, 1894.

———. *Little Folks in Feathers and Fur.* 1875. New York, 1904.

Muir, John. *Our National Parks.* 1901. San Francisco: Sierra Club Books, 1991.

———. *The Writings of John Muir.* Sierra ed. Boston: Houghton Mifflin, 1917–24.

Nuttall, Thomas. *Genera of North American Plants, and a Catalogue of the Species, to the Year 1817.* Philadelphia: D. Heartt, 1818.

Paley, William. *Natural Theology—or Evidences of the Existence and Attributes of the Deity Collected from the Appearances of Nature.* 1802. 2nd ed. Oxford: J. Vincent, 1828.

Phelps, Almira Hart Lincoln. *Familiar Lectures on Botany, Explaining the Structure, Classification, and Uses of Plants, Illustrated upon the Linnaean and Natural Methods, with a Flora for Practical Botanists. For the Use of Colleges, Schools, and Private Students.* 1829. New York: Mason Brothers, 1860.

Pinchot, Gifford. *The Fight for Conservation.* New York: Doubleday, Page, 1910.

Powell, John Wesley. *The Exploration of the Colorado River and Its Canyons.* 1895. New York: Dover, 1961.

———. *A Report on the Arid Region of the United States.* 1878. Ed. Wallace Stegner. Cambridge: Belknap P of Harvard UP, 1962.

———. *Report on the Lands of the Arid Region of the United States, with a More Detailed Account of the Lands of Utah. With Maps.* 1879 facsimile. Intro. T. H. Watkins. Boston: Harvard Common P, 1983.

———. *Selected Prose.* Ed. George Crossette. Boston: David R. Godine, 1970.

Rowlandson, Mary. *The Soverignty and Goodness of God, Together with the Faith-fulness of His Promises Displayed, Being a Narrative of the Captivity and Restoration of Mrs. Mary Rowlandson.* 1682. Republished as *The Captive.* Tucson, Ariz.: American Eagle, 1990.

Sanders, Scott Russell, ed. *Audubon Reader: The Best Writings of John James Audubon.* Bloomington: Indiana UP, 1986.

Siple, Paul. *90° South: The Story of the American South Pole Conquest.* New York: Van Rees P, 1959.

Smith, John. *A True Relation of Such Occurrences . . . in Virginia.* London: John Tappe, 1608.

Stowe, Harriet Beecher. *Uncle Tom's Cabin.* 1852. Boston: Houghton Mifflin, 1923.

"Survival of the Fittest." *Christian Advocate* 20 March 1879. Rpt. in Daniels, *Darwinism Comes to America* 112–14.

Thoreau, Henry David. *Walden.* 1854. Rpt. in *Walden and Other Writings.* Ed. Joseph Wood Crutch. New York: Bantam Books, 1962.

Treat, Mary. *Home Studies in Nature.* New York: Harper and Brothers, 1885.

Ware, Joseph. *The Emigrant's Guide to California.* 1849. Ed. John Caughey. New York: Da Capo P, 1972.

Warner, Susan. *The Wide, Wide World.* New York: Putnam, 1852.

Wells, H. G. *Men Like Gods.* New York: Macmillan, 1923.

Whitman, Walt. *Leaves of Grass.* 1855. Rpt. in *Complete Poetry and Selected Prose by Walt Whitman.* Ed. James E. Miller Jr. Boston: Houghton Mifflin, 1959.

Secondary Works

Aldrich, Michele L. "Women in Geology." Kass-Simon and Farnes 42–71.

Allen, Polly Wynn. *Building Domestic Liberty: Charlotte Perkins Gilman's Architectural Feminism.* Amherst: U of Massachusetts P, 1988.

Ambrose, Stephen. *Undaunted Courage: Meriwether Lewis, Thomas Jefferson, and the Opening of the American West.* New York: Simon and Schuster, 1996.

Angyal, Andrew. *Loren Eiseley.* Boston: Twayne, 1983.

Arnold, Matthew. "Science and Literature." *Nineteenth Century* 12 (1882): 216–30.

Aronowitz, Stanley. "The Production of Scientific Knowledge: Science, Ideology, and Marxism." In *Marxism and the Interpretation of Culture*, ed. Cary Nelson and Lawrence Grossberg. Urbana: U of Illinois P, 1988.

———. *Science as Power: Discourse and Ideology in Modern Society.* Minneapolis: U of Minnesota P, 1988.

Bailey, Thomas A., and David M. Kennedy. *The American Pageant: A History of the Republic.* 6th ed. Lexington, Mass.: D. C. Heath, 1979.

Baym, Nina. *Woman's Fiction: A Guide to Novels by and about Women in America, 1820–1870.* Ithaca: Cornell UP, 1979.

Beer, Gillian. *Darwin's Plots: Evolutionary Narratives in Darwin, George Eliot, and 19th Century Fiction.* 1983. London: Ark Paperbacks, 1985.

———. "Problems of Description in the Language of Discovery." Levine 35–58.

Benjamin, Marina. "Elbow Room: Women Writers on Science, 1790–1840." *Science and Sensibility* 27–59.

———, ed. *Science and Sensibility: Gender and Scientific Enquiry, 1780–1945.* Cambridge, Mass.: Basil Blackwell, 1991.

Benson, Randolph. *Thomas Jefferson as Social Scientist.* Cranbury, N.J.: Association of University Presses, 1971.

Biagioli, Mario, ed. *The Science Studies Reader.* New York: Routledge, 1999.

Black, Ralph W. "John Burroughs." Elder 121–38.

Bloom, Lisa. *Gender on Ice: American Ideologies of Polar Expeditions.* Minneapolis: U of Minnesota P, 1993.

Bonta, Marcia Myers. *Women in the Field: America's Pioneering Women Naturalists.* College Station: Texas A&M UP, 1991.

Botkin, Daniel. *Discordant Harmonies: A New Ecology for the Twenty-First Century.* New York: Oxford UP, 1990.

———. *Our Natural History: The Lessons of Lewis and Clark.* New York: Putnam, 1995.

Branch, Michael. "Early American Natural History Literature." Elder 1059–77.

Branch, Michael, Rochelle Johnson, Daniel Patterson, and Scott Slovic, eds. *Reading the Earth: New Directions in the Study of Literature and Environment.* Moscow: U of Idaho P, 1998.

Brooks, Paul. *The House of Life: Rachel Carson at Work.* Boston: Houghton Mifflin, 1972.

———. *Speaking for Nature: How Literary Naturalists from Henry Thoreau to Rachel Carson Have Shaped America.* Boston: Houghton Mifflin, 1980.

Brown, Gillian. *Domestic Individualism: Imagining Self in Nineteenth Century America.* Berkeley: U of California P, 1990.

Bruce, Robert V. *The Launching of American Science: 1846–1876.* New York: Knopf, 1987.

Brush, Stephen J. *The History of Modern Science: A Guide to the Second Scientific Revolution, 1800–1950.* Ames: Iowa State UP, 1988.

Buell, Lawrence. *The Environmental Imagination: Thoreau, Nature Writing, and the Formation of American Culture.* Cambridge: Harvard UP, 1995.

Burger, Joanna. *Oil Spills.* New Brunswick, N.J.: Rutgers UP, 1997.

Burke, Edmund. *A Philosophical Inquiry into the Origin of Our Ideas of the Sublime and the Beautiful.* 1757. Ed. J. T. Boulton. London: Routledge and Kegan Paul, 1958.

Carlisle, E. Fred. *Loren Eiseley: The Development of a Writer.* Urbana: U of Illinois P, 1983.

Christianson, Gale. *Fox at the Wood's Edge: A Biography of Loren Eiseley.* New York: Henry Holt, 1991.

Commoner, Barry. *The Closing Circle: Nature, Man, and Technology.* New York: Alfred A. Knopf, 1971.

Cotkin, George. *Reluctant Modernism: American Thought and Culture, 1880–1900.* New York: Twayne, 1992.

Cronon, William. *Changes in the Land: Indians, Colonists, and the Ecology of New England.* New York: Hill and Wang, 1983.

Daniels, George H. *Science in the Age of Jackson.* New York: Columbia UP, 1968.

Daston, Lorraine, and Peter Galison. "The Image of Objectivity." *Representations* 40 (Fall 1992): 81–128.

Davidson, Cathy. *Revolution and the Word: The Rise of the Novel in America.* New York: Oxford UP, 1986.

Dawkins, Richard. *The Blind Watchmaker.* New York: Norton, 1986.

Dear, Peter, ed. *The Literary Structure of Scientific Argument: Historical Studies.* Philadelphia: U of Pennsylvania P, 1991.

Elder, John, ed. *American Nature Writers.* 2 vols. New York: Scribner's, 1996.

Ferguson, Robert. "What Is Enlightenment? Some American Answers." *American Literary History* 1 (1989): 245–72.

Fogg, G. E. *A History of Antarctic Science.* Cambridge: Cambridge UP, 1992.

Foucault, Michel. "On Geography." *Power/Knowledge: Selected Interviews and Other Writings, 1972–1977.* Ed. Colin Gordin. Trans. C. Gordon, C. Marschall, J. Mepahn, K. Soper. New York: Pantheon, 1980.

———. *The Order of Things: An Archeology of the Human Sciences.* New York: Vintage, 1973.

Franklin, Wayne. *Discoverers, Explorers, Settlers: The Diligent Writers of Early America.* Chicago: U of Chicago P, 1979.

Gaard, Greta, and Patrick D. Murphy, eds. *Ecofeminist Literary Criticism: Theory, Interpretation, Pedagogy.* Urbana: U of Illinois P, 1998.

Gates, Barbara, and Ann Shteir, eds. *Natural Eloquence: Women Reinscribe Science.* Madison: U of Wisconsin P, 1997.

Gerber, Leslie, and Margaret McFadden. *Loren Eiseley.* New York: Frederick Ungar, 1983.

Giancola, Douglas C. *General Physics.* Englewood Cliffs, N.J.: Prentice Hall, 1984.

Gilligan, Carol. *In a Different Voice: Psychological Theory and Women's Development.* Cambridge: Harvard UP, 1982.

Glotfelty, Cheryll, and Harold Fromm, eds. *The Ecocriticism Reader: Landmarks in Literary Ecology.* Athens, Ga.: U of Georgia P, 1996.

Goetzmann, William. *Exploration and Empire: The Explorer and the Scientist in the Winning of the American West.* New York: Knopf, 1966.

Gould, Stephen Jay. *The Mismeasure of Man.* New York: Norton, 1981.

———. *Time's Arrow, Time's Cycle: Myth and Metaphor in the Discovery of Geological Time.* Cambridge: Harvard UP, 1987.

Green, Martin. *The Great American Adventure: Adventure, Manlinesss, and Nationalism.* Boston: Beacon P, 1984.

Greene, John C. *American Science in the Age of Jefferson.* Ames: U of Iowa P, 1984.

Gross, Alan G. *The Rhetoric of Science.* Cambridge: Harvard UP, 1990.

Gubar, Susan. "*She* in *Herland:* Feminism as Fantasy." In *Coordinates: Placing Science Fiction and Fantasy,* ed. George E. Slusser, Eric S. Rabkin, and Robert Scholes. Carbondale: Southern Illinois UP, 1983. 139–49. Rpt. in Meyering 191–202.

Haraway, Donna. *Primate Visions: Gender, Race, and Nature in the World of Modern Science.* New York: Routledge, 1989.

———. *Simians, Cyborgs, and Women: The Reinvention of Nature.* New York: Routledge, 1991.

Harding, Sandra. *The Science Question in Feminism.* Ithaca: Cornell UP, 1986.

———. *Whose Science? Whose Knowledge? Thinking from Women's Lives.* Ithaca: Cornell UP, 1991.

Hayles, N. Katherine, ed. *Chaos and Order: Complex Dynamics in Literature and Science.* Chicago: U of Chicago P, 1991.

———. *The Cosmic Web: Scientific Field Models and Literary Strategies in the 20th Century.* Ithaca: Cornell UP, 1984.

Herr, Pamela. *Jessie Benton Frémont.* New York: Franklin Watts, 1987.

Ihde, Don. *Technology and the Lifeworld: From Garden to Earth.* Bloomington: Indiana UP, 1990.

Jane, Ann L. Introduction. *Herland.* By Charlotte Perkins Gilman. v–xxiv.

Johnson, Rochelle. "Placing *Rural Hours.*" Tallmadge and Harrington 64–84.

———. "Susan Fenimore Cooper's *Rural Hours* and the 'Natural' Refinement of American Culture." *ISLE* 7.1 (Winter 2000): 47–77.

Jones, David. Introduction. *Rural Hours.* By Susan Cooper. xi–xxxviii.

Jones, Roger. *Physics as Metaphor.* Minneapolis: U of Minnesota P, 1982.

Kass-Simon, G., and Patricia Farnes, eds. *Women of Science: Righting the Record.* Bloomington: U of Indiana P, 1990.

Keller, Evelyn Fox. *A Feeling for the Organism: The Life and Work of Barbara McClintock.* New York: W. H. Freeman, 1983.

———. *Reflections on Gender and Science.* New Haven: Yale UP, 1985.

———. *Secrets of Life, Secrets of Death: Essays on Language, Gender, and Science.* New York: Routledge, 1992.

Kerridge, Richard, and Neil Sammells, eds. *Writing the Environment: Ecocriticism and Literature*. New York: Zed Books, 1998.

Kimball, Lee A. "The Antarctic Treaty System." *Oceanus* 31.2 (Summer 1988): 14–19.

Kolodny, Annette. *The Land before Her: Fantasy and Experience of the American Frontiers, 1630–1860*. Chapel Hill: U of North Carolina P, 1984.

———. *The Lay of the Land: Metaphor as Experience and History in American Life and Letters*. Chapel Hill: U of North Carolina P, 1975.

Kuhn, Thomas. *The Structure of Scientific Revolutions*. 1962. Chicago: U of Chicago P, 1970.

Kurth, Rosaly Torna. *Susan Fenimore Cooper: A Study of Her Life and Works*. Ph.D. diss., Fordham U, 1974.

Latour, Bruno. *Science in Action*. Cambridge: Harvard UP, 1989.

Latour, Bruno, and Steve Woolgar. *Laboratory Life*. Princeton: Princeton UP, 1979.

Lear, Linda. *Rachel Carson: Witness for Nature*. New York: Henry Holt, 1997.

Leverenz, David. *Manhood and the American Renaissance*. Ithaca: Cornell UP, 1989.

Levin, Susan M. "Romantic Prose and Feminine Sensibility." *Prose Studies* 10.2 (Sept. 1987): 178–95.

Levine, George, ed. *One Culture: Essays in Science and Literature*. Madison: U of Wisconsin P, 1987.

Limerick, Patricia Nelson. *Desert Passages: Encounters with the American Deserts*. Niwot: UP of Colorado, 1989.

———. *The Legacy of Conquest: The Unbroken Past of the American West*. New York: Norton, 1987.

Limon, John. *The Place of Fiction in the Time of Science: A Disciplinary History of American Writing*. Cambridge: Cambridge UP, 1990.

Lioi, Anthony. "Coasts Demanding Shipwreck: Love and the Philosophy of Science in Loren Eiseley's 'The Star Thrower.'" *ISLE* 6.2 (Summer 1999): 41–61.

Longino, Helen. *Science as Social Knowledge: Values and Objectivity in Scientific Inquiry*. Princeton: Princeton UP, 1990.

Looby, Christopher. "The Constitution of Nature: Taxonomy as Politics in Jefferson, Peale, and Bartram." *Early American Literature* 22 (1987): 252–73.

Lutts, Ralph. *The Nature Fakers: Wildlife, Science, and Sentiment*. Golden, Colo.: Fulcrum P, 1970.

Maddox, Lucy B. "Susan Fenimore Cooper and the Plain Daughters of America." *American Quarterly* 40.2 (June 1988): 131–46.

Magner, Lois N. "Women and the Scientific Idiom: Textual Episodes from Wollstonecraft, Fuller, Gilman, and Firestone." *Signs* 4.1 (Spring 1978): 61–80.

Marshall, Ian. *Story Line: Exploring the Literature of the Appalachian Trail.* Charlottesville: UP of Virginia, 1998.

Marx, Leo. *The Machine in the Garden: Technology and the Pastoral Ideal in America.* New York: Oxford UP, 1964.

McClintock, James. *Nature's Kindred Spirits: Aldo Leopold, Joseph Wood Krutch, Edward Abbey, Annie Dillard, and Gary Snyder.* Madison: U of Wisconsin P, 1994.

McGregor, Robert. *A Wider View of the Universe: Henry Thoreau's Study of Nature.* Urbana: U of Illinois P, 1997.

McIver, Tom. *Anti-Evolution: A Reader's Guide to Writings before and after Darwin.* Baltimore: Johns Hopkins UP, 1992.

McRae, Murdo William, ed. *The Literature of Science: Perspectives on Popular Scientific Writing.* Athens, Ga.: U of Georgia P, 1993.

Merchant, Carolyn. *The Death of Nature: Women, Ecology, and the Scientific Revolution.* San Francisco: Harper and Row, 1980.

———. *Ecological Revolutions: Nature, Gender, and Science in New England.* Chapel Hill: U of North Carolina P, 1989.

Meyering, Sheryl L., ed. *Charlotte Perkins Gilman: The Woman and Her Work.* Ann Arbor, Mich.: UMI Research P, 1989.

Mitchell, Lee Clark. *Witnesses to a Vanishing America: The Nineteenth-Century Response.* Princeton: Princeton UP, 1981.

Murphy, Patrick. *Farther Afield in the Study of Nature-Oriented Literature.* Charlottesville: UP of Virginia, 2000.

Nash, Roderick. *Wilderness and the American Mind.* New Haven: Yale UP, 1982.

Nevins, Allan. "Introduction: Fremont as an Explorer." Frémont, *Narratives of Exploration and Adventure* 1–23.

Norwood, Vera. "Heroines of Nature: Four Women Respond to the American Landscape." Glotlfelty and Fromm 323–50.

———. *Made from This Earth: American Women and Nature.* Chapel Hill: U of North Carolina P, 1993.

Odum, Eugene P. *Ecology and Our Endangered Life-Support Systems.* Sunderland, Mass.: Sinauer Assoc., 1989.

Oelschlaeger, Max. *The Idea of Wilderness: From Prehistory to the Age of Ecology.* New Haven: Yale UP, 1991.

O'Grady, John. *Pilgrims to the Wild: Everett Ruess, Henry David Thoreau, John Muir, Clarence King, Mary Austin.* Salt Lake City: U of Utah P, 1993.

Opie, John. *Americans and Environment: The Controversy over Ecology.* Lexington, Mass.: D. C. Heath, 1971.

Peyser, Thomas Galt. "Reproducing Utopia: Charlotte Perkins Gilman and *Herland.*" *Studies in American Fiction* 20.1 (Spring 1992): 1–16.

Pitts, Mary Ellen. *Toward a Dialogue of Understandings: Loren Eiseley and the Critique of Science.* Bethlehem, Pa.: Lehigh UP, 1995.

Pratt, Mary Louise. *Imperial Eyes: Travel Writing and Transculturalism.* New York: Routledge, 1992.

Pyne, Stephen J. *The Ice: A Journey to Antarctica.* Iowa City: U of Iowa P, 1986.

Raglon, Rebecca. "Rachel Carson and Her Legacy." Gates and Shteir 196–211.

Regis, Pamela. *Describing Early America: Bartram, Jefferson, Crevecoeur, and the Rhetoric of Natural History.* Carbondale: Southern Illinois UP, 1992.

Reisner, Mark. *Cadillac Desert: The American West and Its Disappearing Water.* New York: Viking, 1986.

Rodgers, Eugene. *Beyond the Barrier: The Story of Byrd's First Expedition to Antarctica.* Annapolis, Md.: Naval Institute P, 1990.

Rolle, Andrew. *John Charles Frémont: Character as Destiny.* Norman: U of Oklahoma P, 1991.

Rossiter, Margaret. *Women Scientists in America: Struggles and Strategies to 1940.* Baltimore: Johns Hopkins UP, 1982.

Rouse, Joseph. "What Are the Cultural Studies of Scientific Knowledge?" *Configurations* 1 (1992): 1–22.

Rousseau, G. S. "Literature and Science: The State of the Field," *Isis* 69 (1978): 583–91.

Schatzburg, Walter, Ronald A. Waite, and Jonathan K. Johnson, eds. *The Relations of Literature and Science: An Annotated Bibliography of Scholarship, 1880–1980.* New York: Modern Language Assoc. P, 1987.

Schiebinger, Londa. *The Mind Has No Sex? Women in the Origins of Modern Science.* Cambridge: Harvard UP, 1989.

———. *Nature's Body: Gender in the Making of Modern Science.* Boston: Beacon P, 1993.

Sheldrake, Rupert. *A New Science of Life: The Hypothesis of Formative Causation.* London: Blond and Briggs, 1981.

Sholnick, Robert, ed. *American Literature and Science.* Lexington: U of Kentucky P, 1992.

Slotkin, Richard. *Regeneration through Violence: The Mythology of the American Frontier, 1600–1860.* Middletown, Conn.: Wesleyan UP, 1973.

Slovic, Scott. "Marginality, Midnight Optimism, and the Natural Cipher: An Approach to Thoreau and Eiseley." *Weber Studies* 9.1 (Winter 1992): 25–43.

———. *Seeking Awareness in American Nature Writing: Henry Thoreau, Annie Dillard, Edward Abbey, Wendell Berry, Barry Lopez.* Salt Lake City: U of Utah P, 1992.

Smith, Henry Nash. *Virgin Land.* 1950. Cambridge: Harvard UP, 1978.

Smith, Marsha A. "The Disoriented Male Narrator and Societal Conversion: Charlotte Perkins Gilman's Feminist Utopian Vision." *American Transcendental Quarterly* 3.1 (March 1989): 123–33.

Smythe, William E. *The Conquest of Arid America*. 1905. Seattle: U of Washington P, 1969.

Squier, Susan M. *Babies in Bottles: Twentieth-Century Visions of Reproductive Technology*. New Brunswick, N.J.: Rutgers UP, 1994.

Stegner, Wallace. *The American West as Living Space*. Ann Arbor: U of Michigan P, 1987.

————. *Beyond the Hundredth Meridian: John Wesley Powell and the Second Opening of the West*. Boston: Houghton Mifflin, 1954.

————. Introduction. Powell, *A Report on the Arid Region of the United States*.

Steingraber, Sandra. *Living Downstream: An Ecologist Looks at Cancer and the Environment*. Reading, Mass.: Addison-Wesley, 1997.

Stewart, Frank. *A Natural History of Nature Writing*. Washington, D.C.: Island P, 1995.

Tallmadge, John, and Henry Harrington, eds. *Reading under the Sign of Nature: New Essays in Ecocriticism*. Salt Lake City: U of Utah P, 2000.

Todorov, Tzvetan. *The Conquest of America: The Question of the Other*. 1984. Trans. R. Howard. New York: Harper and Row, 1987.

Tompkins, Jane. *Sensational Designs: The Cultural Work of American Fiction, 1790–1860*. New York: Oxford UP, 1985.

Turner, Frederick Jackson. *The Frontier in American History*. New York: Henry Holt, 1920.

Unruh, John, Jr. *The Plains Across: The Overland Emigrants and the Trans-Mississippi West, 1840–60*. Urbana: U of Illinois P, 1979.

Upin, Jane S. "Charlotte Perkins Gilman: Instrumentalism beyond Dewey." *Hypatia* 8.2 (Spring 1993): 38–63.

Van Orman, Richard. *The Explorers: 19th Century Expeditions in Africa and the American West*. Albuquerque: U of New Mexico P, 1984.

Walls, Laura Dassow. *Seeing New Worlds: Henry David Thoreau and Nineteenth-Century Natural Science*. Madison: U of Wisconsin P, 1995.

Warhus, Mark. "Cartographic Encounters: An Exhibition of Native American Maps from Central Mexico to the Arctic." *Mapline* Special Issue 7 (Sept. 1993).

Watkins, T. H. Introduction. Powell, *Report on the Lands of the Arid Region of the United States* xi–xx.

White, Lynn, Jr. "The Historical Roots of Our Ecologic Crisis." Glotfelty and Fromm 3–14.

Wilkins, Thurman. *Clarence King: A Biography*. 1958. Rev. and enlarged ed. Albuquerque: U of New Mexico P, 1988.

Worldwatch Institute. *The State of the World: A Worldwatch Institute Report on Progress toward a Sustainable Society*. New York: Norton, 1999.

Worster, Donald, ed. *American Environmentalism: The Formative Period, 1860–1915*. New York: John Wiley, 1973.

———. *Nature's Economy: A History of Ecological Ideas*. 2nd ed. Cambridge: Cambridge UP, 1994.

———. *A River Running West: The Life of John Wesley Powell*. New York: Oxford UP, 2001.

———. *Under Western Skies: Nature and History in the American West*. New York: Oxford UP, 1992.

———. *An Unsettled Country: Changing Landscapes of the American West*. Albuquerque: U of New Mexico P, 1994.

Index

A-Birding on a Bronco (Merriam), 109
Advance Base, Antarctica, 32–35, 37, 40–41, 47–48, 50–52, 189 n. 9
agriculture, 72, 76–77, 81, 92, 95, 101, 128, 131–32, 135, 156, 169, 175–77, 194 n. 10
Allen, Polly Wynn, 72
Alone (Richard Byrd), xiii, 32–34, 38–53, 190 n. 15; connection to *Walden*, 38–42; and gendered rhetoric, 43–44; as life experiment, 32–33, 41, 48, 52; relation to Byrd's other narratives, 38, 189 n. 9; representation of nature, 42–48; and scientific method, 41–42, 47–48, 52; and technology, 33–34, 44, 48–53
American Association for the Advancement of Science, 71
American Naturalist, 109
American Ornithologists' Union, 109
American Philosophical Society, 183 n. 4
American West. *See* West, American
American Women Afield (Bonta), 186 n. 6
Amundsen, Roald, 35–37, 43
Angyal, Andrew, 198 n. 4

animal behavior, 120–26
Antarctica, xi–xiii, 32–53, 139, 154, 171, 176, 186 n. 17; Dry Valleys of, 188–89 n. 1; as energy and information sink, 45–48; exploration of (*see* exploration: of Antarctica); geopolitics of, 34–36, 44, 188 nn. 2, 6; and "Heroic Age" of exploration, 36–37, 43–44; as outdoor laboratory, 37; and science and technology, 36–38, 188 nn. 2, 7; United States' claims upon, 35–36, 43
Antarctic Treaty, 188 n. 6
Antarctic Treaty Organization, 34, 188 n. 6
anthropocentrism, 121, 157, 167–69, 195 n. 12
anthropology, 135, 144
anthropomorphism: in Audubon, 120–21; in Bartram, 120; and Burroughs, 122; in Carson, 147–49; in Susan Cooper (*see Rural Hours:* and anthropomorphism); in Muir, 123–24
Apollo lunar missions, 142
arid region. *See* West, arid
Association for the Study of Literature and Environment, 181 n. 2

Atlantic Monthly, 147
audience, xii, 85, 190 n. 1; of exploration narratives, 8; and the interpretation of data, 11; of natural history, 107–8, 110–11; of popular science, 107–8, 134–35, 145, 147
Audubon (periodical), 109
Audubon, John James, 110, 113, 119–21, 124, 140, 186 n. 19
Auk (periodical), 109
Austin, Mary, 92, 110, 117
autobiography, xiii, 38–39, 107, 110, 140, 189 n. 10

Bacon, Francis, 183 n. 3
Bailey, Florence Merriam. *See* Merriam, Florence
Bartram, William, 8–9, 110, 119–21, 124, 143
Beecher, Catherine, 113, 193 n. 15, 197 n. 12
Bellamy, Edward, 59, 78
Benton, Jessie. *See* Frémont, Jessie Benton
Benton, Thomas Hart, 6–7, 87, 184 n. 5
"big science," 36, 159
biodiversity, xi
biology, xvi, 37, 139, 144, 171, 175
"Bird and the Machine, The" (Eiseley), 157–58
Bird-Lore (periodical), 109
Bird Lover in the West, A (Miller), 109
birds, 112, 120–26, 129, 156–58. *See also* ornithology
Birds in the Grand Canyon County, Among the (Merriam), 109
Birds of Village and Field (Merriam), 109
Black, Ralph, 122
Bloom, Lisa, 186 n. 17, 187 n. 1, 188 n. 6, 190 n. 15
Boas, Franz, 190 n. 2
Bolling Advance Base. *See* Advance Base
Bonta, Marcia Myers, 196 n. 6
Boone, Daniel, 6, 23
botany, 7, 9, 64, 107–9, 130
Botkin, Daniel, 199 nn. 7, 14
Branch, Michael, 110

Brickell, John, 8
Brooks, Paul, 196 n. 6
Bruce, Robert, 71
Buell, Lawrence, 110–11, 198 n. 16, 199 n. 9
Buffon, Georges-Louis Leclerc, 184–85 n. 10
Bumppo, Natty (literary character), 5–6, 17–18, 186 n. 16
Bureau of Ethnology, 85, 97
Bureau of Reclamation. *See* United States Bureau of Reclamation
Burger, Joanne, 164
Burke, Edmund, 28, 185 n. 13
Burroughs, John, 110–11, 117, 119, 121–24, 143, 198 n. 16; critique of anthropomorphism in nature writing, 121–24; views of nature; *Wake-Robin*, 122–23; *Ways of Nature*, 121–22
Byrd, Richard, ix, xi–xii, 32–53, 57–58, 105, 138, 151–52, 171, 189 nn. 9–10; connection with Thoreau, 33, 38–42, 52; contrasted to Frémont, 33, 44, 48–49, 53; controlled by technology, 33–34, 48–53; expeditions' scientific utility, 32–33, 37–38; funding of expeditions, 188 n. 3; philosophy of harmony, 33, 45–46, 48, 52; relationship with nature, 33–34, 39–48, 50–52; role in Antarctic exploration history, 34–38, 43–44; and solitude, 39–41; as tragic hero, 33–34, 47–52. Works: *Alone* xiii, 32–34, 38–53, 190 n. 15; *Discovery*, 37–38, 189 n. 9; *Little America*, 38
Byrd, William, 8, 21

Cabeza de Vaca, Álvar Núñez, 4
Carson, Kit, 21, 23–24, 186 n. 18
Carson, Rachel, ix, xi, xiv–xv, 101, 106, 110, 133, 135–40, 143–50, 152–55, 158–67, 171–73, 176–78; biographical sketch of, 136–37; critique of technology, 144; and ecology, 139, 146, 152–53, 161–67; environmental perspective, 152–53, 159–67, 178, 193 n. 17; and evolution (*see* evolu-

tion: in Carson); and exploration, 138–40, 143–44; and gender, 151–54, 158, 199 n. 9; narrative technique of, 140, 149–51; —, and anthropomorphism, 147–49; as naturalist, 138–40, 144, 152; relation to nature, 143–44, 147, 165; representations of nature, 144–49, 152–54, 158, 160–67; —, critique of mechanistic metaphor, 152–53, 178; views on science, 139, 143–44, 159–61, 165, 178. Works: *The Edge of the Sea*, 137, 139, 153, 162; *Lost Woods*, 148; *The Sea around Us*, 137, 139, 146, 153–54, 160–61, 163–64; *Silent Spring*, 137, 153, 158–59, 162–63, 165–67, 193 n. 17; *Under the Sea-Wind*, 137, 144–48, 162

cartography, ix, 3, 5–6, 9, 12–16

Century (periodical), 85

Ceplair, Larry, 191 n. 10

Champlain, Samuel de, 4

Chicago, 174

Christian Advocate (periodical), 67

cinnabar, 191 n. 4

Closing Circle, The (Commoner), 193 n. 17

"Coasts Demanding Shipwreck" (Lioi), 200 n. 15

Colden, Jane, 196 n. 9

colonialism, 34–36, 60, 62, 187–88 n. 1

Colorado River, xiv, 81–82

Columbus, Christopher, 4, 183 n. 2

Commoner, Barry, 193 n. 17

community, x–xi, 106; in Cooper's *Rural Hours*, xiv, 106, 111–12, 117–19, 124, 126; in Gilman's *Herland*, 57, 69, 71–72, 74, 77–78, 177; in Powell's *Report*, 76, 80, 83–84, 97–101, 177; relationship to nature, 80, 106, 112, 177; relationship to science, xiii, 80, 119, 177; of science, 90; as shaped by attitudes about nature, science, and the landscape, x, 112

Condor (periodical), 109

Congress. *See* United States Congress

Conquest of America, The (Todorov), 183 n. 2

conservation, 58, 78, 135, 176, 178, 194 n. 12; relation to the control of nature, 58, 72, 92, 166, 174; in *Rural Hours*, 106, 111–12, 117, 129–33, 198 n. 17

conservation movement, x, 80, 92, 115

control of nature. *See* nature: control of

Cook, James, 142–43

Cooper, James Fenimore, 5, 17–18, 20, 107, 132, 185 n. 15, 186 n. 19, 187 n. 23. *See also* Bumppo, Natty

Cooper, Susan Fenimore, ix, xi–xii, xiv, 78, 105–134, 136, 143, 147–48, 151, 176–78, 195 n. 1, 196 n. 9; family influences upon, 107; and Frémont, 105, 111; link to Gilman and Powell, 78, 105; literary output, 197 n. 11; *Rural Hours*, xiv, 105–7, 110–120, 124–133, 196 n. 5 (*see also* separate entry); views on gender roles, 113–14

Cooper, William, 107

Cooperstown, N.Y., 107, 112, 131

Cotkin, George, 190 n. 2, 192 n. 10

Crèvecoeur, Hector St. John de, 75, 99

Crossette, George, 194 n. 6

cultural study of science, xvi–xvii, 182 n. 4

Daniels, George, 183 n. 3, 192 n. 10

Darwin, Charles, 4, 8, 67, 109, 112, 122, 143, 168, 192 n. 10, 200 n. 15. *See also* evolution; social Darwinism

Darwinism Comes to America (Cotkin), 192 n. 10

Darwin's Century (Eiseley), 138

Dawkins, Richard, 135

Death of Nature, The (Merchant), 186 n. 20, 199 n. 7

deforestation, xi, 135, 175. *See also* environmental problems

Dekay, James Ellsworth, 113

development, 132, 134–35, 163

Dewey, John, 190 n. 2

Discordant Harmonies (Botkin), 199 nn. 7, 14

Discoverers, Explorers, Settlers (Franklin), 183 n. 2

Discovery (Richard Byrd), 37–38, 189 n. 9

Discovery expedition, 35, 37–38, 188 n. 3

Discovery, Settlement, and Present State of Kentucke (Filson), 23

"Domestic Economy" (Gilman), 74

domestic science, 193 n. 15

Drummond, Willis Jr., 90

Dutton, Clarence, 85, 90

Earth as Modified by Human Action, The (Marsh), 129

ecocentrism, 101, 195 n. 13

ecocriticism, xv–xvii, 92, 110, 178, 181 n. 2, 196 n. 7

ecological community, 118, 124

ecological literary criticism. *See* ecocriticism

ecological perspective, xi, xiv–xv, 124, 133

ecological utopia, 161–63

ecology, ix, xv–xvi, 112, 118, 129–130, 135–36, 139, 146, 153, 155, 173, 175–78, 188 n. 8, 198 n. 18; and evolution, 156–57; and natural history, xii, 110, 112, 178, 196 n. 8; in Wells's *Men Like Gods*, 73. *See also* Carson: and ecology; Eiseley: and ecology; *Herland:* ecological values in; *Report on the Lands of the Arid Regions . . . :* ecological values in; *Rural Hours:* on church-yard ecology, ecological qualities

ecosystem, 72, 130, 146, 175

Edge of the Sea, The (Carson), 137, 139, 153, 162

Einstein, Albert, 135

Eiseley, Loren, ix, xi, xiv–xv, xvii, 101, 106, 110, 133, 135–38, 140–44, 149–52, 154–59, 167–73, 176–78, 199 nn. 10–11; and anthropocentrism, 157, 167–69; and autobiography, 140; biographical sketch, 137–38; and ecology, 154–55, 178; environmental perspective, 167–71, 178; and evolution (*see* evolution: in Eiseley); and explo-ration, 138, 140–44, 170–71; and gender, 152, 154–55, 199 n. 10; and the imagination, 142, 149–50, 167–68, 172; and the journey motif, 142, 168; narrative persona, 140–41, 144; narrative technique, 138, 140, 149–50; —, and metaphor, 149, 168–70; —, and perspective, 149–51; as naturalist, 138; relation to nature, 141, 143–44, 149–51, 158, 167–69, 178, 200 n. 15; representation of na-ture, 152, 154–58, 168–70, 178; —, critique of mechanistic metaphor, 152, 155–58, 171, 199 n. 11; views of science, 141, 167, 170–73, 178, 200 n. 15. Works: *Darwin's Century*, 138; *The Immense Journey* 138, 140–42, 149–50, 155–58, 167–68, 172; *The Invisible Pyramid*, 138, 169–72; *The Unexpected Universe*, 138, 142–43, 149, 168–69

"embodiment relation," 29–30, 49, 187 n. 26. *See also* Ihde, Don

Emerson, Ralph Waldo, 187 n. 23

Emigrant's Guide to California, The (Ware), 8

empiricism, 88–89, 91, 183 n. 4. *See also* scientific method

entomology, 109

environment. *See* nature

environmental ethics, x–xi, xv, 136, 159, 162, 165, 167, 169, 173

environmental history, xvi

Environmental Imagination, The (Buell), 110

environmentalism, x–xi, 176, 193 n. 17, 196 n. 7, 199 n. 8; and science, 135–36, 159–73. *See also* ecology; environmental ethics; environmental problems

environmental problems, 135, 158, 163–64, 171, 175–76, 199 n. 13. *See also* deforestation; global warming; nature: abuse of, exploitation of

evolution, ix, xi, xv, 72, 112, 122, 136, 138, 144, 155, 168, 173; in Carson, 146, 152, 154, 161, 173; and ecology,

156–57; in Eiseley; 141–42, 155–57, 167–68, 173, 199 n. 10; of humans, 155–57, 168, 192 n. 13, 199 n. 10; natural vs. social, 191 n. 10. *See also* Darwin; natural selection; social Darwinism

exploration, ix, xi, 57–63, 107, 177; of Africa, 189 n. 12; of Antarctica, xii, 32–38, 43–44, 186 n. 17; —, and gender, 43–44, 190 n. 15; and aviation, 35–37; of early North America, 3–4; "Heroic Age" of, 36–37, 43–44; as means of connecting to nature, 136, 138–44; nautical, 139, 141; in the nineteenth century, 5, 29, 85; of polar regions, xiii, 34–38, 187–88 n. 1; and sexuality, 6, 24–31, 43–44, 60; of space, 142–43, 170–71; of the Western United States, ix, 4–6, 19, 48, 84–86, 140, 193–94 n. 5. *See also* exploration narratives; scientific exploration

Exploration and Empire (Goetzmann), 5

exploration narratives, xiii, 61, 86, 99, 105, 111, 116, 133, 151, 176, 189 n. 12; and "God's eye" perspective, 15; and heroism, 16–24, 33–34, 86, 190 n. 15; North American, early history of, 4, 183 n. 2; rhetoric of, 5, 8–13, 111, 176, 186 n. 19; theme of physical endurance in, 19–20, 186 n. 17. *See also* exploration; Byrd, Richard; Frémont, John Charles; Powell, John Wesley

Exploration of the Colorado River and Its Canyons, The (Powell), 85, 194 n. 6

exploration science. *See* scientific exploration

explorer: connection to nature, 24, 26–31, 33–34, 40–48, 52–53, 58, 138–44; the expansive gaze of, 15, 20–21, 44, 48; as hero, xiii, 5–6, 16–24, 48–53, 86, 94, 101, 142–43, 171, 177, 179, 190 n. 15; —, in *Herland*, xiii, 57–58, 60–63; as scientist (*see* scientist: as explorer); as tragic hero, 33–34, 47–52. *See also* Byrd,

Richard; Frémont, John Charles; Powell, John Wesley

Familiar Lectures on Botany (Phelps), 108, 195 n. 4

Farther Afield in the Study of Nature Writing (Murphy), 196 n. 7

feminism, 190 n. 2; critique of science, xvi–xvii, 63–71, 182 nn. 5–7, 192 n. 14. *See also* gender; Gilman, Charlotte Perkins: *Herland*; women

Fight for Conservation, The (Pinchot), 92

Filson, John, 8, 23

Fish and Wildlife Service. *See* United States Fish and Wildlife Service

fisheries, 162–64

Flora's Interpreter; or, the American Book of Flowers and Sentiments (Hale), 108

flowering plants, 155–56

"Flow of the River, The" (Eiseley), 150

Ford, Edsel, 188 n. 3

Forerunner, The (Gilman), 58

forestry, 72, 131–32

Forestry, Department of, 195 n. 12

forests, 72, 127–29, 130–34, 175; and conservation, 129, 133

Foucault, Michel, 185 n. 12

Franklin, Benjamin, 121

Franklin, Wayne, 183 n. 2

Frémont, Jessie Benton, 6, 24–26, 184 n. 8; collaboration with John, 24–26; literary output, 186–87 n. 21

Frémont, John Charles, ix, xi–xii, xvii, 3–32, 184 nn. 5, 7–8, 185 n. 13, 186 n. 18; and American expansionism, 7, 11; and Byrd, 43–44, 48–49, 53; and Carson and Eiseley, 138, 141, 151–52, 171, 176–77; and Susan Cooper, 105, 111, 114–15; creative relationship with Jessie Benton Frémont, 24–26; and Gilman, 57–58, 61; heroic description of, 6, 18–19; and maps (*see* maps: in Frémont's reports); political career, 7; and Powell, 80, 83–87, 92, 94; scientific achievements and training, 7. Works: *Memoirs of My Life*, 7, 25; *Narratives of*

Frémont, John Charles (*cont.*)
Exploration and Adventure, 5–6, 8–14,
16–31 (*see also separate entry*); *Report
of the Exploring Expeditions to the
Rocky Mountains in the Year 1842, and
to Oregon and Northern California in
1843–44*, 3, 184 n. 6
frontier, 3; Powell's revolutionary vision of, 86; and *The Prairie*, 17–18.
See also West, American

gender, x; in *Alone*, 43–44; in Carson
and Eiseley, 151–55, 158, 199 nn.
9–10; in Frémont's narratives, 5–6,
16–31; in *Herland* (see under
Herland); and literature, 25–26, 70,
115–16, 185–86 n. 15, 186 n. 19, 187
n. 23, 196 n. 7; as mode of critical
analysis, xvii; and natural history, 18,
107–12; and nature (*see* nature: feminization of; women: and nature); in
*Report on the Lands of the Arid Re-
gions*, 83, 96; in *Rural Hours*, 106–7,
112–17, 196 n. 5, 197 n. 10; and science (*see* science: and gender); sepa-
rate-spheres ideology, 26, 67, 113–
14, 125, 196 n. 5, 197 n. 12; and technology, 29–31. *See also* exploration:
of Antarctica, and gender; masculinity; women
Gender on Ice (Bloom), 186 n. 17, 187
n. 1
genre, 38–39, 107, 110, 126; relation to
book's scope and argument, x, xii
geology, 3–4, 6–7, 9, 28–29, 37, 146,
153, 162, 167
geopolitics, 34–36
Gerber, Leslie, 199 n. 10
"Ghost Continent, The" (Eiseley),
142–43
Gilbert, G. K., 90–1
Gilman, Charlotte Perkins, ix, xi, xiii,
57–80, 105–6, 117, 151, 177, 191 n.
10, 193 n. 16; biography, 57–59; connection to John Wesley Powell, 78,
80; and evolution, 191 n. 10, 192 n.
13; and feminism, 190 n. 2, 193 n.

14; and racism, 63; views on literature and gender, 70. Works: "Domestic Economy," 74; *The Forerunner*, 58; *Herland*, xiii, 57–80, 190 n. 1;
"The Labor Movement," 74; *The
Living of Charlotte Perkins Gilman*,
59; *The Man-Made World*, 68, 70, 72;
Moving the Mountain, 59; "Our
Brains and What Ails Them," 192 n.
12; *With Her in Ourland*, 59; *Women
and Economics*, 59; "The Yellow Wall-
paper," 59
Gilpin, William, 87
global warming, xi. *See also* environ-
mental problems
God, 109, 117, 120, 122; as divine
watchmaker, 45, 190 n. 14
"God's eye" view, 15, 20–21. *See also*
metaphor: in Frémont's reports, and
vision
Goetzmann, William, 5–6
Goodall, Jane, 135
Gould, Stephen Jay, 135
Grand Canyon, 85
Gray, Asa, 109
Great American Adventure, The (Green),
185–86 n. 15
"Great American Desert", 12–13
Great Basin, 5, 7, 13, 27
Great Chain of Being, 14
Great Depression, 138
Great Plains, 5
Great Salt Lake, 7, 15, 93, 96
Green, Martin, 185–86 n. 15
Greene, John, 183 n. 4
Guide to the Wilderness, A (William
Cooper), 107

Haeckel, Ernst, 172, 198 n. 18
Hale, Sarah, 108
Haraway, Donna, xvi, 193 n. 14, 199
n. 10
Harding, Sandra, 192 n. 14
Harper's, 109
Hawthorne, Nathaniel, 17, 187 n. 23
Hayden, Ferdinand, 85, 193–94 n. 5
Herland, xiii, 57–80, 190 n. 1; and

child-rearing, 74; and colonialism, 60, 62; and community, 57, 69, 71–72, 74, 77–78, 177; and the control of nature, xiii, 57–58, 71–73, 75–78; critique of gender roles in, 57, 59–60, 62, 74, 78, 193 n. 15; critique of masculine science in, xiii, 57–58, 60, 63–68, 70; ecological values in, 57–58, 72, 76–78; exploration as narrative frame, 57–60, 191 n. 3; key themes and plot outline, 59–60; and objectivity, 63, 65, 68–69; and population control, 73–74, 76–77; and possibility of feminine science, 69–71; and progress, 57, 66, 68, 71, 74–78; and racism, 63, 76, 191 n. 5; and reproduction, 73–76, 78; as satire, 62–63, 65, 78; and violence, 66–68
"Heroines of Nature" (Norwood), 199 n. 8
Herr, Pamela, 25, 184 n. 8
"Hidden Teacher, The" (Eiseley), 168–69
Hitchcock, Alfred, 60
home economics, 197 n. 12
Homestead Act, 87
Home Studies in Nature (Treat), 109
Hooper, Lucy, 108
Hoover Dam, 81–82, 88
horticulture, 72
"How Flowers Changed the World" (Eiseley), 155–57
Hudson River valley, 111, 121, 197 n. 9
Hughes, Charles Evans (U. S. Secretary of State), 35
Humboldt, Alexander von, 4, 8
Huxley, Julian, 135
Huxley, Thomas, 172
"hydraulic west," 81, 101
hydrographic basin, 93–94

Ihde, Don, 14–15, 29, 187 n. 26
Immense Journey, The (Eiseley), 138, 140–42, 149–50, 155–58, 167–68, 172
"Institutions for the Arid Lands" (Powell), 93

instruments. *See* technology: scientific instrumentation
Interdisciplinary Studies in Literature and Environment, 181 n. 2
International Geophysical Year (IGY), 36, 188 n. 6
Invisible Pyramid, The (Eiseley), 138, 169–72
irrigation, xiv, 80, 86–87, 94–95, 175–76, 193 n. 1, 194 n. 10
Irving, Washington, 185 n. 15, 186 n. 16

Jackson, Donald, 13
Jackson, W. H., 85
James, William, 190 n. 2
Jefferson, Thomas, 6, 8, 88, 99, 110, 183 n. 4, 184 n. 10, 185 n. 13
Joerg, W. L. G., 188 n. 5
Johnson, Rochelle, 111, 197 n. 10
Joliet, Ill., 174
Journals of the First Voyage to America (Columbus), 4
"Judgment of the Birds, The" (Eiseley), 149–50

King, Clarence, 4, 8, 19–20, 27–29, 80, 85, 94, 111, 187 n. 24, 194 n. 5
Kolodny, Annette, 186 n. 19
Kuhn, Thomas, xvii

"Labor Movement, The" (Gilman), 74
Lady's Book of Flowers and Poetry, The (Hooper), 108
Latour, Bruno, 194 n. 11
Lay of the Land, The (Kolodny), 186 n. 19
"Leatherstocking Tales, The" (James Fenimore Cooper), 107, 187 n. 23
Leaves of Grass (Whitman), 187 n. 23
Leopold, Aldo, xv, 78, 92, 101, 106, 117, 128–29
Lewis, Graceanna, 109
Lewis, Meriwether, and William Clark, xii, 4, 8–9, 20, 30, 183–84 n. 4
Linnaeus, 14, 18, 108
Lioi, Anthony, 200 n. 15
literary criticism, xvi, 196 n. 7
literary naturalism, 123

literature: and bioregionalism, 110; conventions in seasonal descriptions, 115–16; and gender (*see* gender: and literature); as metaphor for nature, 146; nineteenth-century American, 25–26, 185 n. 15, 187 n. 23; objectivity vs. subjectivity, 26, 38, 119; relation between technical information and popular literature, 8, 38, 85–86, 119, 123, 134–35; and science (*see* science: and literature); utopian fiction, 72–73. *See also* metaphor; nature writing; rhetoric; science: popularization of

"Literature and Science" (Rousseau), 182 n. 3

Little America, Antarctica, 32, 35, 38, 43, 50–51, 189 n. 9

Little America (Richard Byrd), 38

Little America expedition, 35, 188 n. 3

Little Folks in Feathers and Fur (Miller), 109

"Little Men and Flying Saucers" (Eiseley), 167–68

Living of Charlotte Perkins Gilman, The (Gilman), 59

Long, Stephen, 12

Long, William, 121

"Long Snowfall, The" (Carson), 146

Looking Backward (Bellamy), 59

Loren Eiseley (Angyal), 198 n. 4

Loren Eiseley (Gerber and McFadden), 199 n. 10

Los Alamos, 88

Lost Woods (Carson), 148

Lyon, Thomas J., 196 n. 7

Maddox, Lucy, 107

Maine, 139

Machine in the Garden, The (Marx), 187 n. 25

Man and Nature (Marsh), 129, 194 n. 10

manifest destiny, 6, 8

Man-Made World, The (Gilman), 68, 70, 72

"Map of an Exploring Expedition to the Rocky Mountains in the Year 1842 and to Oregon and North California in the Years 1843–44 . . . " (Frémont and Preuss), 13

maps: as expressions of power and control, 13; in Frémont's reports, 5, 9, 12–16; and Native Americans, 13; relation to natural history, 14; as representations of nature, 5, 12–16; as visual perspective on nature, 12, 14–16

"Marginality, Midnight Optimism, and the Natural Cipher" (Slovic), 198–99 n. 5

Marine Biological Laboratory, 136

Marsh, George Perkins, 129, 194 n. 10

Marx, Leo, 187 n. 25

masculinity, 43, 57–58; and adventure, 19–20, 185–86 n. 15; and civilization, 61–62; and Frémont's scientist-hero, xiii, 5–6, 16–31, 43, 58, 83, 86, 96; and male explorers in *Herland*, 61–66; and science, xvii, 83, 151, 190 n. 15. *See also* explorer; gender

Maury, Matthew Fontaine, 139

McFadden, Margaret, 199 n. 10

Melville, Herman, 187 n. 23

Memoirs of My Life (Frémont), 7, 25

Men Like Gods (Wells), 72–73

Merchant, Carolyn, 13, 95, 186 n. 20, 199 n. 7

Merriam, Florence, 109

metaphor, xvi–xvii, 77, 95, 178; in Carson and Eiseley, 144–58, 168; erotic, 24, 26, 30–31, 44, 53; feminine, xvii, 26, 28, 44, 114–15, 151–54, 158 (*see also* nature: feminization of); in Frémont's reports, 6, 10, 24–26, 30–31; —, and vision, 15, 20–21, 189 n. 12; —, as act of possession, 20, 26, 44; as means of connecting to nature, 21, 86, 148–49; in Muir, 115, 123–24, 198 n. 16; in natural history and nature writing, 119–26; in science, 145, 171. *See also* anthropomorphism; literature

meteorology, 33, 37, 48, 51

Midewin National Tallgrass Prairie, 174

Miller, Olive Thorne, 109
Mind Has No Sex?, The (Schiebinger),
191 n. 8
Moby-Dick (Melville), 187 n. 23
Monod, Jacques, 135
Moran, Thomas, 85
More, Thomas, 78
Mountaineering in the Sierra Nevada
(King), 19–20, 27–28
Moving the Mountain (Gilman), 59
Muir, John, 76, 92, 101, 106, 110, 115,
117, 119, 123–24, 126, 129, 195 nn.
12–13, 198 n. 16
Murphy, Patrick, 196 n. 7

Narratives of Exploration and Adventure
(Frémont): audience, 8, 11; and gender, 5–6, 16–31; heroic narrative persona, 5, 16–24; and metaphor, 6, 10,
20, 24–25; narrative approach, 8–10;
political function, 12, 184 nn. 5, 7;
and Native Americans, 19, 21–23;
representations of nature, 6, 14,
24–31, 185 n. 11; revision of Natty
Bumppo persona, 5, 17–18; scientific
rhetoric and function, 5, 8–13; as
source of information on the American West, 5, 8–9, 184 n. 8; as synthesis of qualitative and quantitative information, 5, 8–12, 14, 16; and
technology, 8, 29–31
National Geographic Society, 188 n. 3
national parks, x
Native Americans, 4, 13, 15–16, 198 n.
20; discussed by Susan Cooper,
132–33; and Frémont, 19, 21–23, 184
n. 5; and maps, 13, 16; and Powell,
15–16, 84–85, 97–99
natural history, ix, xi, 5–6, 14, 17,
105–6, 110–28, 138, 144, 175–77,
185 n. 12, 195 n. 3; and divine order,
112; and ecology, xii, 110, 112, 178,
196 n. 8; and evolution, 112; literary
tradition, 105, 107–12, 178 (*see also*
nature essay; nature writing); —, and
anthropomorphism, 106, 112, 119–

26; —, and gender, 18, 107–12; relation to maps, 14; rhetoric of, 110–12,
119–26; spatial orientation of, 14,
185 n. 12
natural selection, 67–68, 122, 155, 167,
192 n. 13. *See also* Darwin; evolution
Natural Theology (Paley), 190 n. 14
nature: abuse of, 129, 131–32, 134–35,
164–65, 167, 169, 175; as active, 112,
152, 166, 177; adaptability of, 127;
balance of, 132, 164–67, 169, 199 n.
14; character of, xiii, 45–48, 83, 92,
96, 112, 127, 132, 146, 151–58, 160,
164, 166–67, 177, 185 n. 13, 199 n. 7;
vs. civilization, 61, 187 n. 25; and
community, 71–72, 76, 83–84, 106,
112, 118–19, 126–28; and complexity,
xv, 91, 144, 152–54, 161, 166; control
of, xi, xiv, 13, 48, 58, 80, 83, 92,
94–96, 100–101, 118, 143, 151, 156,
159, 163, 165–66, 172; cycles of, xv,
144–45, 153; death of, 95; as divinely
created/ordered, 45, 112, 117–18,
120, 122, 133; as dynamic, 112, 146,
149, 152, 155, 164, 167; exploitation
of, 135, 163, 174; feminization of,
xiii, xv, 5, 24–31, 43–44, 48, 53, 60–
61, 83, 96, 105, 114–15, 133, 136,
151–54, 157–58, 176, 178–79, 186 nn.
19–20; as independent, self-adjusting
system, xiv, 83, 92–95, 101, 151, 166,
195 n. 13; as interconnected, xv, 112–
13, 117–18, 124, 133, 144–46, 154–55,
161, 169, 175, 178; as mechanism, xv,
83, 92, 95–96, 101, 136, 151–53, 155,
157–58, 177–79, 195 n. 14, 199 n. 7;
as passive, xiii, 5, 14, 49, 96, 106,
133, 151, 176, 186 n. 20; as possession, 20, 42–44, 53, 60–61, 106; in
relation to humanity, 106, 110, 112,
117, 126, 128–30, 132–33, 157, 159,
163–64, 176, 178, 193 n. 18, 194 n.
10; in relation to science, xii, 48, 58,
78, 80, 83–84, 101, 106, 112, 133,
134–36, 151–59, 175–76, 178–79;
representations of, x, xv, 5–6, 14,

nature (*cont.*)
   24–31, 42–48, 83, 88, 91–96, 106,
   112–13, 133, 144–51, 151–58, 160,
   163–67, 175–79; as resource, xv, 6,
   14, 31, 58, 79, 83–84, 93–97, 100–
   101, 129, 156–57, 163–64, 170, 174,
   195 nn. 12–13; scientific management of, xi, xiii–xiv, 58, 83, 105, 166,
   176– 77; and time, 146; as vulnerable, 164–66
nature essay, xv. *See also* nature writing
"nature-fakers" controversy, 121–22,
   124
nature writing, xiv, 96, 105, 107, 110,
   119, 137, 147, 196 n. 7. *See also* nature essay; natural history: literary
   tradition
navigation, 139
Nebraska, 137, 150
Nevins, Allan, 6, 8, 18
New England, xi, xv
New York (city), 149
New York (state), 4, 78, 105, 107, 131,
   197 n. 9
New York Times, 35, 188 n. 5
Nicollet, J. N., 7
90° South (Siple), 188 n. 6
Northwest Passage, 139
Norwood, Vera, 109, 111, 195 n. 1, 196
   n. 5, 199 n. 8
Notes on the State of Virginia (Jefferson),
   88, 183 n. 4, 184 n. 10
Novum Organum (Bacon), 183 n. 3
Nutall, Thomas, 113

objectivity, xv–xvii, 24, 38–39, 119, 159,
   167, 171, 189 n. 10, 192 nn. 11–12,
   14, 194 n. 11; in *Herland,* 63, 65,
   68–69. *See also* subjectivity
Odysseus, 142–43
O'Grady, John P., 187 n. 24
oil spills, 164
Oregon Trail, 9, 13
Ornithological Biography (Audubon),
   120–21
ornithology, 109, 135. *See also* birds

Otsego Lake, 114
"Our Brains and What Ails Them"
   (Gilman), 192 n. 12
Our National Parks (Muir), 123–24
Our Natural History (Botkin), 199 n. 14
Owen, Russell, 35

Paley, William, 45, 180 n. 14
pastoral, 28, 112, 132–33, 187 n. 25, 198
   n. 19
pesticides, 166–67, 169, 193 n. 17
Peyser, Thomas Galt, 63, 191 n. 5
Phelps, Almira Hart Lincoln, 108, 195
   n. 4
*Philosophical Enquiry into the Origin of
   our Ideas of the Sublime and the Beauti-
   ful* (Burke), 185 n. 13
Physical Geography of the Sea, The
   (Maury), 139
physics, 171
Pike, Zebulon, 12
Pinchot, Gifford, 92, 95, 194–95 n. 12
Pioneers, The (James Fenimore
   Cooper), 107, 132
Pitts, Mary Ellen, 155, 199 n. 11
Plains, American, 140, 142, 176
Platte River, 141, 150
Polynesians, 139
popularization of science. *See* science:
   popularization of
Powell, John Wesley, ix, xii, xiv, 4, 8,
   44, 49, 71, 76, 78, 80–101, 105–6,
   111, 117, 138, 141, 151–52, 171, 177;
   attitudes toward Native Americans,
   84, 97–99; biographical sketch,
   84–85; Colorado River expedition,
   84–85; debate over historical legacy
   of, 82–83, 85, 194 n. 9; and Frémont,
   8, 84, 86, 92, 94; influence on twentieth-century American West, 82,
   87–88; views on irrigation, xiv, 82,
   86–87; as writer, 8, 85–86, 194 n. 6.
   Works: *The Exploration of the Colorado River and Its Canyons,* 85, 194 n.
   6; "Institutions for the Arid Lands,"
   93; *Report on the Lands of the Arid Re-*

gions of the United States, with a More
Detailed Account of the Lands of Utah,
xiv, 76, 80, 83–84, 86–101 (see also
separate entry); Selected Prose, 93, 194
n. 6
prairie, 128–29
Prairie, The (James Fenimore Cooper),
17–18; character Dr. Battius ("Obed
Bat") in, 17–18, 20
Prairie Schooner, 138
Pratt, Mary Louise, 189 n. 12
preservation, 101, 111, 115, 135, 175,
195 nn. 12–13; vs. cultivation/devel-
opment, 132; in relation to exploitation, xi. See also conservation; environmentalism
Preuss, Charles, 9, 12
Primate Visions (Haraway), xvi, 193 n.
14, 199 n. 10
progress, xii–xiv, xv, 165, 173, 176; and
the control of nature, 71–73. See also
Herland: and progress
Progressive Movement, 194 n. 12
Public Lands Commission, 87
Pyne, Stephen J., 34, 45–46

qualitative vs. quantitative information.
See scientific method: qualitative vs.
quantitative

race and racism, x, 21–23, 63, 76
"Rappaccini's Daughter" (Hawthorne),
17
rationality, xiii, 21–23, 41, 47–48, 53,
58, 68, 75, 96, 200 n. 15; vs. emotion,
22, 26, 29
Reader's Digest, 33, 52
readership. See audience
reductionism, 157
Regeneration through Violence (Slotkin),
186 n. 16
Regis, Pamela, 185 n. 12
Reisner, Mark, 82
Relation (Cabeza de Vaca), 4
Reluctant Modernism (Cotkin), 190 n. 2,
192 n. 10

Report of the Exploring Expeditions to the
Rocky Mountains in the Year 1842, and
to Oregon and Northern California in
1843–44 (Frémont), 3, 184 n. 6
Report on the Lands of the Arid Regions of
the United States, with a More Detailed
Account of the Lands of Utah (Powell),
xiv, 76, 80, 83–84, 86–101; authorship, 90; characterization of science
in, xiv, 80, 83–84, 88–91, 96–97,
100–101; and community, 76, 80,
83–84, 97–101; critique of individualism in, 91, 99–101; ecological values in, 76, 87, 92, 96–97, 195 n. 13;
and economics, 95; and Euro-Americans, 97–101; and irrigation, 86–87,
94–95; and management of nature,
76, 83–84, 86, 94–96, 99–101; and
Native Americans, 15–16, 84–85,
97–99; physical characterization of
the arid region, 86; political and ideological significance of, 83, 86–88;
political reaction to, 86–87; representation of nature in, xiv, 83, 86,
91–96, 105 n. 13; —, and gender, 83,
96; rhetoric of science in, 88–91; scientific method (see scientific method:
in Powell's Report); tensions in, 83,
97; utopian elements of, 84
resource management, 58, 76, 95
rhetoric: of anthropomorphism,
123–24; of Frémont's exploration
narratives, 5, 8–13; of natural history,
110–12, 119–26; of Powell's Report,
88–91; of science, xvi, 88–91, 119,
134–35, 173, 183 n. 4, 190 n. 15, 194
n. 11
Richard, Ellen Swallow, 197 n. 12
Riverby, N.Y., 111
Rocky Mountains, 5, 32, 99, 184 n. 5
Roosevelt, Theodore, 76
Ross Ice Barrier, xiii, 32, 35, 40, 42,
44–45
Rossiter, Margaret, 197 n. 12
Rouse, Joseph, 182 n. 4
Rousseau, G. S., 182 n. 3

Rowlandson, Mary, 198 n. 20
Rural Hours (Cooper) xiv, 105–7,
    110–120, 124–133, 196 n. 5; and an-
    thropomorphism, 106, 112–13,
    119–20, 121, 124–26; and birds, 112,
    124–26, 129; on church-yard ecology,
    126–28; and community, xiv, 106,
    111–12, 117–19, 124, 126, 133; com-
    pared to *Walden*, 105, 110–11, 117;
    and conservation, 106, 111–12, 117,
    129–33, 198 n. 17; contrasted with
    exploration narratives, 105, 111,
    116–17, 133; critique of seasonal
    metaphors in, 115–16; ecocritical in-
    terpretations of, 110–12; ecological
    qualities of, xiv, 106, 112, 118, 126–
    31, 133, 195 n. 5; —, discussion of
    non-native species, 129–30; and
    forests, 118–19, 127–28, 130–33; and
    gender, 106–7, 112–17, 196 n. 5, 197
    n. 10; and genre, 107, 110, 126; liter-
    ary and historical contexts of, 105–
    112, 119; and Native Americans,
    132–33; and natural history, 106, 110–
    12, 119–20; —, integrative method,
    112–29; and nature writing tradition,
    107, 110, 119; and pastoralism, 112,
    132–33; views of nature in, 106, 112–
    118, 127, 132–33, 198 n. 17; —, and
    gender, 112–17; —, and religious be-
    lief, 112, 117–18

Sagan, Carl, 135
*Sand County Almanac, and Sketches Here
    and There, A* (Leopold), 78, 128–29
Scarlet Letter, The, 187 n. 23
Schiebinger, Londa, xvii, 191 n. 8
science: in Antarctica, 36–38; and an-
    thropomorphism, 119; as authorita-
    tive, 49, 68, 83, 159; and communi-
    cation, 134–55 (*see also* rhetoric: of
    science); and community, 69, 71–78,
    84, 97–101; critique of, xv, 136, 159–
    73, 178; and environmentalism, 135–
    36, 159–73; feminist critique of,
    xvi–xvii, 63–71, 182 nn. 5–7, 192 n.
    14; and gender, 152, 192 n. 14, 193 n.

15, 199 n. 10; growth of, 134–35;
    "hard" vs. "soft," 64, 191 n. 7; and
    journalism, 135; limitations of, 48,
    52, 176; and literature, xvi, 3, 8, 116,
    119, 123, 135, 145; masculinization
    of, xvii, 5–6, 24–31, 63–67, 107, 151,
    191 n. 7, 192 n. 14; and metaphor,
    145, 171; and objectivity, xv, 24, 29,
    63, 65–66, 68–69, 158; and the per-
    sonal, 159, 167, 172; popularization
    of, 107–9, 119, 134–36, 173; Powell's
    conception of (see *Report on the Lands
    of the Arid Regions . . .* : characteriza-
    tion of science in); professionaliza-
    tion of, xii, 4, 70–71, 80, 107, 183 n.
    4, 191 n. 8; —, and specialization, 71,
    134–35, 178; pure vs. applied, 70–71;
    in relation to nature, x, xii, xiv, 24–
    31, 48, 78, 80, 83–84, 91–96, 101,
    106, 133–36, 145, 154, 158–59, 175–
    76, 178–79; representations of, 49,
    101, 133, 136, 141; rhetoric of (*see*
    rhetoric: of science); as social
    process, xvi–xvii, 70, 90, 159, 165;
    technical control vs. empathetic un-
    derstanding, xi, xv, 33–34, 135, 158–
    59; and technology (*see* technology:
    in relation to science)
science and literature studies, xvi, 145,
    182 n. 3
Science Question in Feminism, The
    (Harding), 192 n. 14
science writers, 145. *See also* scientist-
    writer
scientific exploration, xi–xii, 4–5, 31,
    57, 85, 94, 142; of Antarctica, 33–38;
    in context of American expansion-
    ism, 31, 35–36
scientific instruments. *See* technology:
    scientific instrumentation
scientific management, xiii, 58, 74,
    83–84, 101, 105, 177, 197 n. 12
scientific method, x, xiii, 96–97, 143,
    159–61, 167, 171, 183 n. 3; as com-
    ponent of Byrd's mission, 33–34,
    41–42, 48; of Herlanders, 58, 68; and
    language, 183 n. 3; in Powell's *Re-*

port, 84, 88–89, 177; qualitative vs. quantitative, 4, 9, 88–89
Scientific Revolution, 95
scientist, x, 183 n. 4; as anthropologist, 140–41, 170; as authority, 21–23, 49; as biologist, 152; as ecologist, 136, 158; as explorer, 5–6, 16–31, 32–34, 49, 53, 57–58, 63–66, 85, 138–44, 151, 179; as hero, 5–6, 16–31, 33–34, 48–53, 83, 85, 105, 116, 176; —, and technology, 29–31, 33–34, 48–53; as natural historian, 105, 136, 151, 177–79; in relation to nature, x, 5–6, 21, 24–31, 33–34, 53, 58, 116–17, 136, 138–44, 149–51, 178–79
scientist-explorer. *See* scientist: as explorer
scientist-hero. *See* scientist: as hero
scientist-writer, 107, 110, 135–38, 145, 176
Scott, Robert Falcon, 36–37, 43, 49, 186 n. 17, 190 n. 15
Scribner's Monthly, 85
sea, 161–64
Sea around Us, The (Carson), 137, 139, 146, 153–54, 160–61, 163–64
Secret History of the Dividing Line (William Byrd), 21
Selected Prose (Powell), 93, 194 n. 6
Seton, Ernest Thompson, 121
Shackleton, Ernest, 36–37, 43, 188 n. 7
Silent Spring (Carson), 137, 153, 158–59, 162–63, 165–67, 193 n. 17
Siple, Paul, 188 n. 6
slime mold, 169–70
"Slit, The" (Eiseley), 140–41
Slotkin, Richard, 186 n. 16
Slovic, Scott, 198–99 n. 5
Smith, Henry Nash, 6, 87
Smith, John, 4
Smith, Marsha A., 191 n. 3
Smith, Neyman, 190 n. 2
Smythe, William, 81–82
Snow, C. P., xvi
social Darwinism, 66–68, 77, 191–92 n. 10
soil, 153

Sovereignty and Goodness of God, The (Rowlandson), 198 n. 20
Speaking for Nature (Brooks), 196 n. 6
"Spore Bearers, The" (Eiseley), 170
Stegner, Wallace, 81
Stowe, Harriet Beecher, 187 n. 23
Structure of Scientific Revolutions, The (Kuhn), xvii
subjectivity, 11, 24, 38–39, 68–69, 88–91, 119, 141, 167, 183 n. 3, 194 n. 11
sublime and the beautiful, 28, 185 n. 13
Sumner, William, 191 n. 10
"Survival of the Fittest" (anonymous), 67

taxonomy, 18, 108
"Taxonomy of Nature Writing, A" (Lyon), 196 n. 7
technology: of Antarctic exploration, 36–37; critique of, 170–72; and gender, 29–31; and nature, x–xi, 48, 53, 101, 135, 144, 158, 187 n. 25; in relation to science, xiii, 49–50, 135, 158, 165, 170–72; of scientific instrumentation, 4, 8, 29–31, 33–34, 48–53, 86; —, and human perception, 187 n. 26. *See also* Byrd, Richard: controlled by technology
Thompson, A. H., 90
Thomson, Charles, 172
Thoreau, Henry David, xii–xiii, 33, 38–42, 45, 48, 92, 105, 110–11, 117, 143, 176, 189 n. 11
Todorov, Tzvetan, 183 n. 2
"Topographical Map of the Road from Missouri to Oregon . . ." (Frémont and Preuss), 9–10, 13–14
Toward a Dialogue of Understandings (Pitts), 199 n. 11
trans-Missouri region, 7–8, 31
Travels (Bartram), 120
Treat, Mary, 109
Treatise on Domestic Economy, A (Beecher), 197 n. 12
trees. *See* forests
True Relation of Such Occurrences . . . in Virginia, A (John Smith), 4

"Truth and the Teachers of Truth" (Lewis), 109
Two Cultures, The (Snow), xvi

Uncle Tom's Cabin (Stowe), 187 n. 23
"Undersea" (Carson), 147
Under the Sea-Wind (Carson), 137, 144–48, 162
Unexpected Universe, The (Eiseley), 138, 142–43, 149, 168–69
United States Antarctic Service, 188 n. 3
United States Bureau of Reclamation, 81, 87, 92
United States Congress, 87, 101, 184 n. 6
United States Fish and Wildlife Service, 137
United States Geological Survey, xiv, 85, 87, 188–89 n. 8
Unruh, John D., 184 nn. 5, 7
Utah, 88, 91, 97
utopian society, xi, xiv–xv, 71–73, 78, 84

Van Orman, Richard, 20
Voyages of Samuel de Champlain, 1604–1618, The, 4

Wake-Robin (Burroughs), 122–23
Walden (Thoreau), 39–41, 105, 110–11, 117
Walden Pond, 39
Ward, Lester, 191 n. 10, 192 n. 13
Ware, Joseph E., 8
Warner, Susan, 187 n. 23
Ways of Nature (Burroughs), 121–22
Wells, H. G., 72–72
West, American, xi, xv, 3–31, 43–43, 48, 53, 71, 80–101, 115, 171, 177, 193 n. 1; expansion of, 6–7, 24, 101; as Garden, 87; mythic values associated with, 80, 99; Powell's influence upon, xiv, 82, 87–88; and science, 5, 88; settlement of, xiii, 3, 5, 8, 11, 14, 44, 53, 83, 96, 115, 177, 193 n. 3

West, arid, xiv, 78, 80–84, 86–91, 93–97, 99–101, 151, 177
"What Are Cultural Studies of Scientific Knowledge?" (Rouse), 182 n. 4
Wheeler, George, 85, 194 n. 5
Whitman, Walt, 187 n. 23
Whitney, Josiah, 194 n. 5
Wide, Wide World, The (Warner), 187 n. 23
wilderness, 6, 18, 20, 26, 107, 110–11, 115, 128, 135, 143, 175–76, 178, 195 n. 12, 198 n. 20
Williamson, Henry, 147
Wilson, Alexander, 110, 113
Wisconsin, 128–29
With Her in Ourland (Gilman), 59
women: excluded from science education, 63, 109; and literature, 24–26, 107; and natural history, 107, 111, 113, 195 n. 3, 196 n. 6; and nature, 61, 109, 114–15, 151, 177, 199 nn. 8–9; and science, xvii, 63–64, 69–71, 107–110, 191 n. 7; —, opportunities for and limits on participation, xvii, 63, 70, 108–9, 113, 136–37, 191 n. 8; and scientific popularization, 107–9, 195 n. 3. *See also* gender; *Herland*
Women and Economics (Gilman), 59
Women in the Field (Bonta), 196 n. 6
Woods Hole, Mass., 136
Woods Hole Oceanographic Institution, 188 n. 8
Work of the Byrd Antarctic Expedition, The (Joerg), 188 n. 5
Worldwatch Institute, 199 n. 13
Worster, Donald, 81–83, 92

Yellowstone, 194 n. 5
"Yellow Wallpaper, The" (Gilman), 59
yeoman farmer, 99–100
Yosemite, 115
Young, Louise, 135

UNDER THE SIGN OF NATURE

EXPLORATIONS IN ECOCRITICISM

Rachel Stein
*Shifting the Ground: American Women Writers' Revisions of
Nature, Gender, and Race*

Ian Marshall
Story Line: Exploring the Literature of the Appalachian Trail

Patrick D. Murphy
Farther Afield in the Study of Nature-Oriented Literature

Bernard W. Quetchenbach
Back from the Far Field: American Nature Poetry in the Late Twentieth Century

Karla Armbruster and Kathleen R. Wallace, editors
Beyond Nature Writing: Expanding the Boundaries of Ecocriticism

Stephen Adams
*The Best and Worst Country in the World: Perspectives on the
Early Virginia Landscape*

Mark Allister
Refiguring the Map of Sorrow: Nature Writing and Autobiography

Ralph H. Lutts
The Nature Fakers: Wildlife, Science, and Sentiment (reprint)

Michael A. Bryson
*Visions of the Land: Science, Literature, and the American Environment from the
Era of Exploration to the Age of Ecology*

AEE- 7030

Gramley Library
Salem College
Winston-Salem, NC 27108